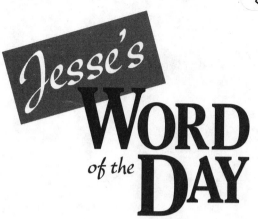

Jesse's
WORD
of the DAY

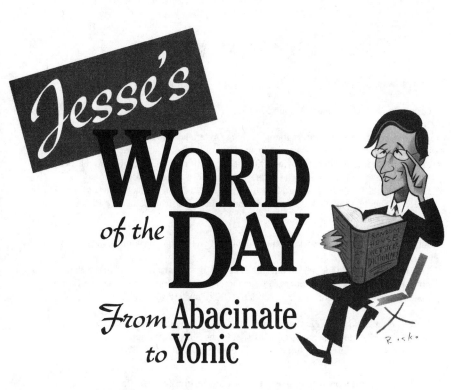

Jesse's WORD of the DAY

From Abacinate to Yonic

JESSE SHEIDLOWER

RANDOM HOUSE   NEW YORK

JESSE'S WORD OF THE DAY

Copyright © 1998 by Random House, Inc.

All rights reserved under International and Pan-American Copyright Conventions. No
part of this book may be reproduced in any form or by any means, electronic or
mechanical, including photocopying, without the written permission of the publisher.
All inquiries should be addressed to Reference & Information Publishing, Random
House, Inc., 201 East 50th Street, New York, NY 10022-7703. Published in the United
States by Random House, Inc., New York and simultaneously in Canada by Random
House of Canada Limited.

All of the material in this work originally appeared on the Random House, Inc. Web site.

This book is available for special purchases in bulk by organizations and institutions,
not for resale, at special discounts. Please direct your inquiries to the Random House
Special Sales Department, toll-free 888-591-1200 or fax 212-572-4961.

Please address inquiries about electronic licensing of this division's products, for use
on a nbetwork or in software or on CD-ROM, to the Subsidiary Rights Department,
Random House Reference & Information Publishing, fax 212-940-7370.

Library of Congress Cataloging-in-Publication Data

Sheidlower, Jesse.
    Jesse's word of the day : from abacinate to yonic / Jesse Sheidlower
       p.   cm.
    Includes indexes.
    ISBN 0-375-70245-8 (pbk.)
    1. Vocabulary   2. English language—Usage.   3. English language—Etymology.
I. Title.
PE1449.S4594   1998
422—dc21   98-16603
                                                     CIP

Visit the Random House Web site at www.randomhouse.com/

Typeset and printed in the United States of America

1998 First Random House Edition

0 9 8 7 6 5 4 3 2 1

ISBN 0-375-70245-8

New York   Toronto   London   Sydney   Auckland

CONTENTS

v

PREFACE

■ Where do people turn with language questions? Dictionaries have many answers, but there are many questions that need more explanation. In the absence of a single, easily accessible source, people often contact the Random House Reference Department with their questions. How old is the slang exclamation *not!*? What does *sthenic* mean? What's the difference between *affect* and *effect*? How do I know when to use single or double quotation marks? What's the third word, after *angry* and *hungry*, that ends in *-gry*? When is it wrong to use *hopefully*? What does the *H.* stand for in *Jesus H. Christ*?

Aside from my regular duties as an editor for the Random House Webster's dictionaries—finding new words, writing definitions, researching word histories, tracking usage—I spend part of every day responding to questions.

The Internet has been increasingly important as a source for language information. The Usenet newsgroup alt.usage.english is one of the most popular of the tens of thousands of newsgroups, and there are Web sites focusing on a huge range of language issues, from the history of Scots to emergency grammar help for students to complex tools for analyzing dialect variation.

In the beginning of 1996, we at Random House decided to use the World Wide Web to bring our everyday questions to a wider audience. Every business day since then, I have answered a question on "Jesse's Word of the Day" page (www.randomhouse.com/jesse or www.jessesword.com) at the Random House Web site (www.randomhouse.com).

This book compiles answers from the first year and a half of this Web page. I haven't invented any questions because I think they are interesting or important; every query you find in this book is one that has really been asked. These are your questions: about etymology, meanings, grammar, style, usage, and more. There are questions here from high-school students and college professors, from foreign learners of English and professional copyeditors. Sometimes I can discern the influence of the Internet itself—the -gry riddle began to circulate widely on newsgroups and through E-mail in 1996, and hundreds of people wrote to ask about it—but more often the questions I receive arise out of real-life language use and genuine curiosity.

People often ask the meta-question of how I do my research. There can be no simple answer to this, since the questions cover such a broad range. I always start by looking up the word in the *Random House Webster's College Dictionary* and the *Random House Webster's Unabridged Dictionary*. The foremost resource at my disposal is the Living Dictionary database of the Random House Reference Department, which consists of millions of examples of language in context, collected by editors and volunteers over the course of fifty years. Evidence from these citations shows exactly how words have been used, and by studying this evidence one can learn a word's age, its associations, its usage. The Living Dictionary database is supplemented by several other computerized data-bases that give access to a vast selection of written English, from literary classics to current journalism.

I will often check other standard dictionaries for comparison, particularly, for historical information, the *Oxford English Dictionary*. Of the thousands of books I use regularly, I should single out the following three: For slang, the *Random House Historical Dictionary of American Slang*, a work in progress of which I am the project editor, is indispensable. For dialect and regional speech the *Dictionary of American Regional English*, also in progress, is likewise unrivaled. Usage issues are comprehensively and wittily treated in *Merriam-Webster's Dictionary of English Usage*, though I also use a range of other usage books for comparison.

My goal has been to explore and explain often-complicated language issues in a thorough, clear, and, hopefully (!), entertaining way. If you have any questions about the English language, or comments on anything discussed in this book, please send them to me by E-mail at jester@randomhouse.com and I will do my best to help.

Jesse Sheidlower
New York
February, 1998

ACKNOWLEDGMENTS

■ Many people have helped me in my daily efforts to answer these questions. In particular, I'd like to thank all of my colleagues at Random House, especially Sol Steinmetz and Enid Pearsons for looking over many of the entries, usually at the last minute; Liz Lesnick and Sandy McCarron in the New Media department for keeping the Web site functional; Charles Levine for letting me spend scarce time on the project.

Sol Steinmetz also read over the entire manuscript and made numerous important improvements. Deborah Fogel did a brilliant job copyediting the manuscript and turning my hastily written prose into a complete and coherent book.

For help researching citations I must especially thank Jeffery Triggs, Director of the *Oxford English Dictionary*'s North American Reading Program, for giving me access to Oxford's computerized corpus of English literature, from which many of my illustrative citations have been drawn. John Simpson, Chief Editor of the *OED*, also helped me with important citations. Joan Hall and Luanne von Schneidemesser gave me access to unpublished material from the files of the *Dictionary of American Regional English*.

For advice on myriad usage and style questions, Mary Beth Protomastro, editor and publisher of the wonderful *Copy Editor: Language News for the Publishing Profession*.

My agent, Bill Clegg, has been incredibly supportive in more ways than I can enumerate.

To Elizabeth Bogner, in thanks for her unending love and support, this book is lovingly dedicated.

All errors that remain are, of course, my own damn fault.

a/an

David Levy writes: **I've noticed a growing usage of "an" preceding words beginning with the letter *h*. I was taught that "an" preceded words beginning with a vowel and "a" preceded words beginning with a consonant. So my question is, when did *h* become a vowel?**

■ Wrong question. The right question is, "Was I taught correctly?" (answer: no, not quite) or perhaps the more direct "What's the correct rule for whether to use **a** or **an**?

The basic form of the correct rule is that **a** is used before words beginning with a consonant *sound* (not, note well, a consonant) and **an** is used before words beginning with a vowel *sound*. Thus, **a** *book,* **a** *car,* **a** *zither,* but **an** *apple,* **an** *election,* **an** *upset.*

The reason to stress the fact that the rule applies to the *sounds* of the letters, and not to the printed or written letters themselves, is that there are many words beginning with a written vowel but pronounced with an initial consonant glide (y) or (w), and these words take an **a: a** *European,* **a** *one-night stand,* **a** *union.*

In addition, the names of the vowels *a, e, i* and *o,* and the consonant letters *f, h, l, m, n, r, s,* and *x* begin with vowel sounds and are used with **an: an** *F in English;* **an** *R-rated movie.* The names of all other consonants, and of the vowel *u,* begin with consonant sounds and are used with **a: a** *B in history;* **a** *U-turn.*

The letter *h* is a special case, partly because it's often silent, and partly because usage has shifted over the years. Words that begin with a silent *h* always take *an,* because they begin with a vowel sound: **an** *hour,* **an** *honor.* In modern use, words with a strongly pronounced *h* take **a: a** *hero;* **a** *horror movie.* But some words beginning with an *h* have an unpronounced or weakly pronounced *h,* especially when they're not stressed on the first syllable, and usage is divided: **a(n)** *historian;* **a(n)** *heroic decision;* **a(n)** *habitual criminal.* The usual choice now is to use **a** with these words, but **an** is often found, particularly in British use.

In the past, it was more common not to pronounce an initial *h,* and examples of **an** *hundred,* **an** *history,* or **an** *hotel* are easy to find, but today such pronunciations or spellings would be regarded as old-fashioned if not erroneous.

■ ■ ■

abacinate

Rasiel Suarez writes: **Have you ever heard of the word "aba-cinate"? Or perhaps "abascinate." It's in the lyrics of a song and by context it should mean something terrible, like geno-cide or some such. Never found the definition in even the big, six-inch-thick dictionary at school.**

■ This has proved to be one of the most interesting questions I've been asked on this site.

First, the context. The song you're asking about must be "Angel of Death," by the death metal band Slayer. The lyrics, which are in general quite repulsive, include this section: "Seas of blood, bury life/Smell your death as it burns/Deep inside of you/**Abacinate,** eyes that bleed/Praying for the end of/Your wide awake nightmare." Believe me, this is one of the milder parts of the song.

Abacinate is a real word. It means 'to blind (a person) by placing red-hot pokers, or metal basins, in front of the eyes'. It comes from Medieval Latin, ultimately from a word for "basin." There's an entry for the word in the *Oxford English Dictionary (OED)*, with no citations at all: it exists solely to support the entry for the nominal form **abacination,** which itself only has one citation, from an obscure source. It's also in some other very, very large dictionaries that few people use today.

Now, the real question about **abacinate** is, if it's so obscure, how did it end up in a rock song like this? One of the nineteenth-century dictio-naries I consulted claimed that it was a technique used in the Middle Ages. Presumably, a lyricist devoted to this sort of thing would be knowl-edgable about medieval torture techniques. So I read through three (count 'em) books about the history of torture. None mentioned *abacina-tion.* I called a professor of medieval history who has written about tor-ture. He'd never heard of it. I found it in a book of obscure words; I called the editor, who said that he had gotten it from the *OED.* I thought that perhaps it occurred in a well-known source that the *OED* didn't include, so I called John Simpson, its chief editor. He said that they didn't have any new evidence for the word in their files.

I asked people who know a lot of obscure things. One of them said, "Oh, yeah, that was a big one in high school. Someone found it in a book somewhere and thought it was neat." This was interesting, but I couldn't go further with it.

I'm assuming that the word was discovered and thought to be inter-esting and maintains some currency among people who remember inter-esting words. I also assume that it really is used by people concerned with torture—although I've searched Web pages devoted to the subject with no luck, the word does appear in the work of Gene Wolfe, a science fiction writer who wrote a notable series about a torturer and who is known for his thorough research.

It's worth noting that in dictionaries, **abacinate** will be found very near the first page, since it occurs so early in the alphabet. (This is also why people know the madeleine story in Proust, or the young-goose-as-toilet-paper bit in Rabelais—they're both memorable things that are found near the beginning of otherwise unreadably long books.)

And that's all I can say. **Abacinate** is a real, albeit extremely rare, word, with a known meaning and etymology. If anyone out there has encountered it before, and knows anything about how it may have been popularized, please let me know.

■ ■ ■

affect, effect

David M. Martin writes: **Now that you've straightened us out on** ENSURE, INSURE, **and** ASSURE, **can you shed some light on the proper usage of "affect" vs. "effect"? I see them used almost interchangeably, but I have a nagging feeling they're not the same thing.**

■ They're not the same thing, although some senses are similar and the words are often pronounced similarly or identically, which leads to a confusion that has been around for five hundred years.

Let's get the noun senses out of the way first: You probably want to use **effect.** The noun **affect** is a technical term in psychology meaning 'an expressed or observed emotional response': "the blunted affect of schizophrenia." It is pronounced with the stress on the first syllable. In all other cases, the noun **effect,** the main sense of which is 'result; consequence' ("the effect of the oil spill") is the right term.

There are two different verbs to **affect.** One means 'to pretend or assume; put on a false or pretended show of': "I affect an English accent"; "She affected an outrageous costume." The second, and the one more likely to cause confusion, is 'to have an effect on; influence': "His poor study habits affected his grades"; "Music affected her deeply." But **effect** has a verb sense too, just to muddle things a bit more, meaning 'to bring about; accomplish': "The administration effected radical changes."

Effect as a verb has been erroneously used in the 'influence' sense since the late fifteenth century, showing that this confusion is nothing new. I've given a rough guide here, but if you're still in doubt, the *Random House Webster's College Dictionary* gives more extensive detail for every sense and subsense of both words.

■ ■ ■

agonistes

Andrew writes: "Agonistes." I have some hazy notions about this, e.g., it comes from "Samson Agonistes" and has something to do with the concept of "agon," but I'd like to know the specifics. Does it mean "the struggles of" or something? (I see it every once in a while in headlines like "Kissinger Agonistes.")

■ The word **Agonistes,** found as an epithet following a person's name, means 'the struggler' or 'the combatant'. It is, as you say, an allusion to Milton's 1671 verse tragedy "Samson Agonistes," which recounts the end of Samson's life, when he is a blind captive of the Philistines (famous line: "Eyeless in Gaza at the mill with slaves"). The struggle that "Samson Agonistes" centers upon is the effort of Samson to renew his faith in God's support.

Probably the most famous post-Miltonic use of **Agonistes** is by T. S. Eliot, who titled one of his dramas *Sweeney Agonistes,* where Sweeney, who appears in several of Eliot's poems, represents the materialistic and shallow modern man. Another well-known example is Garry Wills's 1969 political biography *Nixon Agonistes,* and the word occasionally appears in headlines, as you observe. (Epithets are not especially common today, so you can really only get away with them in headlines or titles, unless you're the old *Spy* magazine and can pull off beauties like "the short-fingered vulgarian," for Donald Trump.)

Agonistes is a borrowing from Greek, of course, where it means 'a contestant in the public games'. This word is derived from *agon,* 'a struggle; contest; assembly' (in English *agon* usually refers to the conflict between the main characters (*protagonists*)in a work). Some related words are *agonist* (the usual English form; **agonistes** preserves the Greek ending), *agony* (originally referring to mental struggle), *antagonist* (the opposite of an agonist), *agonize* (remember John Foster Dulles's "agonizing reappraisal"?), and others.

■　■　■

amathophobe

Gwen Rust writes: I can't find the meaning of the word "amathophobe" anywhere. What does it mean?

■ 'Bout time we had an obscure phobia question around here.

Amathophobia, as any number of dictionaries of obscure words (but few, if any, dictionaries of psychology) can tell you, is the fear of dust. An **amathophobe** is, therefore, a person who fears dust. This should not be confused with *rupophobia, rhypophobia,* or *molysmophobia,* all meaning the fear of dirt, *automysophobia*, the fear of being dirty, or *mysophobia*, the fear of contamination. Isn't it nice that phobias are so minutely observed?

Amathophobia seems to date from the middle of the twentieth century. It derives from the Greek *ámathos* 'sand' and the combining form *-phobia*.

While we're at it, I'll mention that the fear of the number 13 is *triskaidekaphobia*, not to be confused with *paraskevidekatriaphobia*, the fear of Friday the thirteenth, or *triskaidekaphobiaphobia*, which is the dread of idiotic stories about triskaidekaphobia that saturate the media every Friday the thirteenth.

If it seems to you that anything imaginable in the modern world has the companionship of a word denoting its fear, you're probably right. Rather than bemoaning the fact that there are, for instance, four different words meaning 'fear of body odor', we should celebrate the remarkable ability of the Greek language to supply these words, and the remarkable—something—of the modern world that gives rise to a need for them.

■ ■ ■

amnesia

Daniel Bryant writes: We were wondering about the origins of Micronesia and Polynesia, and came up with "nesia" being Greek for "islands," hence "Tiny Islands" and "Many Islands." This led us to wonder about "amnesia" and where it comes from and what, if anything, it's got to do with islands. Can you help? Or have you forgotten . . .

■ I had forgotten, but I looked it up.

The word **amnesia** is indeed a borrowing from Greek, from the word *amnēsía* 'forgetfulness; oblivion', an alteration of *amnēstía*, the source of English *amnesty*. This is ultimately derived from the negative prefix *a-* (as in *amoral* or *atonal*) and the verb *mnásthai* 'to remember', related to the English word *mind*.

Amnesia is a relatively recent borrowing, first found in the late eighteenth century.

The *-nesia* in "Micronesia" and "Polynesia" is also from Greek, as you guess, from the word *nêsos* 'island', which, despite its superficial similarity, is unrelated to the last element in **amnesia**.

■ ■ ■

anal retentive

Dee Werthe writes: I've heard the term "anal retentive" used much too frequently and by people who seem to interpret it differently. Can you clarify the correct meaning, please?

■ The expression **anal retentive** derives from psychoanalytic theory. Sigmund Freud theorized that after birth, a person progresses through a series of stages that allow a healthy individual to reach an adult state of low anxiety, mental stability, the ability to interact with others, the ability to have a sexual relationship, etc. Freud's stages of normal psychosexual development were the *oral stage,* in which the object of gratification is the mouth; the *anal stage,* when the anus is the object, and the child is concerned with the retention or expulsion of feces; the *phallic stage,* when the child shifts its attention to the genitals, but not in an adult, heterosexual way; and the *genital stage,* when a person seeks gratification in a sexual relationship with another person.

The interruption of any of these stages results in a *fixation,* which would have various consequences for the person as an adult. A person interrupted at the late part of the anal stage is an **anal retentive,** and this condition is thought to result in adult personality or behavioral traits that include orderliness, rigidity, obstinacy, obsession with rules, meticulousness, and ungenerousness. The adjective *anal* alone denotes this stage, and hence denotes these traits. Despite its origin in psychoanalytic theory, *anal* is now in broad use, and is sometimes even considered to be a slang term.

The word *anal* is first found in English in a 1930 psychoanalytic text; **anal retentive** appears by the late 1950s. As an adjective, the term is often hyphenated, as in "the **anal-retentive** stage."

■ ■ ■

anfractuous

Robert Davenport writes: My father, who, if alive, would now be 104, often used the term "anfractureosities" (spelling questionable) in the sense of "eccentricities" and told me that it was derived from the German. Was it, or is it, a word?

■ It is probably a word, but I can't be entirely sure from your description. I assume you're thinking of *anfractuosity.* This noun means, in its literal sense, 'the state of having windings or turns; windiness; twistiness'. It is based on the adjective **anfractuous** 'characterized by windings and turnings', as in "an anfractuous path."

Anfractuosity can be used figuratively to mean 'intricacy; obliqueness; complicatedness', especially in phrases like "the anfractuosity of his mind." While this is not exactly the most common word around, it is still in use. We have examples in our files at Random House up to the 1990s, discussing, for instance, the anfractuosities of a translation of a philosophical text. I have never seen the word in the sense 'eccentricity', but it's possible to interpret the 'intricacy' sense as 'eccentricity' if you're not sure what it means. I would suggest that this is likely the case.

Anfractuosity is not from German. It is of Latin origin, perhaps borrowed through French; the *an-* element means 'around; about' and the *fractuous* element means 'breaking; bending' (from the same source as English *fraction, fractious,* and *fracture*).

■ ■ ■

anon

E. A. Rollins writes: **One of my British friends gets chided in L.A. for using the expression "see you anon." People here think it's pretentious, but apparently, it's common where she comes from. I've seen "anon" used in Shakespeare: "The fury spent, anon did this break from her" (speech from *The Winter's Tale*). What exactly does it mean, and where did it come from?**

■ **Anon** is one of our older English words. It comes from elements meaning "in" and "one," that is, 'in one course; straightaway; at once', and is found since the Old English period.

The original meaning is 'immediately; at once', but this sense is now obsolete. The usual sense is 'in a short time; soon'. The expression *ever and anon,* meaning 'now and then; occasionally', is also found.

In current American use, it's safe to say that **anon** is usually self-consciously literary or at least sounds somewhat old-fashioned. An example from an essay in a 1993 newspaper: "The springtimes became autumns, the years became decades, and while nobody was giving the little table a thought it sat there before the long divan, bearing now a bowl of peanuts, now a rosebud, now an advent wreath, and perhaps **anon** a stack of *New Yorkers.*"

The construction *see you anon* is not uncommon: "Good night, Mr. Carraway. See you anon," says a character in Fitzgerald's *Great Gatsby,* for one twentieth-century American example. In current British English, **anon** in other constructions is, as in America, considered something of an archaism, but *see you anon* is not regarded as especially unusual. Even younger speakers would use the expression with no hint of pretension. If you're not British, though, don't try to get away with it here—as you've observed, you'll be in for some raised eyebrows.

■ ■ ■

antsy

Heather Swofford writes: **What can you tell me about the origin of "antsy"? And is "antsily" the appropriate adverbial version? Thanks.**

■ **Antsy,** which means 'restless; uneasy; impatient; anxious; fidgety', has a somewhat questionable origin. Without doubt, it eventually refers to the constant activity of ants, but the real question is whether or not it's the original expression or not.

The familar phrase *to have ants in one's pants* 'to be restless or irritable' dates from the 1930s, though *ant's pants* was a vogue phrase in the 1920s along with *bee's knees, gnu's shoes,* and *cat's pajamas.* The word **antsy** became common in the 1950s, which suggests that **antsy** is derived from the earlier phrase. But there is one example from the nineteenth century that makes the issue murky. An 1838 journal contains the sentence "Minard's talking & Peake's scribbling were enough to drive anyone ancey [sic]." Now, on the one hand this would seem to be the earliest example of our word. However, this is over one hundred years before its next known use. If **antsy**—in whatever spelling—were really in use in the 1830s, it's rather unusual that there's no other example for such a long time.

This could mean that the 1838 example is a coincidence, that it's not the same word as our **antsy.** Or it could be the same word, but for whatever reason, scholars haven't found any other early examples, in which case the "ants in one's pants" phrase would itself be an elaboration of antsy.

The appropriate adverb would be *antsily,* but I've never seen an actual use of this.

■　■　■

apheresis

Liz Blair writes: **What is "apheresis" and why would a person go to the Red Cross for it?**

■ As a medical procedure, **apheresis** is the removal of blood from a person, the separation out of one or more of the elements of the blood (leukocytes, plasma, or platelets), and the reinfusion of the blood back into the donor. This can be done either to treat certain diseases in the donor or to obtain one of the blood elements for medical or research purposes.

The procedure is also called *pheresis,* and can be specifically called *leukopheresis, plasmapheresis,* or *plateletpheresis,* depending on which element is removed from the blood.

While we're here, we may as well mention the original meaning of **apheresis** (also spelled *aphaeresis*), which is 'the loss or omission of one or more letters or sounds at the beginning of a word'. Examples of this process are *squire,* an apheretic shortening from *esquire,* or *'za* from *pizza.* The specific case of apheresis consisting of the loss of an initial unstressed syllable, as *lone* from *alone,* is called *aphesis.*

Apheresis, which is first found in English in the early seventeenth century, is a borrowing of a Greek word meaning 'a removal; a taking away'.

■ ■ ■

-ard

> **Sam Pratt writes: After reading one of your old entries, I started to wonder about nouns ending in -ard that describe people. ("Shard" doesn't count.) You've got "[HOIST WITH ONE'S OWN] PETARD," which you say means "farter." Then there's "retard," in the playground sense. Are there others? Are they also derogatory?**

■ The suffix **-ard** (which also takes the form *-art*) usually denotes people who regularly engage in an (often discreditable) activity, or are characterized in a certain (often negative) way, as indicated by the stem of the word. The suffix is most immediately from Old French, where it formed such words as *mallard* (not applied to people) or *haggard,* and such pejorative words as *bastard, coward,* and our aforementioned *petard.*

The suffix is still productive in English: *dullard, drunkard, sluggard,* and *wizard* are all English coinages, of which only the last is positive.

Ultimately, **-ard** is of Germanic origin, from a word like *hard* or *hart,* related to the English word *hard.* The suffix probably stems from this Germanic word used in personal names, such as *Gerhart,* an older form of "Gerard."

There are other words ending in *-ard* that are not from this suffix, however. *Shard* is one of them, as you suspect, but *retard* is another: it's from Latin *retardare* 'to be slow'; the last element is from *tardus* 'slow'. It's just chance that it ends in **-ard** and has a derogatory meaning. *Hazard, leopard,* and *tankard* are other words, of various origins, whose suffix **-ard** is not the one we're discussing.

■ ■ ■

ass over teakettle

> **Julie Alix Robichaux writes: I wanna know about "ass over teakettle."**

■ **Ass over teakettle** is one of many variants of an expression meaning 'head over heels; topsy-turvy; in confusion'. The usual British version is *ass* (or *arse*) *over tip* (or *tit*), which occurs in James Joyce's *Ulysses*, among other works. This form also occurs in America. For instance, in *The Grapes of Wrath* Steinbeck has a character say, "You jus' scrabblin' ass over tit, fear somebody gonna pin some blame on you."

The earliest known example of the phrase is in an 1899 book about Virginia folk expressions, which defines *ass over head* as 'head over heels; topsy-turvy.' (Note that *ass over head* is a logical expression for a messed-up situation, as opposed to "head over heels," which would seem to be the natural order of things.) However, there must have been many different variants even at that time: a 1943 book about Indiana dialect in the 1890s lists *ass over appetite, ass over applecart,* and *ass over endways.* The common "teakettle" variation is first found in a 1946 book about fighter pilots in World War II, in a euphemized form: "He displayed a rump-over-tea-kettle aggressiveness in seeking dog-fights."

Other objects include *tin cups, teacups,* and *elbow.*

■ ■ ■

augury

Joan Troy writes: **Please, please, please! What is the root meaning of "augury"? I understand the definition, but cannot find the meaning of the root.**

■ Hey, I'm easy—I'll do it for you for only *one* "please"!

Augury, which means 'the art or practice of divination from signs or omens', and hence 'an omen, token, or indication', is a Latin derivative. The immediate source is Latin *augurium,* which is derived from a Latin base form *augur.*

In ancient Rome, the *augures* were official diviners, one of the four main groups of priests. Though they used various methods of divination, an *augur* would often use the flight or behavior of birds as a primary method. (Compare a *haruspex,* originally an Etruscan diviner who divined by examining the entrails of slaughtered animals. I personally find tea leaves a much neater procedure.)

In English, *augur* is normally used as a noun meaning 'a soothsayer; prophet' or as a verb meaning 'to divine or predict' and also 'to serve as an omen of; foreshadow'. The historical meaning 'a Roman augur' is comparatively rare.

The ultimate origin of Latin *augur* is uncertain. It was once considered to be derived from *avi* and *ger(o),* meaning 'directing the birds', but this theory is now usually considered a FOLK ETYMOLOGY. The probable origin is from Latin *augere* 'to increase' (the source of English *augment,* among others), alluding to the growth or prosperity that successful divination would enable.

The word *augury* is first found in English in the fourteenth century.

barbecue

JoAnne Meyers writes: **Where does the word "barbecue" come from?**

■ The word **barbecue** is one of the oldest Americanisms, found in the colonies in the seventeenth century.

It's a borrowing from American Spanish *barbacoa,* which in turn is taken from an Arawakan word, possibly from Taino. Arawakan is a family of Native American languages spoken or formerly spoken in several parts of the Caribbean and Central and South America, and Taino is an Arawakan language of the Greater Antilles. This Native American word referred to a wooden grid on which the meat was roasted or dried. (It actually referred to *any* wooden grid, including one used as a bed, but the idea of sleeping on a barbecue is so unnerving that I refuse to contemplate it beyond this parenthetical note.)

The earliest example of **barbecue** is in 1661, when it is used as a verb meaning 'to cook on a barbecue'. Other early senses include 'the wooden framework for supporting food'; 'a whole animal, or a piece of an animal, roasted on a barbecue'; and 'a social gathering at which food is cooked on a barbecue'.

Many barbecue purists today reserve the word only for specific processes, for example the slow cooking of meat coated in a pungent, vinegar-based sauce, and insist that simply cooking food over a flame be called *grilling.* However, in practice the term **barbecue** is applied widely to any sort of open-fire cooking.

The usual spelling is **barbecue,** but **barbeque** is a frequent variant, and **Bar-B-Q** and other forms are found as well.

■ ■ ■

basket case

Margot Liggett writes: **Some friends and I are sitting around right now discussing where the phrase "basket case" comes from. One person thinks it comes from an old practice of carrying around crippled people in baskets, but I don't buy it. Where does the phrase really come from?**

■ It really does come from an old practice of carrying crippled people around in baskets.

Basket case first appeared as a slang term in World War I meaning 'a quadruple amputee'. Soldiers who had lost all their limbs actually were carried in baskets, because if they were carried on stretchers, they'd be too likely to fall out. This sense, first attested in 1919, was never extremely common, but it still has a small degree of currency.

The usual senses are all figurative developments meaning, broadly, 'anything whose function is impaired'. The most common specific sense is 'a person who is unable to function normally, due to anxiety, stress, or mental illness'; other subsenses are 'a country unable to pay its debts', 'an abandoned vehicle that has been stripped of its parts', and 'an eccentric person'.

■ ■ ■

bated breath

Gregory Sullivan writes: **Today, while perusing a reader-feedback forum on the Internet, I encountered the phrase "with baited breath." The writer probably intended to use the expression "with bated breath." I am curious about the origin of this phrase and the frequency of the above variant.**

■ The often misunderstood and misspelled expression **bated breath** is actually very straightforward.

The word *bate* means 'to moderate; restrain' or 'to lessen; diminish'. It is an aphetic shortening of *abate.* (Aphesis is the loss of an unstressed initial syllable, as in *lone,* from *alone,* or *cute,* from *acute*—see APHERE-SIS.) So *with* **bated breath** means 'with the breath restrained or made gentle, as from excitement', and hence 'in a state of suspense'. Remember "to abate one's breath" and it'll make more sense.

The word *bate* itself, first found around 1300, was once rather common—it appears a number of times in Shakespeare, for example—but is now very rare except in this one set expression. As a result, many people don't know what *bated* means, and change it to *baited* by the process of FOLK ETYMOLOGY—the unclear *bate* is altered to associate it with the common *bait.*

The version *baited breath* is not very rare, and the process that gives rise to it is common and has many parallels, but it's almost always regarded as an error. You should avoid it, lest people wonder what you've baited your breath with, and what you're trying to catch.

■ ■ ■

beadle

Catherine Walker writes: **I'm reading *Oliver Twist*, and there are several references to a parochial "beadle." What the heck is a beadle?**

■ A **beadle** is someone you'd better get really familiar with if you plan to read much more Victorian fiction, because you can find beadles all over the place.

The **beadle** was a minor parish official responsible for various duties, typically including keeping order during a service, waiting on the rector, and punishing petty offenders. In the past, the **beadle** played a reasonably important role in the community, and hence you can find beadles as characters in fiction of various sorts. Dickens seemed especially fond of them, as beadles appear in a number of his books.

Beadles are almost never seen anymore, except in certain ceremonial roles, so the word is effectively limited to historical use.

The word **beadle** is first found in this sense in the late sixteenth century. Earlier—the word goes back to the Old English period—it had various meanings, including 'one who make a proclamation; herald; town crier'; 'a minor messenger of justice; under-bailiff'; and 'a person who walks in front of dignitaries at ceremonies; mace-bearer'. It stems from a root meaning 'to command', and is related to the English word *bid*.

■ ■ ■

beg the question

Del Engen writes: **I've noticed that the phrase "beg the question" is increasingly used in a context where a statement is bursting with an as-yet unasked question. "The statement begs the question: [insert question here]." I thought that "begging the question" was a variety of informal fallacy (*petitio principii,* if memory serves) meaning circular reasoning. Two questions: (1) Is there a better phrase that should be used instead of the incorrect sense? (2) Is this sense now an acceptable use of the phrase? I've seen it in print in reputable newspapers and magazines.**

■ You thought right; this new use of **beg the question** is one that usage experts have only just started to notice.

The traditional use of **beg the question** is, as you note, a rhetorical fallacy known in Latin as *petitio principii,* literally, 'postulation at the outset', which the English phrase "begging the question" translates over-literally, equating *petitio* with "begging." To **beg the question** means 'to assume the truth of the very point being raised in a question'. An example: (Q) "Is capital punishment effective?" (A) "Capital punishment is necessary because without it murders would increase." This "answer" does not address the issue of the effectiveness of capital punishment; it assumes that it is effective and goes on from there. Other examples, well known to interview fans: "When did you stop beating your wife?" "When did you quit smoking?" Both of these again assume the truth of the questions they're asking. As you can see, begging the question can be an effective rhetorical strategy.

The sense that most usage books *do* discuss, and have discussed for many years (usually disapprovingly), is the derived sense 'to avoid the question; evade; sidestep'. This is a somewhat natural development, if you encounter the result of the phrase **beg the question** without knowing what it really means. An example of this: "He simply begged the question by saying that the decisions he disapproved of invented new rights" *(New York Review of Books)*.

The most recent sense is 'to raise the question', which plays on the semantic overlap between *beg* and *ask*—not too surprising a development if you have no idea whatsoever what **beg the question** means. Two examples, both from the *New York Times:* "We have reached the age when brute force can outperform creativity. This statement, of course, begs the question of what creativity is." "Yet the promised technical progress begs the cultural question: What of substance will the Internet add to journalism?" (It's not always possible in context to know whether the writer meant 'to avoid the question' or 'to prompt the question', but there are enough clear examples to demonstrate that 'prompt' is a common intended meaning.)

To address your questions, then, the first is easy: there are any number of better phrases one could use that don't involve a usage problem. "To raise the question," "to force one to ask," "to prompt the question," and others all will do. The second is more complicated, and forces us to grapple with our ongoing problem of what constitutes "correct usage." On the one hand, the new use is found in many highly respectable sources, including the *New York Times,* the *Wall Street Journal,* the *Economist,* the *Times Literary Supplement,* and even some hard-core academic journals. There haven't been any outpourings of rage—yet—amongst the people who usually get upset about such things. One could conclude, on these grounds, that the use is standard. On the other hand, unlike some other usage issues, which depend on natural shifts of senses or arbitrary objections to certain meanings or constructions, this new **beg the question** stems from a complete misunderstanding of what the phrase means. I'd say, therefore, that it is best avoided for now.

■   ■   ■

behead

Bert Fry writes: "Behead"—Why do we use this word to indicate that someone's head is to be removed? Someone who is "bejeweled" has jewels put on on her; "bedecked," and "beguiled" all seem to have structurally similar meanings, exactly opposite in overall effect from removing someone's head. If we mean "dehead" why don't we say it?

■ Because "dehead" sounds pretty silly.

The problem with very common formatives like *be-* is that they can usually be used in a lot of different ways, and not all of them make perfect sense if you don't know the etymological details.

The prefix *be-* derives from the ancestor of the word *by.* It has had various meanings, but most of them are things like 'around', 'about', or 'all over', and thus '(used as a general intensive in various ways)'. It is also used to form transitive verbs from other parts of speech. Examples are your *bejewel, bedeck, beguile,* and also *besiege, befog, befuddle, befriend, beribboned,* and *bespectacled,* all of which may be divided into various specific senses, but none of which means anything like 'away'.

However, *be-* does have 'away' as one of its meanings, and this sense was common in Old English. This use is known as a *privative:* one that indicates negation or absence. Though it is now obsolete, the privative *be-* still survives in a small number of words, including **behead** and *betake.* There are also some parallels in such languages as Middle High German, where *be-* is used with privative force.

Behead is first found in the Old English period. And *dehead,* by the way, is plausible: there are *de-* words in the same sense, including *dehair* and the slangy *denut* 'to castrate'. There's just no need for it with **behead** around.

■   ■   ■

behoove

Don Willmott writes: Why does it "behoove" me? Is there any situation in which I'd be able to "behoove" anyone else? And where the heck does the word come from?

■ **Behoove** (or in the British spelling, *behove*) is an example of a verb that is usually used impersonally. An impersonal verb is one that has no expressed agent, usually taking "it" as an empty subject. Examples are *rain, thunder,* and *lightning,* which are found almost exclusively in third-person constructions with "it" ("it thundered"; "it was raining"); certain senses of words such as *seem* or *appear* ("it seems to me that . . .";

"it appears you are mistaken"); and totally impersonal verbs such as the archaic *methinks.*

There are several constructions with **behoove** that do not take "it" impersonally, but they are very rare in modern English. The only one you'd ever be likely to see is a passive construction like "we are behooved to help." So I wouldn't try to behoove anyone else; it might be dangerous.

Behoove goes back to Old English; it is derived from the noun *behōf,* which means 'profit'.

■ ■ ■

beside oneself

Paul Jackson writes: **How about "beside oneself," as in "He was beside himself with anger"?**

■ How about it? **Beside oneself** is one of several old phrases in which the loss of a mental faculty is explained as being, broadly, away from one's person. The most common phrase is *out of one's mind,* which is first found in the fifteenth century, slightly earlier than **beside oneself.**

Though *beside* now usually means something like 'by the side of; next to', one of its earlier senses was 'outside of; out of'. By around 1500, this developed a figurative sense, parallel to "out of one's mind": 'having lost (a specified faculty); having lost one's senses'. Shakespeare has, iambically, "Enough to put him quite beside his patience" *(Henry IV, Part I).* The more common version with "oneself"—the only current use—is found in the *King James Bible,* Acts 26:24: "Paul, thou art beside thyself; much learning doth make thee mad."

Since the concept is relatively straightforward, other phrases tend to be variants on the same theme. *Out of one's wits, off one's head, on another plane,* and any number of slangy alterations all represent this family of expressions.

■ ■ ■

betide

Jay Ackroyd writes: **Now that you mention archaic-sounding words, I've never really understood what "betide" means, as in "Woe betide the man who touches one hair on the wee lass's head." Nor have I ever heard it without the leading "woe." Are we just talking flows of a sea of woe in this construction?**

■ **Betide** is yet another word that has pretty much gotten locked into an archaic formula, and rarely appears any other way.

Betide means 'to happen; come to pass', or more often as a transitive verb 'to happen to; befall'. It is quite old, first appearing in the twelfth century, and is based on the prefix *be-* and Old English *tidan,* also meaning 'to happen'. The word is always found in the third person, but has seen a wide range of use over the years: "As if some euill were to her betight" (Spenser, with deliberately archaic spelling); "A strange adventure, that betided/Betwixt the Foxe and th' Ape" (Spenser again); "If he were dead, what would betide on me?" (Shakespeare, *Richard III*); "What is betide/Of th' Argive threats" (Hobbes).

The only use that is at all common now, however, is as a subjunctive in the expression of a wish. The subjunctive can often have an archaic flavor, and so it does here. Subjunctive **betide** has been found in various constructions (e.g., "A happy Morning betide you Lady"—Thomas Heywood, 1633), but now *woe betide* is all you see. This formula is as old as Shakespeare, naturally ("Now help, or woe betide thee evermore"—*Titus Andronicus*).

Some other examples: "Woe betide him unless his skill should prove some apology for his insolence!" (Sir Walter Scott, *Ivanhoe*); "Woe betide the tyro; the foolhardy, Heaven preserve!" (Melville, *White-Jacket*); "He will be pitiless and cruel. Woe betide poor Catherine!" (Henry James, *Washington Square*); "Woe betide anyone that looks crooked at him" (James Joyce, *Ulysses*).

The *New Shorter Oxford English Dictionary* points out that the *woe betide* formula was originally used as a threat, meaning something like "May woe happen to . . .", but now appears most often as a warning.

■ ■ ■

between you and I

Mellennesse Mountain writes: **You know, I've insisted that "between you and I" was incorrect for so long that I'm not ready to give it up—but given its popularity, it must be considered "standard," right?**

■ It depends on what philosophical viewpoint you take toward usage. Briefly, there are two main approaches: prescriptive and descriptive. The prescriptive approach involves the handing down of rules by those claiming to have a special knowledge of or feeling for a language. Prescriptivists tend to be conservatives who regard language change with suspicion, if not disdain. The descriptive approach involves the objective description of the language as it is actually used. Descriptive advice is based solely on usage, rather than on any feeling about what "should" be correct.

These categories are not very firm. There are few prescriptivists who would *always* reject a usage regardless of how common it is and what sort of people use it. Conversely, few descriptivists would argue that *any* construction is acceptable as long as it can be found in the writing or speech of a native speaker.

Now, **between you and I** is a usage issue that has been much discussed. The overwhelming majority of people who comment on it, and all the prescriptivists, reject it outright, for the reason that the preposition *between* should take a pronoun in the objective case, namely *me*. The usual explanation for the substitution of *I* in this phrase is that it is an example of *hypercorrection*. This is the process of introducing erroneous forms in an effort to replace seemingly incorrect forms that are really acceptable. The assumption is that since various uses of *me* are considered incorrect—as a subject (e.g., "John and me went to the store"), as an object of "to be" (e.g., "It's me")—and are often criticized, people tend to use "I" even when "me" is correct.

It takes a lot of work to defend **between you and I,** but there are those who try to do so. The standard approach is first to cite a few important sources. Shakespeare uses it in *The Merchant of Venice,* and it is also found in the works of the Restoration playwrights William Congreve and Sir John Vanbrugh, to name a few early users. The use of "'tween you and I," one scholar notes, "seems to have been a regular Elizabethan idiom." Then, look at modern examples, showing that it's reasonably common in the speech of even educated persons. It is not difficult to collect examples from the speech of teachers, lawyers, broadcast announcers, and so forth. Finally, make some grammatical arguments: coordinated phrases often show syntactic peculiarities, and the use of subject pronouns where object pronouns are expected is not uncommon; the phrase *you and I* can be considered to be a "notional subject," even where it is grammatically an object; the entire phrase **between you and I** can be considered an idiom and so not bound by traditional grammatical rules.

Despite these various arguments, it remains true that **between you and I** is almost always considered wrong. Even if you accept some (or all) of the above points, it is unlikely the phrase could be regarded as "standard." The strongest descriptivist argument in favor of the phrase would be that there's ample historical precedent for the use, and it's not that uncommon in informal speech. But in modern use it is very, very rare in print of any sort, and comparatively rare in formal speech. That does not constitute a ringing endorsement of a judgment of "standard."

■ ■ ■

beyond the pale

fredgm@pacbell.net writes: **Where is "beyond the pale"? I've heard that it is "beyond death," or beyond an actual geographical place, possibly Russia?**

■ Several geographical locations are named *Pale:* One is in Burma, one is in Bosnia, near Sarajevo, and one was a city in ancient Greece. None of these has anything whatsoever to do with the expression **beyond the pale.**

There are two etymologically unrelated words *pale*. One is an adjective that means 'lacking intensity of color; colorless or whitish' and derives from the Latin word *pallidus*, also the base of our English word *pallid*. The other is a noun that means 'a stake or picket, as of a fence'; it derives from the Latin word *palus* 'a stake', which also gives us the word *pole*.

It is this second *pale* that is the source for the expression **beyond the pale**. An extended sense of *pale* is 'a fence made of pales', and therefore 'a fence of any sort' and then figuratively 'a limit; boundary'. **Beyond the pale,** then, means 'beyond the limits of propriety, courtesy, good sense, etc.'. This parallels other expressions such as "you've really crossed the line this time." Since this word *pale* is relatively uncommon today, the origin of the phrase with "beyond" is unclear to most of us.

This *pale* is used to refer to real geographical boundaries, for example the Pale of Settlement, which was a territory in czarist Russia (your mention of "possibly Russia" suggests that you have heard of this) where Jews were permitted to live; it covered about 400,000 square miles and was abolished in 1917. There were other such pales, but the expression **beyond the pale** does not come from them.

This *pale* is first used in the Middle English period; the figurative sense 'a limit; boundary' is first recorded about 1400.

■ ■ ■

bi-

Robert Degerberg writes: **What is the skinny on using "bimonthly" or "biweekly"? Some of my dictionaries say it means "every other," some say "twice" and some say to use either or don't use it at all. What is your opinion?**

■ **Bi-** is a potentially ambiguous prefix because it really can be used to mean 'every two' or 'twice each', whatever your dictionaries say. The two senses have been current for a very long time, and part of the problem is that people usually assume you know what sense is being used. In publishing, for instance, **bi-** almost always means 'every two', so a *biweekly* magazine comes out every two weeks and a *bimonthly* magazine comes out six times a year. In other contexts, *biweekly* is equally commonly assumed to mean 'twice a week'. If you encounter an example where there isn't any way to tell what the author meant, there's not much you can do—both senses are current.

There are a few solutions you can adopt for your own writing. One is to use *semi-*, which always means 'twice each', when that is what you mean. Another is to avoid use of **bi-** altogether, specifying "every other month," "twice a year," and so forth. Finally, you can use **bi-**, but give enough context in your writing to show exactly what you intend: "We'll be having biweekly meetings on Mondays and Thursdays"; "Elections will be held biannually in November of even-numbered years."

■ ■ ■

Bildungsroman/Entwicklungsroman

Sarah Burnes writes: Could you tell me the difference between a "Bildungsroman" and an "Entwicklungsroman"? What's the deal with the latter word, anyway?

■ Well, the most important differerence is that **Bildungsroman** is relatively common in English and **Entwicklungsroman** is so rare that only a few hard-core types will know what it means.

The words, which are so close in meaning as to be almost synonymous, both refer to types of novels common in German literature that discuss the personal development of a single person, typically in youth. A **Bildungsroman,** from German *Bildung* 'education; formation' and *Roman* 'novel', focuses especially on the moral and spiritual development of the main character. The definitive example is Goethe's *Wilhelm Meisters Lehrjahre* (in English, *Wilhelm Meister's Apprenticeship*), which greatly influenced later German novels. A more recent example is Thomas Mann's *The Magic Mountain.*

If an **Entwicklungsroman,** from German *Entwicklung* 'development', is any different from a **Bildungsroman,** then the difference is so slight as to be not worth worrying about. Some sources call them synonymous; some say just that "the differences are slight," and some give them different but effectively synonymous definitions, e.g., "a novel of development" versus "a novel showing the development of its protagonist." I'd say that you probably don't have to worry about this one, unless you're a German-lit expert, in which case you probably know what it means anyway.

The other variant worth consideration is the *Künstlerroman,* or 'artist novel', which is a **Bildungsroman** in which the protagonist becomes an artist, musician, or poet. Important examples are Joyce's *Portrait of the Artist as a Young Man* and Thomas Wolfe's *Look Homeward, Angel.*

Entwicklungsroman has some slight fame for being the longest word in English (it is found in a few English dictionaries) having each of the five vowels once and only once.

■ ■ ■

bleachers

Don Willmott writes: When I go to a Yankees game, I sit in the "bleachers." Why?

■ Because you can't afford the good seats. But that's probably not what you're asking.

The **bleachers** were originally a section of unreserved, backless benches at a ballpark that were uncovered. The word *bleacher* is often said to come from the jocular notion that people sitting in them would be bleached by the sun. (We'll pass over the fact that people would actually tend to get darker by sitting in the sun; these things don't always make sense.) The actual reason was that the benches themselves were bleached from the sun, and were hence also called *bleaching boards,* referring to the plain boards (rather than individual seats) on which people sat. The boxes and the grandstand, in contrast, had a roof over them so that spectators (and seats) were out of the sun.

The word is first found in the late nineteenth century. The **bleachers** were always the cheapest seats (in the mid-1950s at Ebbets Field, a ticket for the **bleachers** was only 50 cents, compared with $1.75 for the grandstand and $3 for the lower boxes). As a result, the **bleachers** is now used figuratively to refer to the cheapest, most distant seats at any event or venue, whether covered or not.

■   ■   ■

bootleg

Thomas Willshire writes: **I've heard of "bootleg" gin, "bootleg" records, and the play a quarterback runs in the NFL called a "bootleg." The latter is a play designed to deceive the opposition. These uses of the term all carry some suggestion of phoniness or inauthenticity. OK. What does that have to do with a boot and a leg?**

■ The original meaning of **bootleg** in the seventeenth century was a rather boring one: 'the upper part of a boot'. It becomes relevant to your senses when people began to smuggle liquor by hiding the hooch in their boots. (Strange as this may seem, it was apparently a real practice in the late nineteenth century.)

Rather than "phoniness or inauthenticity," as you suggest, the main meaning is something like 'illegal; unauthorized; unregulated'. In early use, around 1890, the usual context was liquor, with **bootleg** as a noun being more or less equivalent to *moonshine,* and as a verb meaning 'to smuggle liquor'. The broader application to *anything* smuggled or made illicitly, such as **bootleg** cigarettes or a **bootleg** recording, arose by the 1920s. Still later senses, such as the **bootleg** *play,* which was in use by the 1940s, bring the idea of simple deception to bear.

■   ■   ■

booze

Don Willmott writes: **I have a hangover, which makes me wonder why liquor is also known as "booze."**

■ Blame the Dutch.

Booze, meaning 'alcoholic drink, especially hard liquor', was originally a verb—*bousen* in Middle English—meaning 'to drink alcoholic liquor, esp. to get drunk', and it is a direct borrowing from Middle Dutch *būsen,* which meant 'to drink to excess'. The Dutch word is related to Middle High German *būsen* 'to carouse; revel', but the ultimate origin of these words is unknown.

The word *bous[e]* is first found in English in the early fourteenth century as both a verb and the more familiar noun. The spelling **booze** is from the seventeenth century, a different pronunciation that probably reflects dialect variation.

Some other *booze*-related words include *boozed,* first recorded from Benjamin Franklin; *boozefest* from the 1920s; *boozehound* from the 1910s; and *boozy* from the sixteenth century.

■ ■ ■

Brodie

Coleen Corbitt writes: **OK, here's a challenge for you (I know the answer to this one and wondered if I could get you). What does the phrase "to take a Brodie" mean and what's its origin?**

■ To take (or do) a **Brodie** is to fall, leap, or dive. The phrase is also used in figurative senses, such as '(of a play or movie) to fail utterly; flop'; '(in boxing) to throw a match; take a dive'; or '(of a car) to spin around; do a 180 or 360', and as a verb in identical senses.

The expression comes from the name of Steve Brodie, who claimed to have leapt from the Brooklyn Bridge on July 23, 1886. This claim, which could not be verified, sparked huge media interest in New York and was talked about for many years afterwards.

To do a Brodie is first recorded in the late 1890s, and is still current.

■ ■ ■

brouhaha

stacyjm@aol.com writes: **Well I am not really sure how it is even spelled, which is probably why I can't find it in the dictionary. The word is "brewhaha." I have heard it a lot and not always in the same context. Most commonly used as "that was some brewhaha last night." So, I assume it means a get-together or party. What do you know about this word?**

■ **Brouhaha,** as it is usually spelled, means 'turmoil; clamor; uproar; hubbub; confusion'. So it could certainly be applied to a busy party, but that would be a specific application of the word. Furthermore, **brouhaha** is normally used of unpleasant examples of confusion; using it to talk about a noisy but fun party would be considered unusual.

Brouhaha is a borrowing from French; it is first found in English in the late nineteenth century. In French the word goes back to sixteenth-century drama, where characters dressed up as the devil cried "brou, ha, ha!" Its earlier history is uncertain. It may simply be an expressive or echoic coinage.

One theory, proposed by the etymologist Walther von Wartburg, is that it comes from the Hebrew phrase *bārūkh habbā* 'blessed be he who comes', frequently used both in prayers and to welcome people to public ceremonies such as weddings, and that the sense 'confusion' arose by association of the phrase with noisy celebrations. Unbelievable as this etymology may seem, it is well supported and has been widely accepted. The Hebrew phrase is in fact common; it appears several times in the Book of Psalms, for example. Most notably, a dialectal form of Italian has the word *barruccaba,* also meaning 'confusion', and clearly borrowed from the Hebrew phrase. Other words in other languages also show that words from Hebrew prayers were used in senses like 'confusion' or 'chattering', thus supporting the semantics of the suggestion.

Brouhaha is relatively common today, but can sound somewhat old-fashioned. It does pop up in a brilliant slang word which you are all encouraged to use: *brewhaha* 'a beer', punning on **brouhaha** and *brew* 'a beer'. It sounds much more fun than *brewski,* and this way you'll get to talk about the Hebrew text of the Bible. What could be better?

■ ■ ■

buck

Richard Clare writes: **Doesn't the word "buck" in "the buck stops here" refer to "buck slips"—the forms used in the government to forward documents (and problems) to higher-ups, rather than to dollars?**

■ Actually, it's the other way around. The expression *buck slip,* govern-mentese for 'routing form', is almost certainly derived from the expression *pass the buck,* but you are correct that the 'dollar' sense of **buck** is not involved.

The origin of these expressions comes from the language of poker. The **buck** was an object used to indicate the dealer of a particular hand, apparently so called because a knife with a buckhorn handle was once used for this function. (In modern casino poker, where an employee of the casino physically deals for all the players, the object indicates the position of the player who represents the dealer. This object is now usually called the *button.*) To *pass the buck* meant literally to give another person the chance to deal, and figuratively to pass responsibility on to someone else.

The expression *the buck stops here* was Harry Truman's way of saying "the responsibility ultimately lies with me," and alludes to *pass the buck.*

The literal use of **buck** as an indicator of the dealer in poker dates from the 1860s. The sense 'responsibility', especially in the phrase *pass the buck,* dates from the 1900s, with *buck passer* first found in the 1920s. But *buck slip* is a term that arose in World War II, by which point *pass the buck* was quite common.

The origin of **buck** 'a dollar', which a number of people have asked about, is uncertain. A common explanation is that it derives from *buckskin,* after the use of deerskins as units of exchange on the frontier. Two problems with this etymology are that a deerskin was worth more than a dollar, and that *buck,* first attested in the 1850s, is quite rare until the twentieth century. But this is still the most likely explanation, so I'll stick with it.

■ ■ ■

bugaboo

Ben Arbogast writes: While the dictionary has a definition of "bugaboo," the origin is indeterminate. Any clues?

■ This is an uncertain one. **Bugaboo,** which means 'something, especially an imaginary thing, that causes fear or worry; goblin; bugbear; bogey', has a few complications. The earliest form of the word, found in the middle of the eighteenth century, is *buggy-bow;* the form **bugaboo** is not found until later in the eighteenth century.

The second element is usually assumed to be from *boo!,* the interjection used to frighten. One problem with this assumption is that *boo* by itself is not found until the early nineteenth century. However, *boo* seems to have developed from *bo,* a similar interjection that is centuries older; the fact that the first form of **bugaboo** is *buggy-bow* suggests that the second element may be a form of *bo(o),* one way or another.

The first element is the tough part. It is undoubtedly related to such words as *bugbear and bogy* (as in *bogeyman,* now a more familiar form). The original word that these are based on is the Middle English *bug* 'an object of terror; goblin', but this word is of uncertain origin. (It is probably not related to *bug* 'an insect', which is itself of uncertain origin.) An origin in a Celtic language is often suggested—especially Welsh *bwg* (the *w* in Welsh is a *u*-like vowel)—but for various reasons this cannot be proved; the Welsh word may simply be a later borrowing from English. The existence in the late nineteenth century of a word **bucca-boo** 'a ghost; bugbear' in Cornish English is interesting, but does not by itself prove that Cornish (the Celtic language) is involved. In short, while this word *bug* is involved, there's no definite way to move beyond it.

■　■　■

bummer

John Sabo writes: **Please explain the origins of the word/expression, "bummer."**

The ultimate origin of **bummer** is uncertain, as with many interesting words. I should also point out that there are two different words **bummer,** and the relationship between them is indirect at best.

The first **bummer** broadly means 'a person who bums; a beggar; bum'. This word, which has several related senses, is first found in the 1850s, and apparently comes from the German *Bummler* 'loafer'. It is now largely obsolete.

The second **bummer,** which I assume is the one you have in mind, means 'a terrifying or unpleasant experience induced by a hallucinogenic drug; bum trip', and hence 'anything that is unpleasant, difficult, dangerous, etc.'. Both senses arose in the late 1960s, as did the interjectional use **bummer!**

This **bummer** is probably formed from *bum (trip)* and the *-er* ending, or directly from *bum* (adjective) in the sense 'bad' (which is the origin of *bum steer* 'bad advice' and *bum trip,* in any case) with the same ending. This *bum* adjective derives from *bum* 'a contemptible or despicable person'; (also) 'a beggar'; the change in meaning from 'a contemptible person' to '(of anything) contemptible' is pretty straightforward. However, this *bum* is of uncertain origin.

The probable answer is that it is simply a shortening of the first **bummer** we discussed above. A difficulty with this conclusion is the existence of several earlier examples (going back to 1540 in Scots use) of *bum* in semantically related senses. The most likely explanation is that these earlier *bum* words are of different and unrelated origin, and all the *bums* we've been discussing stem from the 1850s German *Bummler.*

■　■　■

cache

Arun Thomas writes: **I just read the spot about the word CASH and its origins. Does the word "cache," which I have always heard with respect to money (for example, "the old widow added the coins to her secret cache") come from the same origins?**

■ No, it's just a coincidence.

CASH, as we have seen, comes one way or another from French *caisse* 'a money-box'. This French word derives, by way of Occitan (the language of southern France), from Latin *capsa* 'a case'.

Cache, on the other hand, is also from French, but it's a direct borrowing of **cache** 'a hiding place', a sense we also find in English. The French word is a noun derived from *cacher* 'to hide'. With assorted twists and turns not worth delving into, *cacher* derives from the Latin verb *cogere* in its sense 'to collect'.

Cache is first found in English in the late eighteenth century. The first examples generally had to do with a hiding place for provisions or ammunition, rather than money. While **cache** certainly can be used to describe a hiding place for money, that's not its primary sense, so both the identical pronunciation and the possible semantic overlap with cash are just coincidences.

■ ■ ■

cake-hole

Brendan Pimper writes: **"Cake-hole": I've seen this word crop up in a few places lately. It sounds old, but my (feeble) dictionary doesn't have it. Is it old? If not, can we pin the credit (blame) on anyone in particular?**

■ **Cake-hole** is a slang term for 'the mouth', and it's mainly British, which is probably why it doesn't show up in most American dictionaries, feeble or otherwise. The first documented appearance of the term is in 1943, in an small book of British military slang, although sources claim it was used in the RAF throughout World War II, and was originally a Yorkshire dialect term in use since at least 1914.

The term seems to have been popularized in such expressions as *shut your cake-hole!,* which is the only form I've seen in the United States.

The earliest American example, to my knowledge, is only in the 1970s, though it's likely that it was in use earlier.

■ ■ ■

call a spade a spade

psather@aol.com writes, **along with a number of other people asking the same basic question: What is the origin of the expression "call a spade a spade"? Is this a politically correct expression?**

■ Let's get two things straight here: first, the expression to **call a spade a spade** is thousands of years old and etymologically has nothing whatsoever to do with any racial sentiment. The second is that in spite of this, some people *think* it is a racial statement, and therefore it should be treated with some caution.

To **call a spade a spade,** which means, ironically for this discussion, 'to speak plainly and bluntly; to speak without euphemisms', is first found in ancient Greece (in its Greek form, of course). The exact origin is uncertain; the playwright Menander, in a fragment, said "I call a fig a fig, a spade a spade," but Lucian attributes the phrase to Aristophanes. Later, Plutarch notes that "The Macedonians are a rude and clownish people who call a spade a spade." (It is worth noting that the Greek word translated as "spade" seems actually to mean something like "bowl" or "trough"; the "spade" may be based on a Renaissance mistranslation. In this case the original expression was *to call a bowl a bowl,* and thus the "spade" expression is "only" 500, rather than 2,500, years old.)

After it first appeared in English in the sixteenth century, the saying became quite common, and was used in various forms and allusions. My favorite English example:

Cecily: When I see a spade I call it a spade.
Gwendolen: I am glad to say I have never seen a spade. It is obvious that our social spheres have been widely different.
                    —Oscar Wilde, *The Importance of Being Earnest*

Spade meaning 'a black person' is far more recent; it is first found in the early twentieth century. It derives from the black color of the suit of spades in a deck of playing cards.

Clearly our expression to **call a spade a spade** was very well established long before the word *spade* had any racial sense. However, today the word *does* have a racial sense. If the expression is assumed to be offensive, it should be used with caution even if there's no real basis for the assumption. This is not an unusual event. The word *bloody,* for example, does not derive from a profane oath such as "by our lady," but that's what people thought, and the word was once considered quite offensive.

The incorrect etymological assumption did not change the word's offensiveness. Not many people today would object to **call a spade a spade,** but some might, and one should at the very least be aware of that.

■ ■ ■

callipygian

Marvin writes: **I came across the word "callipygian" in a book about writing. The author was discussing words that interested him for their sound, meaning, whatever. This example struck a chord in me, but I can't figure out or find out what it means. Can you help?**

■ In the ranks of words that people think are really cool, **callipygian** stands rather high. It means 'having well-shaped buttocks'. Because of this excessively useful meaning, and its formal appearance, **callipygian** tends to be a word people remember, and one that appeals to word-obsessed authors: "Those dusky Afro-Scandinavian buttocks, which combine the callipygian rondure observed among the races of the Dark Continent with the taut and noble musculature of sturdy Olaf, our blond Northern cousin" (Thomas Pynchon, *Gravity's Rainbow*).

Callipygian is from Greek *kallipýgos*, where it was an epithet of Aphrodite. The word is formed from *kalli-* 'beautiful' (as in *calligraphy* 'beautiful writing'), and *pygé* 'buttocks'. It is sometimes found in the variant *callipygous*, which seems to have been a favorite of Aldous Huxley.

Callipygian is first found in English around 1800.

■ ■ ■

canard

Eva Yaa Asantewaa writes: **Please tell me the origin of the expression "canard" as in "It's a canard." Someone told me that "canard" means 'duck' in French. True?**

■ Yes, **canard** does mean 'duck' in French. The question here is whether the French word is related to the English word you're curious about, **canard** meaning 'a false or baseless, usually derogatory story, report, or rumor'. The answer is yes.

While the connection between ducks and false stories would seem to be an unusual one, the explanation is simply that a part of a French idiom has made it into English, and the idiom doesn't translate well. Just as *kick the bucket* meaning 'to die' wouldn't make sense if it were literally translated into another language, the French idiom doesn't make sense in English.

Canard means 'a false story; hoax' in French, which is where the English sense directly comes from. But the full phrase, in use since Middle French, is *vendre un canard à moitié* (literally "to half-sell a duck"), which means 'to cheat or swindle', since to half-sell a duck is the same as not selling it at all. And something—the duck—used for swindling can be considered a false or deceptive thing, which is how it all gets tied together. In English we preserve only the 'duck' word, without the rest of the idiom—which, as said, wouldn't make sense in English anyway.

This sense of **canard** is first found in English in the middle of the nineteenth century. The French word is based on a word meaning 'to quack; cackle', which is of imitative origin.

■　■　■

cash

Ross Olsen writes: **Cash. I know everyone wants it but where did the name come from? Is it related to the surname 'Cash' as in Johnny?**

■ The basics of the origin of **cash** are pretty well set, but there is some slight argument about specifics. The word is usually said to come from French *caisse,* which means 'a money box'. The earliest example of **cash** in English is 1596, in the standard sense 'money, esp. in the form of coin or banknotes'. The sense 'a money box' is found in English also, but very slightly later.

The only problem with this is the semantic connection between 'a money box' and 'money': the sense 'money' is an English innovation—it's not found in French—and getting from 'a money box' to 'money' is not necessarily obvious. So some have suggested that **cash** is a back formation from *cashier,* meaning 'a person in charge of cash at a bank or business', which is also first found in English in 1596, borrowed from French *cassier* 'a treasurer' (which itself derived from *caisse*). If *cashier* is 'a person in charge of cash', extracting **cash** itself is logical, more logical than a sense shift from 'money box' to 'money'. In either case, English is borrowing from related words in French. (Dutch may be involved as well, but there's no need to get into that here.)

The surname *Cash* is of English origin. It is a variant of *Case,* and is originally an occupational name (like *Smith*) for a person who makes boxes or chests—cases. Since the word *case* is ultimately related to the word that's the basis of **cash,** one could say that the surname *Cash* is related to **cash** 'money', but it's not a direct connection. *Johnny Cash,* by the way, is the singer's real name; if he had changed it from something else, it would be more likely to be a direct borrowing of **cash.**

■　■　■

catholic

Max Fine writes: **In conversation I heard, "As far as food is concerned, she has catholic tastes." I asked for clarification and was told that "catholic" in this context meant "narrow; limited." The person in question is a meat and potatoes person who avoids exotic cuisines. Didn't "catholic" used to mean just the opposite?**

■ It still does mean just the opposite. I haven't encountered this interpretation before, and I have to assume that this is just an error.

First, let's get the ecclesiastical uses out of the way as quickly as possible. In current American usage, and usually in Britain as well, *Catholic* with an uppercase *C* refers to the Roman Catholic Church. The history of the ecclesiastical use of *Catholic* is very complicated; the main definition *Random House Webster's College Dictionary* gives for these other senses is 'of or pertaining to the Christian Church that was formerly undivided or to all the modern orthodox churches that have kept the apostolic succession of bishops'. Suffice it to say, though, that unless you have a deep interest in theology, you can almost always take *Catholic* to mean *Roman Catholic* unless otherwise indicated.

The lowercase, nonecclesiastical use of **catholic** has always been in senses of the sort 'universal in extent; all-encompassing; wide-ranging'. A clear example from the essayist Charles Lamb: "I bless my stars for a taste so catholic, so unexcluding." Another example, from E. M. Forster's *Room with a View*: "For her taste was catholic, and she extended uncritical approval to every well-known name."

The example you cite is, as you say, the opposite of this usual meaning of the word **catholic.** This sense of 'narrow' should be regarded as an error, perhaps arising from the perceived rigidity in the Roman Catholic Church.

Catholic derives, through Late Latin, from Greek *katholikós* 'universal; general'.

■ ■ ■

cat's fur to make kitten britches

Dayna K. Shah writes: **When I was small, whenever I asked my father a question he did not want to answer, he would say "Cat's fur to make kitten britches," that is, "None of your business." I never found anyone else who had heard the expression until last month when I was visiting Pennsylvania, when I overheard someone using the same phrase. Have you ever heard this expression and do you have any insights as to its origin?**

The phrase **cat's fur to make kitten britches** is a joking nonsense reply to the question "What for?" or "What's that for?" It's a pun on the words *for* and *fur,* which are often pronounced identically.

There are other examples of this sort of wordplay in response to certain common questions: "So what?" "Sew buttons" and "Well?" "The well is deep" (or "dry") are two good ones.

I've only encountered the "cat's fur" phrase in response to questions ending with "for." I'd guess that your father used it only to answer those questions, but that you just assumed it was an expression he used to avoid answering in general, because you didn't know what the connection was.

Although hard evidence is lacking, the expression **cat's fur to make kitten britches** seems to date back to the nineteenth century. It isn't specifically associated with any region of the country.

■ ■ ■

chicanery

***Tim Ellis writes:* Can you please discuss the origin of "chicanery"?**

■ The word **chicanery** is one of those that is easy to explain superficially, but difficult to get to the bottom of.

Chicanery means 'the use of sly or evasive language, reasoning, etc. to trick or deceive', and also 'a tricky or deceitful maneuver; subterfuge'. Example from Literature: "There emerged gradually a picture of stupid chicanery and petty corruption for stupid and petty ends, conducted principally in hotel rooms into which bellboys whisked with bulging jackets upon discreet flicks of skirts in swift closet doors" (William Faulkner). It is a borrowing from French *chicanerie,* and is first found in the early seventeenth century. The French word is based on the verb *chicaner* 'to use chicanery; pettifog'.

(There's also an English word *chicane* 'to use chicanery' or as a noun equivalent to **chicanery** itself, but it is comparatively rare and is not found until the later seventeenth century. This later date is what suggests that the English **chicanery** is a borrowing from French *chicanerie,* rather than an English coinage based on English *chicane* and the *-ery* noun suffix.)

The ultimate origin of French *chicaner* is uncertain. It, like the English word, is first found in the early seventeenth century. The most likely explanation is that it is a borrowing of Middle Low German *schikken* 'to arrange; bring about'.

■ ■ ■

cleave

Charles Levine writes: **Why does "cleave" seem to mean two totally opposite things? You can cleave to something, to stick to it, but you can cleave something, meaning to cut it in two.**

■ There are two main ways that a word can have contradictory meanings. In one case, exemplified by *overlook,* a word can develop in two different directions semantically. One way is 'to look (something) over; scrutinize; peruse; supervise', and the other is 'to look over and thus not see; disregard'. Both of these meanings developed logically, but they are opposite. (Since this can be confusing, the result in English is that the sense 'scrutinize' is now somewhat rare. The word *oversee* is normally used instead to mean 'scrutinize' or 'supervise'—but *oversee* itself once had a sense 'disregard'!)

The second case is exemplified by **cleave:** two totally different, etymologically unrelated words have fallen together. One word is from the Old English *cleofian,* and means 'to adhere closely and faithfully; cling', as in "to cleave to one's principles." The other word is from the Old English *clēofan,* and means 'to split or divide by or as if by cutting blow', as in "to cleave wood," or figuratively as in "that issue will cleave the Republican Party." In this case, though the two words were originally distinct, natural language changes have made their forms in Modern English identical, so they appear to be the same word. This is a common process in English, but only attracts much notice when it results in such obviously divergent meanings.

Words with such contradictory senses are called "Janus words," after Janus, the Roman god who faces in opposite directions. Another example of a Janus word is *sanction,* which can mean either approval or penalty.

■　■　■

cock a snook

Abby Tannenbaum writes: **Have you ever heard of the term "to cock a snook"? A friend of mine thinks it's a variation on "to thumb one's nose" and asked me where I would look to see if that was true. I said I'd ask you.**

■ To **cock a snook** is primarily a British expression, which is why it is unfamiliar to most Americans. A *snook* is a derisive gesture made by putting one's thumb on one's nose and waving the fingers; to **cock a snook** is to make such a gesture. While this is the same action as "thumbing one's nose," it is an entirely different expression, not a variant.

To **cock a snook** is often used figuratively to mean 'to express contempt or derision', as in the made-up sentence "The Tory party cocked a snook at the idea of European unity." This figurative use parallels the American expression *to give one the finger*: this expression is found much earlier in the figurative sense 'to hold in contempt or derision' than in the literal sense 'to extend one's middle finger as an obscene gesture of contempt'.

Snook is first attested in the late eighteenth century. Its origin is unknown. It is unrelated to two different *snook*s, one referring to a type of fish, the other a Scottish word for 'a promontory', and is also unrelated to *snooker*, the game similar to billiards.

■   ■   ■

compleat

> *Raymond Chen writes:* **This one falls into the category of "A word that doesn't mean what you thought it did." A recent *Slate* article [which collects a series of earlier articles] is entitled *The Compleat O. J. by the Sea*. The usage here seems more in the sense of "complete; entire" rather than "expert; accomplished," which is what I thought. Does this word not mean what I thought it meant?**

■ No, **compleat** usually means what you thought it means. In this case it's being used, probably unintentionally, as a jocular spelling for *complete* in its usual sense.

The original, and usual, sense of *complete* is 'having all parts or elements; lacking nothing; entire; whole'. This sense is derived from Latin *complētus*, a participle of *complēre* 'to fill up; fulfill', which is made up of *com-* (as in *combine*, *compare*) and *plēre* 'to fill'.

Another sense of *complete* is 'highly skilled and accomplished in all aspects; expert'. This sense became archaic, but was revived in imitation of Izaak Walton's book *The Compleat Angler* (1653), a treatise on fishing. The title means 'the skilled angler', not 'a guide to fishing that has every possible detail', as it is often incorrectly interpreted today. When this sense of *complete* was revived, it was first used in titles equivalent to Walton's in both spelling and form: *The Compleat Batchelor* (1900), *Come and Get It! The Compleat Outdoor Chef* (1942), *The Compleat Imbiber* (1953), and others. It then began to be used in running text, where it maintained the archaic spelling **compleat** and the meaning 'accomplished; expert'.

When you look up **compleat** in dictionaries, they usually give a definition such as 'accomplished; expert' and an etymology noting that it's an archaic spelling of *complete* alluding to Walton's *Compleat Angler*. But my impression is that many, if not most, people think it's simply an archaic spelling of *complete* (in the sense 'whole; entire'), and use it accordingly. People don't understand what the word means in Walton's title. In the *Slate* title you cite, the word is clearly just a spelling variant of *complete*.

Depending on your philosophical bent, this is either an example of ignorance, or language change in progress.

■　■　■

conjunction beginning a sentence

mbasps@usa.nai.net writes: **At the risk of opening a PANDO-RA'S BOX, whatever happened to that ol' grammar rule about not beginning a sentence with a conjunction? Today's newspapers routinely use an incomplete sentence which begins with a conjunction instead of creating a phrase with the perfectly serviceable comma or semicolon. The words would read in the same way, so why use incomplete sentences?**

■ This question actually raises two issues. One issue is the validity of the traditional rule against beginning a sentence with a conjunction. The other, more important one is the use of incomplete sentences or thoughts.

The rule against beginning a sentence with a conjunction is an old and pervasive one, and most people remember having been taught it in grade school. But very few usage writers have recommended avoiding the practice; most seem to think that it's fine, for effect, as long as it's not overdone. H. W. Fowler goes so far as to call the rule an "ungrammatical piece of nonsense." The rule is probably meant to prevent examples such as "I have a cat. And a dog." When dealing with young children, it is easier to say "don't begin a sentence with 'and' or 'but'" than it is to say "Don't use incomplete sentences," which is a more difficult concept for the very young to understand.

Sentences beginning with "and" or "but" are found in English as early as the ninth century, in the *Old English Chronicle,* and such sentences can also be found in Shakespeare, the King James Bible, John Locke, Edmund Burke, Lord Macaulay, Charles Dickens, and others. There's nothing inherently wrong with the practice.

If a sentence is incomplete, or if so many sentences begin with "and" that its overuse is notable, that is indeed a problem, but one that should be treated on its own merits. The problem with "I have a cat. And a dog." is not that the part after the period begins with "and," it's that the part after the period is an incomplete sentence, and should be criticized for that reason. Also, the practice is rhetorically conspicuous, and if used in inappropriate contexts it can seem jarring. Thus, there's nothing ungrammatical about "I have a cat. And it is a nice cat." But it's inappropriately strong, since there's not enough disjunction to justify a new sentence. But consider this example: "I have a cat. And I'd do anything to save her life." It seems, to me at least, to be both grammatically and rhetorically appropriate. So if a newspaper does use an incomplete sentence, that is fitting grounds for criticism, whether it begins with "and" or not.

One final comment: in the construction you're discussing, semicolons are used to separate independent clauses of a compound sentence. An incomplete clause is as bad as an incomplete sentence. As far as the grammar is concerned, semicolons in these cases are no different from periods; they only change the emphasis. Thus changing a period to a semicolon would avoid an incomplete sentence but create an incomplete clause.

■ ■ ■

cool, groovy

A. *Sebastian Fox writes:* I interchangeably use the words "cool" and "groovy" for playful affirmation. My boss, who regularly uses "cool," has requested my not saying "groovy." Is there negative history associated to it?

■ Quite a bit, actually, and one of the more interesting things about both words is how their reception has varied over the years.

Cool is rather remarkable in the length of time it's been a common slang word. There are related senses of **cool** that date back to the early nineteenth century, but the current senses—'clever; sophisticated'; 'fashionable; stylish'; 'superlative; enjoyable; satisfactory', and others—began to appear among African-Americans in the 1920s, and were popularized in mainstream society by jazz musicians after World War II. Since then, it has been extremely common, it has consistently been in favor, and it has always been considered slang. The usual trend is for very common slang words to become dated—try saying that something's *swell* and you'll get the picture—or to become standard, rather than slang, words.

Groovy, despite a similar origin, has had a markedly different sociolinguistic history. The word is first recorded in the 1930s; it's derived from the phrase *in the groove.* **Groovy** was heavily used throughout the 1940s and 1950s, especially by jazz musicians. But the popular perception now ties it to the late 1960s, where it is considered one of the characteristic words of the hippie movement. **Groovy** today is most often used in derisive reference to the attitudes popularly associated with the hippies (although it's worth pointing out that it has made something of a comeback in the last few years).

There's a good chance that someone using **groovy** today without any suggestion of irony will be considered a bit foolish. There's no good reason why **cool** should still be an almost universally popular term indicating enjoyment while **groovy**—not to mention, say, *marvy, fab,* or *far out*—have fallen out of fashion, but that's the way things go.

■ ■ ■

coolie

Bao Chu writes: **The word "coolie" is used offensively to refer to an unskilled laborer in the Far East. The word has the same meaning in Vietnamese, though it is spelled differently. Please tell me the origin of the word.**

■ The word **coolie** is a borrowing from Hindi, one of the main languages of India, where it means 'a day laborer'. The Hindi word is probably borrowed from Tamil, another language of India. There is also the possibility that the word is influenced by *Kuli,* the name of a people from Gujarat who were often employed as laborers.

Coolie is first found in English in the early seventeenth century, but similar words are found in Portuguese and French in the sixteenth century, which suggests that the word was common among Europeans in India at that time.

Though **coolie** is usually used to refer to unskilled Indian or Chinese laborers, the word was first used in India; it was not applied to Chinese laborers until the mid-eighteenth century. I'm not familiar with Vietnamese, and can't explain the origin of the word in that language, but I'd assume that the Vietnamese word is either a coincidence, or a later borrowing from a European language. Vietnamese didn't have much influence on European languages in the sixteenth to seventeenth centuries, and the early association of the word with India shows that **coolie** cannot be a borrowing from Vietnamese.

The use of **coolie** to mean 'an Asian laborer' is not normally considered offensive as a word; it's more the practice of imperialism it suggests that can be offensive. At this point it is found almost exclusively in historical use. **Coolie** is, however, used as a racist term to refer to 'an Asian person' (with no suggestion of laboring), especially in South Africa, and this use is of course quite offensive.

■ ■ ■

cootie

Mitch Mitchell writes: **Last night my six-year-old asked me what "cooties" were because a boy in her class told her she had them. I remember saying similar things to girls in my elementary school thirty-five years ago. How long has this imaginary germ warfare gone on?**

■ It's hard to say, because this sort of thing doesn't get written down very much. But we can start at the beginning and cover what we can.

The earliest sense of **cootie** is 'a body louse'. This sense was especially common in World War I, and was popularized by journalistic accounts of soldier life. There aren't any known examples of the word before the war. Other figurative senses used in the war were 'a small vehicle' and 'a repulsive person'.

The origin of **cootie** is uncertain. It is often suggested that it derives from the Malay *kutu* 'a biting insect', and while this is both semantically and phonetically plausible, there's no evidence that the word was first used in Southeast Asia. Malay is a difficult language to propose without a good explanation of how the word got to the United States. If some early connection with Southeast Asia could be demonstrated, that would make a strong case, but otherwise we have to say "origin unknown."

The sense your young daughter is asking about has been defined by Jonathan Lighter in the *Random House Historical Dictionary of American Slang* as 'an imaginary microbe or repulsive quality thought to be transmitted by slovenly or obnoxious people', with "obnoxious people," at least in the elementary school context, meaning 'anyone of the opposite sex'. The earliest written example of this sense that anyone has discovered is in the 1970s, but that's unquestionably much later than its first use. Several of the examples refer to the 1950s or 1960s, and you're familiar with it from about 1962, so it seems very likely that the sense existed in the 1950s and probably earlier. Anyone doing research on children's folklore is invited to send in early examples of it, in return for which I'll give the informant a box of soap, courtesy of Random House, Inc.

■   ■   ■

cop

mmoldtha@expert.cc.purdue.ed writes: **I would like to know where the word "cop" comes from when used in phrases such as "cop a walk," "cop a plea," or "cop an attitude."**

■   The origin of **cop** in the broad sense of 'to catch; take' is unknown; there are two widely accepted but competing theories, neither of which is necessarily correct.

The very earliest relation in English is *cap,* in sense of 'to arrest' or 'to seize', found in two examples around 1600 and also found in Scots. The form **cop,** probably a dialectal variant, first appears in 1704 in a slangy sense, although there's a gap of 140 years until the next known example. The word becomes relatively common in the 1850s. This long gap could mean that the 1704 example is a coincidence, unrelated to the recent word; it more likely means that the word was not in common written use until the nineteenth century.

The two likely possible origins for *cap* are Dutch *kapen* 'to take or steal', of Germanic origin; or dialectal Old French *caper* 'to take', ultimately from Latin *capere*. There's no convincing reason for preferring either of these origins.

The noun **cop** 'a policeman', about which someone is bound to ask, is related to this. The 1844 example of **cop** means 'to arrest', and by the 1850s we had evidence of *copper* 'a policeman', which surely comes from this **cop** and the agentive suffix *-er.* **Cop** as a noun, also found in the 1850s, is just a clipping of *copper.* The word *copper* does not come from the fact that policemen had prominent copper (or brass) buttons on their uniforms, and **cop** does not come from "Constable On Patrol," or any other acronym.

Of the specific phrases you mention, *cop a plea* 'to plea-bargain' is first found in the 1920s; *cop a walk* 'to take a walk; go away' is first found in the 1950s; and *cop an attitude* 'to grow belligerent' is first found in the late 1960s.

■ ■ ■

copacetic

> *dxmatz@mail.wm.edu writes:* **An etymology question: Where does the word "copacetic" come from? The Kerouacs claim it for the Beat Generation, though the Fitzgeralds are fit to be tied, insisting that its birth was in the Jazz Age. I'd put my money on the latter, but even my unabridged *Random House* thinks its origin is "unknown." But you know better, n'est-ce pas?**

■ I wish I did know better.

The one thing not open to debate is the dating: **copacetic,** first found in 1919, and its variant *copasetty* were in reasonably frequent use by the 1920s. Examples of it from that period appear in novels, in the magazine *Variety,* in books about the criminal underworld, and in essays about African-American culture. So it dates at least from the Jazz Age, if not earlier—some later examples suggest that it was in use among blacks in the South in the late nineteenth century.

The origin, unfortunately, remains unknown. There have been various proposed etymologies, including origins in Louisiana French (Creole or Cajun), Italian, and most pervasively Hebrew (which is unlikely based on assorted phonological, semantic, and sociolinguistic grounds too complicated to discuss here). There's even been the ridiculous suggestion that it comes from a gangster phrase "the cop's on the settee," meaning 'the coast is clear'. None of these etymologies is accepted by scholars, and there's just not much more I'm able to say.

Here's the earliest example, from a 1919 novel:

" 'As to looks I'd call him, as ye might say, real copasetic.' Mrs. Lukins expressed this opinion solemnly . . . Its last word stood for nothing more than an indefinite depth of meaning."

■ ■ ■

could care less

Susan Ralston writes: How did "I could not care less" come to be replaced by "I could care less"—a virtually meaningless statement?

■ The phrase I **could care less** has been repeatedly condemned in recent years for its illogic: if you *could* care less, surely that means that you *do* care to an extent. But it's not meant to be taken literally. I **could care less** is sarcastic. When it is spoken, the stress is "I could CARE LESS," not the way one would stress a serious declaration. It's the same as saying "I really give a damn," when you don't, or "Nice move!" when someone makes a clumsy mistake—yes, they mean the opposite of what they say, but they're deliberate. The sarcasm allows you to express more disdain than simply saying "I couldn't care less." In addition, the phrase, whether with "couldn't" or with "could," is expressing indifference, so a strict interpretation is even less justified. Finally, idioms often fail to make sense—ever think hard about *head over heels?*

The expression *I couldn't care less* became common in England in World War II and was apparently based on an earlier catchphrase "I couldn't agree with you more." The "could" variant is first found in the mid-1960s and was being objected to by the 1970s.

■ ■ ■

crone

Chris Bonneu writes: I love your Web site. I just discovered it and couldn't get away from it for well over an hour. Now a question: isn't it true that the word "crone" comes from the Dutch and is related to the word "carrion"?

■ Yes, it is true, proving conclusively that reading this page makes you smarter.

OK, OK, it *might* be true. That is, **crone** is definitely related to *carrion,* but the Dutch connection is less certain.

Crone, which means 'a withered, witchlike old woman; hag', is first attested in Chaucer in the late fourteenth century (although there are earlier uses as a name). The word comes from the Anglo-French word *carogne,* itself from Old North French, which literally meant 'carrion' but also meant 'a cantankerous woman', and to which we'll return in a bit. The question is whether the English word **crone** was borrowed directly from the French word, or if it was borrowed through the Dutch word *croonie* (found in various spellings). This Dutch word meant 'an old ewe', and the English sense 'hag' could be a transferred use of the Dutch 'old ewe' sense. This is a plausible semantic change, and might be more likely than a shift directly from the French 'cantankerous woman' to 'hag'. The problem is that the sense 'an old ewe' isn't attested in English until the sixteenth century, two centuries after the 'hag' sense appears. So although it is very likely that the English sense 'an old ewe' is borrowed from the Middle Dutch word, it is less certain that the original English sense 'hag' is also borrowed from Dutch.

To restate the etymology, **crone** 'a withered old woman; hag' was borrowed from Anglo-French *carogne,* perhaps directly or perhaps by way of Middle Dutch *croonie* 'an old ewe'.

To return to the Old North French *carogne,* that word comes from an (assumed) Vulgar Latin form *caronia.* This *caronia* became, in a different dialect of French, *careine,* and this was the source for the Middle English word that gives us the modern *carrion.* So the same word went through French one way and came out **crone** and another way and came out *carrion.* The ultimate source of the Vulgar Latin word is the same root that gives us *carnivore.*

■ ■ ■

cut to the chase

Phil Mercurio writes: **Some online friends and I were wondering where the phrase "cut to the chase" originated. The best that we could come up with was that it had to do with movies, as in "cut to the chase scene" (get past the boring part). But looking up "chase" in the dictionary suggests that it might have to do with metalworking. What do you think?**

■ I think that your best guess is the right one.

Cut to the chase, which means 'get to the point; get on with it; get down to business', is unquestionably a reference to chase scenes in action movies.

The literal use—as a director's instruction to go to a chase scene—is quite old. A 1929 novel about Hollywood, for example, has "Jannings escapes . . . Cut to chase." The figurative use, which is now quite common, is fairly recent; it seems to date only from the late 1970s.

While there is a verb *chase* in metalworking, meaning 'to ornament (metal) by engraving' or 'to cut a screw thread with a chaser' (from French, ultimately related to the English word *case*), this is not connected to **cut to the chase.** The occurrence of *cut* and *chase* in the metalworking definition is coincidental.

■ ■ ■

darb

Michael Mele writes: "A real darb." My mom, born near Danville, IL in 1926, uses this phrase, which puzzles all of my friends now that I find myself using it as well. The expression is almost always used to describe unsplendid sartorial achievements. Striped pants with plaid shirts. Hillary's plaid coat and blue hat at the [first] Clinton inaugural (or was it the other way around?). Not always disheveled but inventively pulled together. Once upon a time a suit with tennis shoes would certainly have elicited this description, but fashions change. Any guidance would be appreciated. Is this a regionalism, or just one of those nonsense family words?

■ This was a fascinating question, because it seemed to be totally the opposite of what I expected. **Darb** was a fairly common slang term in the 1920s meaning 'a person or thing that is attractive, superior, or remarkable; "a peach"'. The word was used in both world wars, in several different showbusiness books and magazines, and by Ernest Hemingway in a letter. It seems to have been used through the 1950s, but then becomes rather rare.

I had never seen an example of it being used in a negative way, and was about to write it off as an idiosyncrasy, but I did manage to find a few examples. A word list from the 1930s gives **darb** as a "term of disparagement" and later in the same list as a synonym for "a stupid person." Since this negative sense is so poorly attested, I can only assume it's very rare. It probably arose as an ironic comment—any positive statement can be used disparagingly in the right context, and sometimes these uses acquire lives of their own.

The positive sense of **darb** is first found in 1915. A slightly earlier sense is 'money', which was used by criminals, and is a clipping of *darby,* used as underworld slang since the late seventeenth century.

■　■　■

D-Day

Rick Pike writes: What does the *D* in the World War II term "D-Day" stand for?

■ The *D* in **D-Day** stands, boringly enough, for "day." It was British military code for the day on which any military operation was planned to begin. The time of day for the start of an operation was called—as you will not be shocked to discover—*H-Hour*. These terms were in use during World War I. The specific use of 'June 6, 1944, the date of the invasion of Western Europe by the Allies in World War II', is the only one most people know about now.

■ ■ ■

dead

> *Charles Levine writes:* **How did "dead" get teamed up with other words in such pairs as "dead right," "dead reckoning," and "deadeye"? Collocations like "dead weight" bear an obvious relation to the meaning of "dead," but how did the other collocations with dead get their meaning?**

■ **Dead** is used in a vast number of figurative senses, some of which make sense and some of which are a bit more obscure. Following the *Oxford English Dictionary* for the development, the most obvious sense is 'deprived of life', the main sense, which has figurative uses such as 'asleep', 'numb or insensate', and '(of languages) no longer spoken'. From there we go to the sense 'deprived of a vital quality', such as '(of something normally burning) extinguished', as in "holding a dead cigar in his hand," '(of sound) muffled', '(of color) dull'. Then we have 'without vigor; lifeless; dull' ("it was a dead party").

These meanings are all fairly obvious developments. The next development is a larger one: broadly, 'absolute; complete; utmost', in reference to death being the final step in life. Your *dead reckoning,* or 'the determination of geographical position based on internal factors only, rather than astronomical navigation', is an example of the "absolute" meaning (it is not, as some have claimed, a shortening of *deduced reckoning*); others are *dead giveaway* and *dead ringer.* This sense is also used adverbially, meaning 'completely; absolutely; thoroughly', hence *dead right* and a number of other collocations, such as *dead perfect, dead broke,* and *dead serious.* Other examples maintain some of the original sense: *dead tired* and *dead drunk* both imply 'to an extent suggesting death'. *Deadeye* in the nautical sense 'a wooden disk with holes through which ropes are drawn' is a shortening of the earlier *deadman's eye,* which is probably suggested by the appearance of the disk.

With some exceptions, most of the obscure formations can be explained by applying the 'absolute; complete' meaning to the phrase.

■ ■ ■

deasil

Mia Shinbrot writes: **Would you tell me the derivation of the word "deosil"? It means 'moving in the same direction as the sun', i.e., 'clockwise.' Is it related to the Greek "deos," meaning 'god'? And I've been pronouncing it DAY-oh-sill; is this correct?**

■ The word **deasil,** as it is usually spelled, is one of the relatively few words in English that derive from Scottish Gaelic. It comes from the word *deiseil* (the form is the same in Irish Gaelic, but all the early examples of the word in English contexts are from Scotland, not Ireland), which also means 'clockwise'.

This *deiseil* derives from the Middle Irish words *dess,* which means 'right' or 'south', and *sel* 'turn' or 'time'. This first element *dess* is not related to any word for god (it would be *deus* in Latin; the Greek would be *theós*), but is related to Latin *dexter* 'right', which is the origin of the English *dexterous.*

Deasil is pronounced "DEE-zl," identical to *diesel,* the type of engine. The word is first found in the late eighteenth century.

Deasil is usually contrasted with *withershins* or *widdershins,* which means 'counterclockwise', and is of Germanic origin. *Withershins* is first found in the early sixteenth century and comes from elements meaning 'the opposite way'.

■ ■ ■

decimate

jswhite@win.bright.net writes: **Words seem to change their meanings over time. When we were reading Caesar's *Gallic Wars,* we knew that decimation was merely an object lesson. The guilty group would be lined up and every tenth man would be eliminated. A Web search for "decimate" yields many interesting examples, none referring to anything as small as 1/10. A search of the *N.Y. Times* was less fruitful; at least I haven't caught William Safire using "decimate" for complete destruction.**

■ Your search could lead you to two conclusions. One is that absolutely everyone is wrong and you can't find a single example of someone using **decimate** correctly. The other, which could follow from this, is that **decimate** doesn't mean what you think it means. Let's look at the history of the word.

As you note, the Latin word *decimāre* means 'to select by lot and kill every tenth person of', and it refers to the method of discipline the

Romans used to keep rebellious military units in line. The other nine-tenths of them, at least. It derives ultimately from *decem* 'ten'. The earliest sense of **decimate** in English, found about 1600, is a historical reference to this Roman practice.

The next sense, 'to exact a tithe of one-tenth from', applies chiefly to a tax that Oliver Cromwell levied on the defeated Royalists. This sense is of historical interest only.

The only sense that's ever been common in English is the figurative 'to destroy a great number, proportion, or part of', first found in the mid-seventeenth century. Despite repeated claims that this sense is erroneous, on the grounds that **decimate** should refer only to a destruction of one-tenth, that is how the word is used. In fact, it seems to be the *only* way the word is used; despite the insistence of various usage critics, a real example of **decimate** meaning 'to destroy one-tenth of' has never to my knowledge been found in actual running text.

For reasons that have never been clear to me, some people are quite strongly opposed to this particular figurative sense, without being equally bothered by other words whose meanings have changed over the past two thousand years. The opinion of H. W. Fowler on this issue is notable. Fowler, we recall, is the generally conservative English usage writer whose *Modern English Usage* (1926) is the most important English usage guide ever published. Fowler was a classicist by training, and sometimes objected quite strongly to English words that he thought violated principles of Latin or Greek. For instance, he thought the innocuous word *amoral* was "inexcusable" (it combines a Greek prefix with a Latin stem), and *bureaucrat* was "so barbarous that all attempt at self-respect in pronunciation may perhaps as well be abandoned." But Fowler calls the figurative use of **decimate** "natural" and does not object to it; certainly he wouldn't have hesitated to offer criticism of the word if he felt it were even slightly deserved.

As far as the English use of the word is concerned, the important aspect of the ancient Roman practice of decimation was not the exact proportion of people killed, but the arbitrary viciousness of the punishment. There is nothing wrong with using **decimate** to mean 'to destroy a great number, proportion, or part of', and there never has been. It is worth keeping in mind that some people will disagree with this statement, but in my opinion there are no firm grounds for doing so.

It is also worth mentioning that some critics (Fowler included, here) warn against **decimate** used with specific numbers ("the disease decimated 70 percent of the population"). This does not seem to be a common usage in English.

■   ■   ■

defenestrate

> *Spontaneous Bob writes:* **I've been searching for the history behind "defenestration" (my all-time favorite word) meaning roughly "to throw or be thrown through a window." Please help me lest I defenestrate (???) myself out of frustration.**

■ **Defenestrate,** which means exactly 'to throw out of a window', is one of *everyone's* all-time favorite words. It's the epitome of the "hard word" that many people know, everyone finds amusing, and lends itself to all sorts of good use.

For the key to the word *defenestration,* we must look at political history, a subject largely untouched in these pages. In 1617, Catholic officials in Bohemia closed Protestant chapels that were under construction, despite guarantees of religious freedom that the Protestants had been granted under an earlier emperor. A group of Protestants called an assembly, and two imperial commissioners were found guilty of violating the guarantee of religious rights and were thrown from a window of the palace in Prague. This event, on May 23, 1618, became known as the *Defenestration of Prague,* and touched off the Thirty Years' War, as Protestants from Bohemia and neighboring lands joined in a revolt against the authority of the Hapsburg Emperor Ferdinand II.

It is a little-known fact that the two defenestrated commissioners were booted out of a low window and suffered no injuries. Nonetheless, it's a great story, and since we will like our history enlivened with Great Stories, the Defenestration of Prague is one that many of us were forced to learn about in high school. That's why the term is familiar to most people.

Although **defenestrate** has been used for centuries referring to this event, the current, somewhat jocular use seems to have become popular relatively recently (early twentieth century). It is still frequent, especially in the figurative sense 'to take harsh action against; fire (a person) (from a job)', etc. Two examples: "The rapper went on to make the odd declaration 'I don't throw babies out of windows,' no doubt prompting nationwide police-data-base searches for unsolved baby defenestrations" (*New York,* 1994), and the useful figurative "He and Ed Fancher were defenestrated by Clay Felker in 1974" (Nat Hentoff, in the *Village Voice,* 1996).

Defenestrate comes from Latin, formed from *de-* 'out of; away from' and *fenestra* 'a window' (French *fenêtre*). It is first found in English in 1620, right after the Prague example.

■   ■   ■

deipnosophist

> *A whole bunch of people have written:* **OK, just what does "deipnosophist" mean anyway? And where's it from?**

■ *The Deipnosophists* was the title of a Greek work in fifteen books (of which ten survive in full) by Athanaeus, a grammarian who lived around 200 C.E. It was set as a symposium in which a number of wise men sit at a dinner table and discourse learnedly on everything from literature, art, and politics to the food in front of them.

The word **deipnosophist** is derived from Greek elements meaning 'meal' and 'wise man'. The usual use of the word in English is 'a person who is an adept conversationalist at table', though it is occasionally used to mean simply 'a gastronome'. I guarantee that if you use it in any way, no one will challenge you on what you say it means.

The work by Athanaeus is available in an edition in the Loeb Classics series, if you should get a hankering to plow through seven volumes of third-century dinner party chitchat. It's really good, actually. Give it a shot.

■ ■ ■

dickens

Several people have written: **What is the origin of the expression "the dickens," and what exactly does it mean?**

■ **Dickens** is used, usually following *the,* as a euphemism for "the devil" in mild oaths having various forms.

The earliest example known is found in Shakespeare: "I cannot tell what the dickens his name is" *(The Merry Wives of Windsor).* Some other examples to show you the range of use: "What a dickens is the Woman always a whimpring about Murder for?" (John Gay, *The Beggar's Opera*); "What the dickens is wrong with you?" (Stephen Crane, *The Red Badge of Courage*); "How the dickens could he let the public know how truly great his president was?" (Sinclair Lewis, *Our Mr. Wrenn*); "I thought the vein or whatever the dickens they call it was going to burst though his nose" (James Joyce, *Ulysses*); "That hurt like the dickens!" (my father, a few weeks ago).

Dickens is almost certainly an application of *Dicken,* a diminutive of *Dick,* itself a diminutive of the male given name *Richard,* with **dickens** and *devil* having the same initial sound. Compare the slightly later *deuce* used in the same way, or, for another example of a euphemistic use of a name with the same initial sound, the substitution of *Jehoshaphat* for *Jesus.* Another example of an *altered* name as a euphemism for "devil"-type words is *Sam Hill,* as in "Who in Sam Hill are you?," an Americanism based on **Sol(o)mon** as an oath and *Hill* as a euphemism for *Hell.*

■ ■ ■

dicty

Dean Kinter writes: I was sitting at home reading the James Baldwin short story "Sonny's Blues" and came across the word "dicty" used as an adjective. Other than as a Greek prefix to the name of several cellular slime molds, I can't find a meaning. Apparently it's Harlem slang for strict, uptight, conventional, or some such. Can you shed any light on the question? Apparently it hasn't survived into today's slang of rap music.

■ Hey, never underestimate the power of slime molds on street slang.

Dicty, though quite common at one time, is now rather rare, and when it does appear it's usually in historical reference. There are three main senses: '(of people) wealthy or fashionable', and by extension 'haughty; conceited; snobbish', which is the most common sense, and then '(of things) attractive; fancy; pleasing'.

Dicty, almost exclusively black slang, is first found in the early 1920s, and was frequent throughout the Harlem Renaissance. The word occurs in works by Claude McKay, Countee Cullen, Arna Bontemps, and Carl Van Vechten; later users include James Baldwin, Billie Holiday, and Duke Ellington.

The origin of **dicty,** sometimes spelled *dickty,* is unknown. I'd bet DOLLARS TO DOUGHNUTS, though, that it's unrelated to the scientific prefix *dicty-* 'net', derived from a Greek word meaning 'to throw', and found, as you say, in the names of families or genera of various slime molds, fungi, spiders, lungworms, brown algae, and other nasties.

■ ■ ■

didgeridoo

Oliver Hutto writes: What is a dijeridu? How do you spell it?

■ The **didgeridoo,** to use its most common spelling, is a type of musical instrument used by Australian aborigines. It is, in effect, a long hollow wooden or bamboo trumpet that produces low resonant sounds.

The didgeridoo has become popular recently among musicans who use it in non-Australian music, and examples of it can be found in various mainstream recordings.

The word is most commonly spelled **didgeridoo,** although many other spellings are found, including *didjeridoo, didjeridu, dijeridoo, dijeridu, dijiridu,* and others.

The word is a borrowing from Yolngu, an Australian aboriginal language group spoken in the Northern Territories. It first appears in English around 1920.

■ ■ ■

(the) die is cast

Andrew Kuten writes: **In today's paper, Sylvester Stallone says of his continuing career as an "action picture" star, "The die has been cast for me." What do we say when we use that cliche—the gambling cube has been thrown? or the mold has been set? I've heard both explanations, and they both sound plausible. But I've never seen a definitive definition or origin.**

■ The expression **the die is cast,** which means 'a decisive step has been taken; an irrevocable decision has been made; fate has taken charge', is a reference to the gambling cube. A derivation from the setting of a mold is indeed sensible, but in this case demonstrably wrong.

The person we're quoting, in translation, when we say that **the die is cast** is none other than Julius Caesar, who, according to Suetonius, phrased it as *iacta alea est,* although one also sees *alea iacta est* and versions where *iacta* is spelled *jacta.* (We won't even get into Plutarch, who has Caesar saying it in Greek.)

Caesar is supposed to have said this in 49 B.C.E. at the Rubicon, the river that separated Cisalpine Gaul, which Caesar ruled, from Italy, which Caesar was invading to start a civil war. Successfully, I might add. His point was that once you've decided to gamble, you must abide by the result, good or bad. (This belief, taken to an extreme, is delightfully explored in the remarkable '70s cult novel *The Dice Man,* by Luke Rheinhart, which is really worth checking out.)

The other linguistic result of this river crossing is that *to cross the Rubicon* is also used to mean 'to take a decisive, irrevocable step'. And one's *Rubicon* is the point at which one has to make an important and irrevocable decision.

■　■　■

dis

Jim Gallant writes: **I've just discovered your wonderful Web site from a reference in *Slate* magazine. Have you discussed the word "diss" ('disparage') yet? It's not included in the latest dictionaries, and its origin is not clear to me.**

■ The verb **dis** in the sense 'to disparage; belittle' or 'to show disrespect to; affront' may not be in most of the "latest" dictionaries, but it has been in the *Random House Webster's College Dictionary* since 1991.

Dis is a clipping of a word beginning with *dis-,* probably *disrespect,* but perhaps *disparage* or *dismiss.* It is a slang term originally used in rap music; the first examples are found in the early 1980s, and it started to achieve mainstream popularity by the late 1980s, peaking around 1990 or so. There is also a noun **dis,** meaning 'an expression of disrespect'.

The past and participial forms are *dissed* and *dissing.* **Dis** itself is found in that spelling or as *diss;* we give **dis** as the main variant because of its origin in words spelled *dis.*

■ ■ ■

disgruntle

Mike James writes: **Recently in the news I've heard stories of disgruntled former employees taking hostages. "Disgruntled" seems to be used to describe people much more upset than it would have been used for in the past. Where does it come from and why don't we hear of people who are "gruntled"?**

■ **Disgruntle,** which almost always appears as the participial adjective *disgruntled,* means 'to put into a state of sulky dissatisfaction; make discontent'. It has more force than simply 'upset'; the ongoing resentment is the main factor—which may be why the word has been common recently.

Disgruntle is first recorded in the late seventeenth century. It is based on the real word *gruntle* 'to grumble; complain', which is the frequentative of *grunt* in its usual sense. A "frequentative," also called "iterative," is a verb form that expresses repetition of the action of the verb; the *-le* suffix is often frequentative in English. Other examples are *sparkle* and *suckle. Gruntle* is found around 1400 meaning 'to grunt', and around 1600 meaning 'to grumble', which is the sense used in **disgruntle.**

The *dis-* prefix in **disgruntle,** which in English usually has negative meanings *(disarm, disconnect, disobey),* functions here as an intensive. Though rare, *dis-* has this meaning in a few other words, such as *disembowel.*

Gruntled itself, meaning 'content; pleased', does exist in English, but only as a back formation from *disgruntled* as if the *dis-* were indeed a negative prefix, which it's not, as we've just seen. It is almost always found in jocular or facetious uses. The classic example, from Jack Winter's hysterically funny piece in The *New Yorker* wherein Winter drops negative prefixes from words that usually take them: "It had been a rough day, so when I walked into the party I was very chalant, despite my efforts to appear gruntled and consolate."

■ ■ ■

dog, v.

Andrew Kuten writes: **What does it mean to dog somebody?**

■ There are a lot of *possible* meanings for **dog** as a verb—not all of which can be discussed on a family Web site—but the most common sense is 'to follow or track like a dog, especially with hostile intent'. A rather clear example from Shakespeare: "I have dogged him like his murderer" *(Twelfth Night)*.

This sense of **dog** is first found in the early sixteenth century, and is still widely current. Another common sense is the figurative use 'to harass' (that is, to harass as if by setting dogs on someone). Some other related senses include 'to follow close' and 'to chase with a dog'.

There are various parallels for this type of development. The closest is the use of *hound* in the same way, which is also first found in the early sixteenth century. A more recent example is *bird-dog,* from the twentieth century. You'll find, in fact, that many animal names can be used as a verb in the rough sense 'to behave like (the specified animal)', so you can *cat* around, *bulldog* someone to the ground, and *hawk* a person's every move.

A few other verbal uses of *dog* are '(used as a mild oath)' (e.g., "dog it!" or "dog my cats!"); (in the phrase *dog it*) 'to do something lazily; shirk; loaf'; and 'to taunt or tease'.

■ ■ ■

dollars to doughnuts

Kelly Bahmer-Brouse writes: **Where did the phrase "dollars to doughnuts" come from? This has driven me crazy for years, and none of the standard reference sources have helped. (None of the nonstandard ones have, either.)**

■ **Dollars to doughnuts** means 'most certain' or 'most assuredly'. It comes from the idea of betting. Betting a dollar to a half-dollar, for instance, means that you're giving 2 to 1 odds—you're willing to risk a dollar to win only a half-dollar. Being willing to bet dollars against doughnuts (viewed essentially worthless) means that you're totally confident that you're right, so confident that you'll bet money against practically nothing.

The expression is also found in a number of variants, including *dollars to buttons, dollars to dumplings, and dollars to cobwebs,* each of these objects also being considered worth little or nothing.

Dollars to doughnuts as an adjectival or adverbial phrase is first found in the late nineteenth century in America. The first explicit reference to betting is not found until the 1920s, in a story by "Ellery Queen"—"I'll bet dollars to doughnuts Field played the stock market or the horses"—but betting is unquestionably the origin of the expression.

■ ■ ■

(the) dozens

fredgm@pacbell.net writes: **A phrase from Black English that I heard going some twenty-five years or so ago, was "doing the dozens," meaning to exchange (mostly) friendly insults, in a kind of rap rhythm. How the heck does "dozens" play into this?**

■ **The dozens** is a game, especially common among urban blacks, of exchanging insults, usually about the mother of the opponent. Skilled playing of **the dozens** displays verbal improvisation of great originality and wittiness. It also requires a thick skin: you lose the contest if you get upset. The game is often in a stylized, rhythmic form, and **the dozens** is considered one of the percursors of rap music. Some excellent examples of **the dozens** can be seen in the 1992 movie *White Men Can't Jump.*

    The dozens is usually used in such phrases as "to play the dozens" or "to do the dozens"; the form *dirty dozens* is also common. The word dates at least to the 1910s, but the game was probably played considerably earlier. There are examples of this type of game in several other cultures; in sixteenth-century Scotland, a *flyting* was a battle between poets who exchanged abusive poems; and in the late nineteenth century, American cowboys engaged in "cussing contests," where a saddle would be awarded to the most abusive participant.

    The origin of the term is unknown. Some conjectures: it refers to a throw of 12 in craps, twelve being a difficult number to match; the original form had twelve verses, each one referring to a different sex act; and inferior slaves were sold in lots of twelve, so the number 12 itself came to mean 'wretched; inferior.' None of these hypotheses has any solid proof, and the origin is likely to remain a mystery.

    Some other terms for this type of stylized insulting are *capping, jiving, joaning* (or *joning*), *sounding, snapping,* and *signifying.*

■ ■ ■

dram

Joseph C. Kim writes: **The lyrics of my favorite Bob Dylan song, "Moonshiner," has the word "dram" in it: "The whole world's a bottle, and life's but a dram." My dictionary says that it means a small amount of something to drink, but I'm curious as to its origin.**

■ **Dram** has two meanings referring to fluid measure: one is the specific one, 'a fluid dram', equal to 1/8 of a fluid ounce. The far more common meaning is the broader 'a small drink of liquor'.

These meanings derive from the use of **dram** as a unit of weight, equal to 60 grains, or 1/8 of an ounce, in apothecaries' weight (3.88 grams metric) or 1/16 of an ounce in standard avoirdupois weight (1.77 grams metric; apothecaries' and avoirdupois ounces are not identical).

The original weight from which this measure comes is the ancient Greek *drachma* (in Greek *drachmḗ*), which was both a unit of currency and a unit of weight. *Drachma,* going through Latin and French, ended up in fourteenth-century English as *dragme.* Since this is somewhat difficult to pronounce, it was phonetically reduced to the form **dram,** which is what we use today.

The form *drachma,* which now is used only to refer to the Greek weight or coin, was reborrowed in the sixteenth century. The Greek word literally means 'handful', and is derived from the verb *drássesthai* 'to grasp'.

■ ■ ■

dribs and drabs

George Bredehorn writes: **Why do things that trickle come in "dribs and drabs"?**

■ Because it sounds good. Really.

Both **drib** and **drab** mean 'a small quantity or amount'; the phrase **dribs and drabs**, which first appears in the nineteenth century, means 'small and usually irregular amounts'. The earlier word is **drib**, which is first attested in the early eighteenth century. **Drib** is probably a back-formation from *driblet* or *dribble,* both of which come from the verb **drib** 'to fall or flow in small amounts; trickle'; **drib** is probably an onomatopoeic variant of *drip.*

The word **drab** is first recorded in the early nineteenth century. It is probably a gradational variant of **drib**, that is, one based on a change in the vowel.

The emphatic use of two words with a similar meaning is common in English. Established phrases such as *time and tide* ("tide" having an archaic sense equivalent to "time") or *without let or hindrance* are part of our stock vocabulary.

More relevant here is the use of repeated or reduplicated forms. When a compound consists of a base word repeated with a difference in the vowel, it is called a *gradational compound.* These compounds are old and well attested in English; examples are *ding-dong,* where both words represent the sound of a bell; *mishmash,* based on *mash; tip-top,* based on identical meanings of *tip* and *top;* and *wishy-washy,* based on *washy.* **Dribs and drabs,** therefore, while considerably more recent than these other examples, represents the same type of word formation.

■ ■ ■

driveway and parkway

rcarter@virtu.sar.usf.edu writes: **I certainly may need help with words. But first, to check out your credentials. Why do we drive on a "parkway" and park on a "driveway"?**

■ One of the classic illustrations of the supposed illogic of English is the fact that we *park* on a **driveway** but *drive* on a **parkway.** There are two explanations for this particular conundrum: (1) the meanings of words change over the years, and (2) the same word can have more than one meaning.

A **driveway** originally *did* refer to a road you drive on: a driveway was a private road leading from a main road to a house. (Imagine the stereotyped long, winding driveway leading up to a huge manor house and you'll get the idea.) But nowadays, when driveways are thirty feet long and lead only to a garage—if anything—their purpose is just to store cars next to a house. That's why we park on driveways.

A **parkway,** in contrast, was (and still is) a thoroughfare meant to suggest a park: rather than just being a plain road, it has trees planted on the sides or on a median divider, it's usually smaller than other highways, it twists and turns—a scenic road, in short. So the *park* part of **parkway** is the word meaning 'a nice-looking piece of land in a natural state', *not* the word meaning 'to leave (a vehicle) in a place'. And that's why we drive on parkways.

■ ■ ■

druthers

Maria Boylan writes: **I would like to query the origins of the word "druthers." I've heard it used in the following context: "If I had my druthers, I'd go fishing." Am I right in assuming that it is connected to the phrase "I'd rather . . ."? Am I also right in assuming that it is peculiar to the American Midwest? (I am just as interested in finding out where it originated and where it is still used—if at all—as I am in finding out its etymology.)**

■ The word **druthers** means 'choice; preference' and is almost always found in the phrase "to have one's druthers." The word, as you guess, comes from a vowel alteration of *'d rather,* a contraction of "[I, he, etc.] would rather."

In its early history, **druthers** was primarily a southernism. Now the word, which is indeed still in use, is quite widespread. It may even be best to consider it "informal" or "colloquial," since it can't really be attached to any particular dialect area. It does not seem to have ever been peculiar to the Midwest. Another interesting point is that, according to the *Dictionary of American Regional English*, **druthers** is used more frequently among speakers having a college education.

Druthers is first found in the United States in the late nineteenth century.

■ ■ ■

dudgeon

George Bower writes: **I read a column the other day— probably George Will in the** *Washington Post***—in which he referred to certain persons being "in high dudgeon," i.e., a state of angry indignation. Can you tell me the origin of the word "dudgeon"? And is there a term for people who use uncommon words when better-known words would serve the same purpose?**

■ Wait—let me get this straight. George Will referred to *someone else* as being in high **dudgeon**? That's a good one. George Will is the archetype of high **dudgeon**, it seems, what with all of his "The radicalism of the 1960s is what caused the Great Depression"-style rhetoric.

Ahem. Anyway, **dudgeon** means, as you say, something like 'a feeling of offense or resentment; anger; indignation', and is almost always found in the phrase "in high dudgeon." The word is first recorded in the late sixteenth century.

I cannot, unfortunately, tell you the origin of the word. It is yet another in that large category labeled "origin unknown." One can make a few observations: an *-udgeon* ending is found in some other words *(bludgeon, curmudgeon)*—which are also of uncertain origin.

Perhaps more significant, there is another English word **dudgeon,** which means 'a type of wood [unknown, but sometimes assumed to be boxwood] used to make the handles of daggers', and hence 'a dagger-handle made of such wood' and 'a dagger' itself. This word is found most famously in *Macbeth*: "I see thee still;/And on thy blade and dudgeon gouts of blood." This **dudgeon,** first found in English in the early fifteenth century, is a borrowing from Anglo-French, although the ultimate origin is unknown. There is no obvious conjecture tying the 'anger' word to the 'hilt-wood' word. One proposal has been that a phrase such as "(take) in dudgeon" is meant to refer to the hand on a dagger-handle, with one grabbing a dagger in anger, but this proposal has not been generally accepted.

As for a term for people who use overly complicated words, it really depends on your point of view. "Pedant" or "show-off" are possibilities, but so is "great writer." Defenders of using complicated words usually cite among their justifications: that the word in question was not something the writer considered difficult; that the word was the only one, or the best one, that expressed what the writer wanted to say; that the word was especially appropriate on other stylistic grounds (e.g., it sounded "literary"); that the writer enjoys challenging the reader by using unusual words. In the case of **dudgeon,** I'd say that while it's not a very common word, it's certainly not so rare that its use should be considered unusually noteworthy.

Especially coming from George Will.

■　■　■

duff

terramere@aol.com writes: **The expression "off my duff" is used in a children's song. What is a "duff"?**

■ A **duff** is what you sit on; it means 'the buttocks or rump'. It's often used in the phrase *to get off (one's) duff* 'to get moving; become active', but occurs in other phrases as well.

The origin of this **duff** is unknown. There are some other **duff** words: **duff** meaning 'dough', and 'a dessert made with dough', which comes from a dialectal pronunciation of *dough* (compare *laugh* and *enough*); there's **duff** as British thieves' slang meaning 'something worthless or counterfeit' and hence adjectivally 'worthless; of poor quality', of unknown origin; there's *duffer* 'a swindler or hawker of contraband', from this last **duff** and *duffer* 'an incompetent person' which may be of different origin again; and others. While people have drawn various conjectures on the relationship between various of these **duff** words, no one has any good idea where **duff** 'the buttocks' comes from.

This sense of **duff** is first attested about 1840, in several bawdy English music hall songs which I can't quote on a family Web site.

■　■　■

dukes

Don Willmott writes: **In the wake of the recent Tyson/Holyfield fight: Why are fists called "dukes"?**

■ As with so many slang terms, no one is entirely sure. There is one widely accepted theory, but it raises some large questions that need to be answered.

The word **dukes** referring to the hands is first recorded in an American slang dictionary published in 1859. This dictionary is heavily derivative of several earlier English dictionaries, but the word does not appear in its English sources. **Dukes** is also found in an American boxing memoir in about the same year.

The usual explanation for **dukes** bases the word in rhyming slang. Rhyming slang, we may recall, is a style where a word is replaced by a phrase that rhymes with the word; often the rhyming element of the phrase drops out. Thus *apples and pears* is rhyming slang for *stairs,* and often the "pears" drops out, leaving *apples* as a synonym for "stairs." Though rhyming slang is very common in certain parts of England and Australia, it has never held much appeal in America; the only familiar example is *raspberry* 'a sputtering sound made with an extended tongue, used to indicate derision or contempt', based on *raspberry tart* as rhyming slang for *fart.*

Since the rhyming phrase doesn't have to have any connection to the word it rhymes, rhyming slang is a convenient way to explain the origin of otherwise inexplicable words. In the case of **dukes,** there is at least a plausible source: the well-attested rhyming slang *Duke of York* 'a fork' (that is, the eating utensil; there are other interpretations of *Duke of York,* including 'walk' and 'cork', but these don't need to concern us). The argument goes that **dukes** is used for "forks," *forks* is an early-nineteenth-century term for 'fingers', and *fingers* represent the hands. Thus, **dukes** are hands.

This theory has two main problems. First, it's a few steps from "Duke of York" = 'a fork' to **dukes** = 'hands', and though these steps are plausible, we have to take them all on faith. Second, **dukes** is first attested in America, and rhyming slang was not a big part of mid-nineteenth-century American slang. It's possible that we've just missed earlier English examples, or that it is an American development, but we have some explaining to do either way.

Other theories are that **dukes** is derived from a Romani (Gypsy) word, which is somewhat plausible—*dooking* 'fortune-telling' (also 'palmistry') is found in the nineteenth century and the spelling *dook* was fairly common for 'hand'—or that it's just a metaphorical application of the standard *duke* 'powerful nobleman'.

■ ■ ■

eighty-six

Jim Kohli writes: I've got a friend who says that the phrase "eighty-six" means something like 'to discard' (perhaps with some amount of prejudice). My dictionary says that the slang expression means only to refuse to serve an undesirable in a restaurant. Do you know if this expression has acquired more widespread meaning, and/or the etymology of this expression?

■ Yes, **eighty-six** is used in the widespread sense 'to reject; discard', among other senses. The etymology is a more difficult question.

The earliest related use of **eighty-six** was as a restaurant code word meaning that an item was out of stock. Number-codes were widely used in restaurants, both for brevity and secrecy. Some other codes were *eighty-two*, an order for two glasses of water, *ninety-five*, which meant that a customer was walking out without paying, and *ninety-nine*, which meant that the head soda fountain manager was around. **Eighty-six,** first attested in the 1930s, was extended in the 1940s to mean 'an undesirable customer who is to be denied service'.

By the 1950s, **eighty-six** was used as a verb in various senses, including 'to eject or dismiss', 'to stop or quash', and 'to discard'. (A specific sense 'to murder' is first attested in the 1970s.) These senses are all common to an extent today, and most good dictionaries, including the *Random House Webster's College Dictionary,* include them.

The ultimate origin of **eighty-six** is unknown. The most widely accepted theory is that **eighty-six** is rhyming slang for *nix*, which has various meanings like 'no', 'nothing', and 'to reject' (as in the famous, and often misquoted, headline in *Variety* in 1935, "Sticks Nix Hick Pix"). As discussed under DUKES, however, rhyming slang has never been very popular in the United States. Another problem is that it doesn't account for the origin of other numeric codes such as those given above, which would seem to be related to **eighty-six.** Another theory connects it to Chumley's Bar, an establishment at *86* Bedford Street in New York, but this would seem to be a coincidence. There are still other theories, some based on explanations that a certain place (as a specific restaurant, or a ship) only had room for eighty-five people, so the eighty-sixth person was rejected, but these are largely conjectural with little or no supporting evidence.

■　■　■

enquire, inquire

Michelle Williams writes: **Perhaps it's only because I've read entirely too many British novels, but what the hell difference is there between "enquire" and "inquire?" Being the snob that I am, I always use the former. The latter just doesn't seem right anymore. Are they really the same, and will I ever overcome my need to be pretentious and smug?**

■ The difference between **enquire** and **inquire** is that one is spelled with an *e-* and the other is spelled with an *i-*. That's really about it.

In America, **inquire** is notably more common than **enquire,** which typically appears in more formal uses; in England, they're about even. The main American dictionaries all give the former as the preferred spelling but do not consider the latter to be wrong. But note that several British sources, including the Oxford dictionaries and the generally conservative H. W. Fowler, also recommend the spelling **inquire.**

Both forms developed from the Latin *inquīrere* 'to search out; investigate'. This word came into Old French as *enquerre* and was then borrowed into Middle English as *enqueren,* thus making the *e-* form the first one in English. In the fifteenth century, the word was consciously respelled to conform it to the spelling of the original Latin word. But the *e-* spelling continued to be used in English, and that's the situation we're in today.

If you want to adopt the more common American spelling, and not sacrifice your pretension and smugness, you can vigorously claim that the **inquire** spelling, by alluding to Latin, is more conservative. If you want to maintain your current state, and justify your resulting pretension and smugness, you can vigorously claim that that the **enquire** form, being the original form used in English, is more conservative. The choice is yours.

■ ■ ■

ensure, insure, assure

Cary & Gail Porter write: **When does one use "ensure" and when does one use "insure"? Are they interchangeable?**

■ The distinction, if any, between **insure** and **ensure** is one of the frequent usage issues that gets raised. We'll thrown in **assure,** too, just to round things out.

These three words all mean, in the broadest sense, 'to make certain'. Two distinctions are *usually* observed: **Assure** is used of people, in the sense 'to declare earnestly so as to guarantee confidence': "She assured him that she was serious." And in the financial sense 'to guarantee property or people against risk', **insure** is the most common word.

In general senses, however, **insure** and **ensure** are largely inter-changeable in American English: "My recommendation will insure/ensure you get a good table." The main question, then, is which word to use in these general senses. Many usage writers suggest that **insure** be restricted to financial uses and **ensure** be used for the other senses. If you are going to follow a rule, this might as well be the one.

■ ■ ■

excogitation

Mark Sanders writes: **I was wondering if "exocogitation" is a word, and if it is, what does it mean and what are its origins.**

■ "Exocogitation" is not a word I've seen before, but **excogitation** certainly is, albeit a somewhat uncommon one.

Excogitation means 'the act of thinking or studying intensely', and hence 'the result of thinking; a contrivance'. A couple of examples: "The labour of excogitation is too violent to last long; the ardour of enquiry will sometimes give way to idleness or satiety" (Samuel Johnson, *Rasselas*); "To the excogitation of this problem, [he] had devoted many anxious hours" (Dickens, *Our Mutual Friend*).

Excogitation is from *excogitate* 'to think out; devise; study intensely', derived ultimately from Latin *excogitare.* It is first found in English in the early sixteenth century. A slightly more common related English word, also from the early sixteenth century, is *cogitation* 'reflection; meditation', ultimately from Latin *cogitāre* 'to cogitate; powder; meditate.'

■ ■ ■

extravaganza

Don Willmott writes: **Is "extravaganza" an artificial word crafted from "extravagant" (and invented by P.T. Barnum perhaps), or does it have its own legitimate lineage? And how old is it? What was the first extravaganza?**

■ Hey—be careful about those claims of bastardy. Why can't **extravaganza** be crafted from *extravagant and* be legitimate? There's no reason to call it artificial.

In this case, **extravaganza** is closely related to *extravagant,* but it's not a direct borrowing. **Extravaganza** is taken from Italian *estravaganza* (the usual form is *stravaganza*), which means 'an extravagance' or 'peculiar behavior'. The spelling with x is presumably adopted from the existing English words *extravagance* or *extravagant,* from the same ultimate source.

This ultimate source is Latin *extrāvagant-*, the stem of the present participle of *extrāvagārī* 'to wander beyond' (the second element is also the source of English *vagary*); both *extravagant* and the later *extravagance* are probably borrowed through Middle French.

Extravaganza is first found in English in the 1750s, when it had the sense 'extravagant language or behavior'. The usual sense 'a dramatic, musical, or literary work marked by extravagance' is found by the 1790s. The first production described this way is a play about *The Courage of Sir John Falstaff,* which seems mild to me, but things were kind of busy in the 1790s.

■ ■ ■

feckless

> *Chester Zenoe writes:* **How about exploring the roots and meanings of "feckless," as in "Oh, sharper than a serpent's tooth is a feckless child"?**

■ OK. **Feckless** has two main senses, depending on whether it is used of people or of things. Of people, by far the more common use, **feckless** means 'irresponsible; indifferent; lazy'. Of things, it means 'ineffective; futile'.

Feckless is of Scots origin, and was for some time used mainly by Scots writers. (Example from Sir Walter Scott: "Ye'll no do for Steenie, lass—a feckless thing like you's no fit to mainteen a man.") It is now, though perhaps not common, no longer regionally limited. (Example from Willa Cather: "Let people try to stop her! She glowered at the rows of feckless bodies that lay sprawled in the chairs. Let them try it once!")

Feckless is first found in the late sixteenth century. It is formed from the Scots *feck* 'efficiency; vigor', a clipped form of *effect,* and the standard suffix *-less.* You should not be surprised to hear that in Scots there is also the word *feckful,* meaning 'efficient; vigorous'.

By the way, the actual quote is "How sharper than a serpent's tooth it is/To have a *thankless* child" (Shakespeare, *King Lear* 1.4).

■ ■ ■

fell swoop

> *Don Willmott writes:* **Here's a phrase I've been wondering about: "one fell swoop." I know it means "all at once," but I wonder about its origins. Dive-bombing pelicans? Hawks? Shakespeare?**

■ Why can't it be hawks *and* Shakespeare? (You knew it had to be Shakespeare, didn't you?) The phrase stems from a passage in *Macbeth.* Macduff has just been told that his wife and children have been killed:

All my pretty ones?
Did you say all? O hell-kite! All?
What, all my pretty chickens and their dam
At one fell swoop?
(*Macbeth* 4.3.216ff)

Macduff is speaking metaphorically, with Macbeth as the bird of prey ("hell-kite") and his wife and children as chickens. **Fell** means 'fierce; cruel; savage; deadly', and **swoop** is just 'an act of swooping, as by a bird of prey' (and this passage is the first use of **swoop** in that sense in English), so the line literally means 'in one fierce pounce'.

The line began to be used figuratively early on to mean 'by or as if by one blow; all at once; all together', which is now the only meaning; the literal sense has been largely forgotten.

The word **fell** in this sense, now rare or archaic, comes from the same Old French word that gives us the English word *felon*. **Swoop** is a variant of the Old English word that gives us the modern word *sweep*.

■ ■ ■

fin

Brendan Pimper writes: Fin. I was delighted to find out the origin of SAWBUCK (a $10 bill) in a previous posting. The only time I had seen "fin" used was in a song with the line ". . . a fin or even a sawbuck." From the context, I think "fin" meant a $5 bill, but I'm not sure. Slangmeister?

■ A **fin** is indeed a slang term for a $5 bill, or $5. (Or, I should point out, in early British or Australian usage, a 5-pound note.)

This **fin** is a clipping of *finif*, also meaning a $5 bill. *Finif* (the word is spelled in many different ways) is a borrowing from Yiddish *finef* 'five', of Germanic origin and related to English *five*. *Finif* is first attested in the 1850s and is now rather rare. **Fin** itself is first found in England in the 1860s; it does not seem to have become common in America until the 1920s.

Though **fin** may not be as common as it once was, it is still in use. My favorite recent example is from that brilliant TV show *The Simpsons:* "Driver, here's a fin. Get us home and don't spare the whip!" Other 1990s sources include the TV show *Donahue* and *Rolling Stone* magazine, showing that it's not really that obscure a term.

Some related senses include 'a five-year prison term', and the gambling sense 'five hundred dollars'—both senses are paralleled by equivalent semantic developments of other terms for money. A derived form, parallel to *sawski*, is *finski*, which is found in that '80s classic film *Ferris Bueller's Day Off*.

■ ■ ■

fixing to

Beth McCullough writes: **Having lived more than a few years in the South, I have often wondered about the origin of the expression "fixing," which seems means something on the order of "about to" as opposed to "repairing." Example: I'm fixin' to feed the chickens.**

■ The verb **fix** has had a great many senses in American English, some of which have come under harsh criticism. It may interest you to know that the sense 'repair', which you regard as standard—and it is totally standard—was frowned upon at the beginning of this century.

The earliest use of **fix** in a sense like this came in the early eighteenth century in America, when the word meant 'to get ready; prepare'. This particular sense was used throughout the colonies. (It is part of a broad set of meanings of the word roughly in the sense 'to get into order; establish; settle definitely'.)

The use you're asking about, 'to be about [to]; to plan [to] imminently', is an extended sense of this. (The difference is that the 'plan' sense does not involve any preparation. Your example of "fixin' to feed the chickens" could go with either sense; an expression like "It's fixin' to rain" could only go with the 'be about to' sense.) It is first found in the 1930s, and is used mostly in the South Atlantic and Gulf states. Note that in this use, the verb is always found in progressive tenses followed by the infinitive—that is, it's always in the construction *fixing to* [verb]. Also, the verb is only used with actions that are going to happen immediately: you wouldn't say, "I'm fixing to get married in five or ten years."

Though *fixing to* is starting to be used more widely, it remains one of the best-known indicators of Southern speech, along with such words as *reckon* and *y'all*.

■ ■ ■

flivver

Loren Marshall writes: **My father used the slang term "flivver" to mean a car. (The spelling is a guess.) I've never known where it came from. Do you?**

■ No, I don't have a clue. No one really does; "origin unknown" is the phrase to keep in mind when discussing this word, because it appears in almost every reference.

The earliest use of **flivver** is 'a small, cheap, or old automobile', and in the early days it referred especially to a Ford Model A or Model T. This sense is first found in 1910. Nowadays this use is typically historical or jocular; it's rarely found when discussing current cars. Two derived senses that are now obsolete are the naval sense 'a 750-ton destroyer' (the full-size model was 1,000 tons), which was only used during World War I, and the aviation sense 'a small plane'.

The other important sense is 'a failure or disappointment; something inferior'. This is first found in 1915, but its related verb 'to fail; fizzle' is first found in 1912. It is therefore quite possible that this is the original sense, the 'lousy car' sense being just a narrowing that became very popular, and its slightly earlier attestation merely an accident of the historical record. However, even if true, we still have no idea where this sense of **flivver** comes from.

Some other related words are **flivver** as a verb meaning 'to drive in a flivver'; *fliv* as a noun usually meaning 'something inferior' and rarely meaning 'a lousy car'; and *fliv* as a verb in both senses of **flivver** verb.

■ ■ ■

floccinaucinihilipilification

Madeleine Isenberg writes: **I'm wondering about "floccinaucinihilipilification." Can you confirm that this means more or less "making much ado about nothing"? I believe there are four prefixes that all mean "small" at the beginning of the word. What is the origin of this word? Who used it first? Does it qualify as the longest word in English? Also, how would you actually use this in conversation? "You are making a mountain out of a molehill—stop floccinaucinihilipilificating!"**

■ The word **floccinaucinihilipilification,** which is usually encountered only as an example of one of the longest words in English, means something like 'the estimation of something as valueless'.

The word is formed from four Latin words, all of them meaning 'of little or no value; trifling', and the noun suffix *-fication,* as in *classification.* The *Oxford English Dictionary (OED)* tells us that the Latin 'trifling' words are "enumerated in a well-known rule of the Eton Latin Grammar."

The word is first recorded in 1741, in a letter of William Shenstone, an eighteenth-century English pastoral poet and landscape gardener. The *OED* records other uses in the early nineteenth century from Sir Walter Scott (who spells the second element "-pauci-" instead of "-nauci-") and the poet Robert Southey.

The question of the longest word in English is a difficult one; suffice it to say that **floccinaucinihilipilification** is one of the longest that's been seriously used; it's also the longest word in the first edition of the *OED.*

If one were going to use it in conversation, the most likely sentence would resemble, "Do you know that 'floccinaucinihilipilification' is one of the longest words in English?" But it is not without a useful meaning, and one could imagine something like "I can't believe that critic's floccin-

aucinihilipilification of the new Jim Carrey movie! I thought it was great!"
If you try it, however, be warned that your friends will think you very
weird.

■　■　■

flotsam and jetsam

**Kristine Kern writes: Is it redundant to use the terms "flot-
sam" and "jetsam" together (as in "He was surrounded by
flotsam and jetsam")? Do they have different meanings?**

■ In the technical sense, **flotsam** and **jetsam** have different meanings.
Flotsam is the part of the wreckage of a ship or its cargo found floating
on the water. **Jetsam** is cargo or parts of a ship that are deliberately
thrown overboard, as to lighten the ship in an emergency, and that subsequently either sinks or is washed ashore. (While we're on the subject, we
might as well mention *lagan*, which is goods thrown into the sea but
attached to a buoy so they can be recovered.) The common phrase **flotsam and jetsam** is used to refer to the entire residue of a shipwreck, and
is not redundant.

Both words have also developed equivalent broad senses, meaning
'useless or unimportant items; odds and ends'. The set phrase **flotsam
and jetsam** is also used in this sense, and while it is redundant when
used this way, there's no real reason to object to it. After all, there are a
number of other phrases linking two effectively synonymous words such
as *without let or hindrance* or KIT AND CABOODLE. Some people do object
to the figurative use of either word, believing they should be used strictly
for the nautical senses, but they're being needlessly rigid.

Flotsam comes from the Anglo-French *floteson,* derived from Old
French *floter* 'to float', which is related to the English word *float.* It is first
attested in the early seventeenth century. **Jetsam** is an altered and abbre-
viated version of *jettison,* and is first found in the late sixteenth century.

■　■　■

fluke

**Craig Klampe writes: The high point of our day here at the
aquarium is finding out your word of the day. A couple of
workmates are curious about the word "fluke." There is a
whale's fluke and then there is the surprise fluke. Just a coincidence?**

■ Probably, but who knows with stuff like this. **Fluke** is another one of
those words whose dictionary etymologies are peppered with "of uncertain origin"–type statements.

The one variety of **fluke** for which the origin is known for sure is the one you didn't mention, strangely, since you're in the aquarium business. **Fluke** meaning 'a type of flatfish' goes back to Old English. This Old English word is etymologically related to words meaning 'flat' in several languages, including Latin *plaga* 'a flat surface', Greek *pélagos* 'the open sea', and German *flach* 'flat'.

The next **fluke** is the one meaning 'the part of an anchor that catches in the ground' (first attested in the mid-sixteenth century), which then has the figurative sense 'one of the triangular lobes on the tail of a whale' (early eighteenth century). It's possible that this word is a special use of the 'fish' word, after the resemblance of the fish to the flat triangular part of an anchor. I personally favor this theory, but most dictionaries consider them separate words. One would expect that if this were an extension of the 'fish' word, it would be found much earlier than the sixteenth century.

Finally we have the word **fluke** that means 'a stroke of luck'. This sense is first found in the mid-nineteenth century, with the specific nuance 'an accidentally successful shot in billiards'. It is of unknown origin, though it is sometimes connected to an English dialect word **fluke** meaning 'a guess' that is not recorded until later in the nineteenth century. There have been attempts to connect it to the 'flatfish' word (by way of the earlier English slang *flat* 'a victim of swindling; sucker'), but these theories strike me as being rather unlikely.

■ ■ ■

flume

Roy Murphy writes: The first episode of the ABC drama *Relativity* used the word "flume" to refer to the indentation on the upper lip below the nostrils. A well-known George Carlin sketch from the early '70s claims that part of the body has no name. Is this a new usage to fill the gap that GC identified?

■ I *think* it's new—at least, I've never encountered **flume** before in this meaning, though it certainly makes sense.

As for the vertical channel on the upper lip, it certainly does have a name, George Carlin notwithstanding, and that name is *philtrum*. *Philtrum*—the word has existed in English since the seventeenth century—is one of those words that is well worth knowing, because some smart aleck is always going around saying that there's no name for the thing.

Some other parts of the body that you probably didn't know had names are the *uvula*, which is the small fleshy thing hanging down at the back of your throat; the *lunulae*, which are the white half-moon-shaped areas at the base of your fingernails; and best of all, the *perineum*, which is the small area between your—er, um—between your two most private parts. (Also known, in slang, as the *t'aint,* for reasons that must remain secret. This is a public space, after all.)

There. Now you're all set to win a bar bet. Just don't challenge a doctor.

■ ■ ■

folk etymology

Ryan Call writes: **In an entry or two on your absolutely enjoyable "Word of the Day" site, you mention that a folk etymology is the process of altering an uncommon word or element to conform it to one that's better known (for instance, the "cater" in catercorner becoming "kitty" in** KITTY-CORNER**). However, in my university days majoring in linguistics, it seems to me that the definition I found most common was "an explanation for the origins of a word or phrase which, though quite logical or popular, is untrue." Was I hallucinating, is this an alternate usage, or are you (gasp) mistaken in your application?**

■ We'll go with door #2, "an alternate usage," thus making sure we both look good.

Though one could define the linguistic term **folk etymology** broadly as 'any popular misconception about the origins of a word or phrase, esp. one resulting in modification', it would be best to divide it up into two separate senses.

The one that I believe is more common is the one I've used in several columns: 'a modification of a linguistic form according either to a falsely assumed etymology, as "Welsh rarebit" from "Welsh rabbit," or to a historically irrelevant analogy, as "bridegroom" from "bridegome" '. In other words, a modification to make a word seem as if it's related to a more common or more easily understood word. In the case of *bridegroom,* for example, the original form of the second element was *gome,* based on an Old English word for 'man'; when this word became obsolete, the last element was changed to *groom,* as if it were related to the very common *groom* 'person who cares for horses'. Other examples are *cockroach,* from Spanish *cucaracha* (a word of imitative origin), assimilated to *cock* 'a male chicken' and *roach* 'a freshwater fish'; and *shamefaced,* originally *shamefast* 'bound by shame', with the second element altered to *-faced* as if meaning 'showing shame in one's face'.

The other sense, which I believe is less common in linguistics, is 'a popular but false notion of the origin of a word'. Thus, the idea that *posh* is an acronym for "Port Outward, Starboard Home," referring to the cooler and therefore more desirable cabins on the England-India sailing route, which is demonstrably untrue, can be called a **folk etymology.** There is some overlap in these senses, since a popular but false notion of the origin of a word can give rise to a modification of the word.

The expression **folk etymology** is first attested in the late nineteenth century.

■   ■   ■

fortnight

> *sarankina@aol.com writes:* **Not having been born here, but across the Atlantic, the word "fortnight" for a two-week period was common usage (until I moved here, where I hardly ever hear it). Where did it come from?**

■ **Fortnight** comes from the Middle English form *fourtenight,* which is a contracted form of the Old English *fēowertēne niht,* meaning 'fourteen nights'. Pretty descriptive, doncha think? (One side question raised by the term is why "night" is used for 'a period of twenty-four hours', when the usual practice is to measure time by "days." This reckoning by "nights" is an ancient Germanic method; it was considered unusual even two thousand years ago, when Roman historians mentioned it.)

While the term **fortnight** is, as you say, in very common use in Great Britain, in America it is rather uncommon, and is considered more of a formal or literary term.

■   ■   ■

four-flusher

> *Ken Kurson writes:* **I'm wondering about the derivation of the pejorative "four-flusher." I know it means exactly what you'd expect: someone dishonest or untrustworthy. But my belief is that it evolved from someone who cheats at cards (holds four of the same suit, then produces a fifth from "up a sleeve" to fill out the flush). But others have posited that it refers to the popular concept of "mercy flushing"—giving the toilet an extra swish after a particularly nasty emission, something a dishonest person would presumably have to do often. Can you clear this up?**

■ The "toilet" etymology has to be one of the more bizarre suggestions I've ever heard. Why would a dishonest person be more likely to need the extra flush? Why wouldn't he be referred to as a "two-flusher"? And wouldn't a dishonest person be more likely *not* to be helpful by giving the extra flush?

Four-flusher (often spelled solid as **fourflusher**) is unquestionably from poker. A flush is a hand consisting of five cards of the same suit; a four-flush is a hand with only four cards of the same suit—that is, a nearly worthless hand. The concept of "cheating" doesn't seem to be part of the development of the term. Rather, "worthless" and "ungenuine," straight-forward applications of what an actual four-flush is, are the ideas represented. As a noun, *four-flush* means 'an incompetent or worthless person; something false or insincere'; and as a verb it means 'to bluff, especially by pretending knowledge'. A **four-flusher**, then, is 'a pretentious person; fraud; bluffer'.

The technical poker sense of *four-flush* is first found in the late 1880s. The figurative senses all developed around 1900.

■ ■ ■

freelance

Don Willmott writes: **I work with freelance writers all day. Does the etymology of the word go all the way back to King Arthur and the Knights of the Round Table?**

■ No, as with most aspects of the Middle Ages, it only goes back to the nineteenth-century medieval revivalists. The earliest use of **free lance** (in early use, it was usually spelled as two words) meant 'a mercenary soldier of the Middle Ages', and goes back to the medieval novel *Ivanhoe* (1820), by Sir Walter Scott, who also effectively invented the concept of clan tartans and most other aspects of the Scottish Highlanders. This use pops up in various historical novels of the Victorian era.

The word was being used figuratively by the 1860s to mean 'a person (as a politician) who contends in various causes without being attached to a particular group'. The use of **freelance** referring to a writer arose by the 1880s, and the verb **to freelance** by around 1900.

■ ■ ■

f*ck

Les Aldridge writes: **I've always wondered about the Anglo-Saxon word which is sometimes attributed to 'found under carnal knowledge' which I'm sure has no such origin. What I'm confused about is how did a word which stands for an obviously pleasurable activity become a curse? How the f*** did this f***ing word show up with so many negative connotations?**

The very interested may want to look at my book entirely about this word, called, predictably enough, *The F-Word* (Random House, 1995). For now, a brief discussion will have to suffice.

The word which we'll spell **f*ck** is neither Anglo-Saxon (at least in the technical sense) nor an acronym. The common acronymic origins are usually variants of "forced unlawful carnal knowledge," shortened to our word and forced to be worn by convicted rapists in mythical Olden Tymes, or "fornication under consent of the King," reflecting some desire of a medieval monarch to repopulate his country after a plague. These etymologies, like a great many suggested acronymic explanations, are entirely false.

Words related to the English **f*ck** are found in a number of Germanic languages, including Norwegian, Swedish, Dutch, and (probably) German. These words all have sexual meanings as well as meanings like 'to strike' or 'to thrust'. There have been various attempts made to connect these words to words in other, more distantly related languages, but none of these attempts has been convincing, due to complicated linguistic factors beyond the scope of our discussion.

The first example of any of these words is actually in English itself, in the late fifteenth century (thus well past the Anglo-Saxon period), when **f*ck** appears, encyphered, in a brief English passage in a Latin satirical poem. The cypher suggests that the word was already considered taboo. The offensiveness of the word accounts for its strength even though the activity it denotes is usually considered pleasurable. It is not always easy to tell how certain expressions developed; the use of *f*cking* as a synonym for 'damned', for instance, may derive from opprobrious use of such literal expressions as *f*cking whore*. The expression *f*ck you* is probably a variant of the earlier *go f*ck yourself,* which is certainly a plausible candidate for a truly offensive sentiment, however pleasurable the act in question may be in nonreflexive contexts.

Most of the examples of the word in figurative or extended uses, or in various phrases or compounds, are not attested until the twentieth century.

■ ■ ■

full-court press

> *E. A. Rollins writes:* **What does the expression "full-court press" mean, and where did it come from? I gather, from the context in which I heard it used, that it means "with great fanfare," but I don't want to use it until I'm sure I understand what I'm saying.**

■ **Full-court press** is originally a basketball term. In this literal sense, it refers to a defense in which the team without the ball applies player-to-player pressure to the offensive team the entire length of the court. The usual practice is to allow the offensive team to get halfway down the court (a *half-court press*) or near the basket before applying strong defensive pressure. A full-court press takes a great deal of effort, but can be an effective tactic. The *press* in **full-court press** refers to defensive pressure, not to the journalistic press, which your (incorrect) inferred sense suggests.

The figurative sense is 'a vigorous attack or offensive; strong pressure', and is often found in political contexts: "a full-court press for health reform."

The basketball sense of **full-court press** is first found around 1950; the figurative sense dates from the late 1970s.

■　■　■

G-2

Mark Grannis writes: **I recently ran across the term "G2" meaning "intelligence" (in the military sense), or more broadly perhaps, "inside information." I have been unable to discover its origin, though some have guessed that it is of World War II vintage and may refer to a U.K. intelligence organization (or organisation, as the case may be). Do you have any G2 on "G2"?**

■ The **G-2** is the intelligence staff of a large U.S. Army organization, one that's commanded by a general. It dates to 1903, when the War Department—now euphemistically renamed the Department of Defense—organized the General Staff into three groups; "Military Information," which evolved into the intelligence staff, was the second group.

The basic staff of a general-commanded group (normally including the entire army or marines; a specific army (1st Army, 2nd Army) or corps (I Corps, II Corps, etc.); a division; and a brigade). Eventually, it had four sections: G-1, Personnel; **G-2**, Intelligence; G-3, Operations; and G-4, Supply. During World War II there were two additional staff functions at regional headquarters: G-5, Civil Affairs and Military Government; and G-6, Public Relations and Psychological Warfare—an interesting mix, that.

Groups commanded by a lower-ranking officer than a general, as regiments and battalions that are part of a division, use an S-series of staff designations (S-1, S-2, etc., with the *S* standing for "staff"); here S-2 refers to intelligence.

Companies, separate companies, and detachments are too small to have these staff groupings.

The G-series of staff designations originated in the French army in the late nineteenth century.

The U.S. Army Air Corps, and subsequently the U.S. Army Air Forces, used A-series designations for staff functions, A-2 being the intelligence staff.

■　■　■

geek

Ben Davis writes: In a department correspondence, I wrote, "Department geek is a John Smith at x54321 for information." My boss criticized me for this use of "geek," which he thought was demeaning, especially if someone outside the department saw the memo. I do not think this is pejorative in this context. Can you address this issue?

■ There are a few issues to address here; let me start by addressing one that you did not ask about: the origin of the word **geek.**

It is not true, though it is often claimed, that the original sense of **geek** is 'a carnival performer who performs sensationally morbid or disgusting acts, such as biting the head off a live chicken'. This sense, while real, does not arise until the late 1920s. The original sense is still the usual one, 'a peculiar, eccentric, or offensive person, esp. one who is overly intellectual'. Depending on how one interprets the evidence and the definition, this word is first found either in the 1870s or the 1900s, but it's clear that it had a reasonable degree of currency in America by the 1910s. It is probably a variant of the earlier, now obsolete word *geck* 'a fool', of Dutch or Low German origin.

Now, on to your real question, which concerns the appropriateness of using **geek** to describe another person. It is true that there has been something of a trend lately to use **geek** as a positive term of self-description, in a sense like 'a dedicated, knowledgeable computer user'. In a way, this parallels similar developments of other originally offensive or derogatory terms, such as the use of *nigger* by blacks in self-reference, or the adoption of *queer, dyke,* and *fag* by homosexuals. As with these terms (which are, of course, generally considered far more offensive than **geek**), whatever the status of their use by group members, their use by nonmembers is best avoided. To whatever extent **geek** is becoming an acceptable, broadly used term, it does remain potentially derogatory.

(You do not specify whether you yourself are a self-described computer geek, but even if you are, your application of the term in this case to another person, where outsiders could encounter it, is not recommended. Your claim that you are not being pejorative is beside the point, if others are likely to take offense. The only way I'd say such a use would be acceptable is if John Smith were himself encouraging others to call him "the department geek," but I assume from your boss's reaction that this is not the case.)

■ ■ ■

get-go

Rob Ewen writes: I've often come across the phrase "from the get-go" where I would normally use "from the word go," meaning "right from the start of something." From where was "the get-go" got?

■ The **get-go** in the phrase *from the get-go,* which means 'from the start; from the very beginning', is a nominalization of the verbal phrase *to get going* 'to begin'. This use of "get" as a noun has other precedents; Australian slang has seen the word *get* 'an act of leaving or fleeing' for about one hundred years. The imperative verb *get!* 'Leave! Go away!' is also worth mentioning.

Get-go is a rather new expression; it is an Americanism first recorded in the mid-1960s. In its early history, it was used primarily by black speakers, but now it is more widespread. One variant is the shortened *from the get;* the expression also appears in the form *git-go,* reflecting a common pronunciation.

The colloquial expression *from the word go* is also an Americanism, but a much older one; it is first found in the 1830s. *Get!* (also spelled "git!") is first found in the 1860s.

■ ■ ■

gewgaw

Chris Molanphy writes: On the front page of a recent *New York Times,* an article posited that Thanksgiving is the one remaining American holiday not besotted with "geegaws." In other words, one is not obligated to buy a loved one trinkets or put up decorative tchotchkes in celebration of Thanksgiving. Coincidentally, a *Wall Street Journal* article the same day about home security notes that the home security industry preys on homeowners' fears by selling them "security bells, whistles and gewgaws." I've seen this word occasionally and still can barely pronounce it, much less use it comfortably in a sentence. My dictionary lists both spellings of the word, but the *Times*'s "geegaws" is listed only as an alternate spelling of the *Journal*'s "gewgaws." A definition is given for gewgaws, but no known origin. I was wondering which spelling is more correct, and whether you have any better sources on the origins of geegaws/gewgaws.

■ First of all, **gewgaw** is usually pronounced "GYOO-gaw," rhyming with "raw," although "GOO-gaw" is almost as common, and is how I pronounce it. Allegedly the word is sometimes pronounced "GEE-gaw," a pronunciation probably associated with the *geegaw* spelling, but I've never heard this myself. The usual meaning is 'something gaudy and useless; a trinket; bauble'.

Gewgaw is of unknown origin. It is first found in English in its current form in the early sixteenth century. The earliest appearance in any form was in the early thirteenth century, when it was written *giuegoue,* leading some scholars to argue that this represents "give-gove" (*us* and *vs* were then represented by the same letter in writing) and positing a Dutch origin on complicated grounds. Another school suggests a relation to *gogue,* an Old French word meaning 'a joke; jest' that appears to be the origin of the modern *à go-go.*

All one can say with certainty, however, is that **gewgaw** is a gradational compound. *Gradational compounds,* discussed under DRIBS AND DRABS, are reduplications where the vowel is changed, such as *mish-mash* or *heehaw,* and in English can often indicate derision or contempt.

A synonum of **gewgaw** that is also a gradational compound is the better-known *knickknack.* The spelling of the word has been, as you might expect, highly variable over the years. Some recorded variants include *guegaw, guy-gaw, gugaw, gwegawe* [sic], *gewgaie, gugae,* and *gewgow,* so we shouldn't be too surprised that there are two versions common enough now to make it into dictionaries. I think that **gewgaw** is significantly more common, but *geegaw* is certainly out there. We've collected several examples from the *New York Times,* so it could be a house style or the preference of an editor there. Nonetheless, should you have occasion to use the word yourself, I'd recommend **gewgaw.**

■　■　■

gift horse

chucho@worldnet.att.net writes: **"Don't look a gift horse in the mouth"—A friend of mine says this admonition is a reference to the Trojan horse. I contend it refers to the practice of some who look at a horse's teeth for signs of age (or disease) before purchasing the animal. If those people had looked in the Trojan horse's mouth they would have been surprised, but maybe not vanquished.**

■　This proverb indeed refers to the practice of gauging a horse's age by the condition of its teeth. The proverb warns against questioning the value of something received by luck or chance. It doesn't allude to the Trojan horse—after all, as you observe, it would have been a good idea if the Trojans *had* looked that gift horse in the mouth! (For a proverb that *does* refer to the Trojan horse as a gift, we have "Beware of Greeks bearing gifts," an adaptation from the Roman poet Virgil.)

Don't look a gift horse in the mouth is a well-established proverb. It is first found in the United States in the mid-nineteenth century, and in England in several proverb collections in the sixteenth. But it was in wide circulation a millennium before that; in the fifth century, St. Jerome, in a biblical commentary, wrote "Noli . . . ut vulgare proverbium est, equi dentes inspicere donati," or "Don't, as the common proverb has it, look at the teeth of a gift horse."

■ ■ ■

gird one's loins

Roger Grow writes: What is the meaning of "gird one's loins"?

■ The phrase **gird one's loins** means 'to prepare oneself for something requiring strength and endurance; ready oneself for action'.

The main meaning of *gird* is 'to encircle or bind with a belt or band'; *loins,* though often used to refer to the genitals, actually refers to the part of the human body between the hips and the lower ribs, regarded as the seat of physical strength. To **gird one's loins** literally means 'to wrap a belt around one's waist', the point being that in the days of loose garments, belting oneself would confine one's clothing and allow freer motion of the body.

In general, *gird* is used chiefly in figurative ways. **Gird** *(up)* **one's loins** is one such example, and the phrase's currency stems from its frequent use in the Bible. The King James Version (the phrase is found in other translations as well) has, among a number of other uses, "Gird up thy loins, and take my staff in thine hand, and go thy way" (2 Kings 4.29); "Gird up now thy loins like a man; for I will demand of thee, and answer thou me" (Job 18.3); and, for an obviously figurative example, "Wherefore gird up the loins of your mind, be sober, and hope to the end for the grace that is to be brought unto you at the revelation of Jesus Christ" (1 Peter 1.13). Lastly, an example without "up": "She girds her loins with strength, and she makes her arms strong" (Proverbs 31.17).

Some other uses of *gird* include 'to surround; enclose; hem in'; 'to prepare oneself for action; brace' (that is, the same thing we've been discussing, but without "loins"); and 'to equip or invest' (as "to gird oneself with a sword" or "to gird oneself with endurance"). The word goes back to the Old English period, and is ultimately related to the Modern English word *yard* through the idea of 'something enclosed'.

■ ■ ■

gist

Gary Knapp writes: In the phrase "the gist of it all," just what does "gist" mean, and where does it come from?

■ The word **gist** in this example—and in most examples you're likely to encounter—means 'the main or essential point of a matter; the essence'. It is a broadening of the earlier, and now rare, legal sense 'the ground of a legal action'.

This sense comes from a legal phrase in Anglo-French, *(cest action) gist,* literally '(this matter) lies' ("lies" in the sense 'is founded on; consists of'). In the phrase, **gist** is the third person singular, present indicative of *gesir* 'to lie'. In other words, the word that English borrowed from the French phrase is *not* the word that means in French what the English word means. English in effect borrowed the "wrong" word. This process is fairly common when borrowing from compounds and phrases. Another example is *church,* for a Greek phrase meaning 'the Lord's house'; *church* comes from the word for 'Lord; master', not the word for 'house'.

Gist is first found in the legal sense in the early eighteenth century, and in the broader sense in the early nineteenth century.

■ ■ ■

gonna

John Benz Fentner, Jr., writes: It's the most ubiquitous (at least in the East) verbalism that never sees print . . . the use of "gonna" for "going to." Given that it probably doesn't have much of a written history, how are we gonna find out where "gonna" comes from?

■ There are a few things we can do. The first is to explain what **gonna** is: a pronunciation spelling. *Pronunciation spelling* is spelling based on how a word is actually pronounced (usually informally), rather than on what the traditional spelling is. **Gonna** for "going to" is one example, others are *of* for "have" ("She could of done it") and *lemme* for "let me."

These examples all show the process of *assimilation,* where a speech sound is modified to become identical or similar to a neighboring speech sound. For instance, the Latin source for *aggression* began *adgre-;* the *d* was assimilated to the following *g.* In *grandpa,* the *d* drops out entirely and the *n* is assimilated to an *m* because *m,* like *p,* is vocalized with the lips touching (these sounds are called *bilabials*), giving the standard pronunciation "grampa."

So the short answer is that the written form **gonna** represents a pronunciation spelling of an assimilated version of *going to.* Note also that **gonna** is only used when the *to* is introducing an infinitive; when the *to* is a preposition, we do pronounce it, which is why we don't say "I'm gonna the store." A similar form is *wanna*, which also represents an assimilation of "verb + to + infinitive."

Regarding the written history of **gonna,** it's not quite as rare as one would think. There are examples almost two centuries old in Scottish use: "Now, Willie lad, I'm ganna gie you twa or three directions." Written use in the United States starts in the early part of this century. Many examples are spelled **gonna** or *gunna,* but some are spelled *gointa* or *gonter,* showing intermediate stages where the *-g* of *going* is not pronounced but the *t* of *to* still is.

Finally, I'll mention the ultimate reduction, where *going to* is leveled all the way to the neutral vowel schwa: "Well, baby, if you just give me a chance, Ima have it together pretty soon" (a 1970s example of Black English); "I'm a stand on this corner where she can see me," (*New York Press,* 1996).

■ ■ ■

goombah

Glenn Tornell writes: **What's the origin and meaning of the word "gumba," which I've heard in old Godfather-type movies to refer to a leg-breaker or enforcer?**

■ **Goombah,** to use its usual spelling, is an English rendering of a dialectal Italian pronunciation of *compare,* which can mean 'godfather', 'friend', or 'accomplice; crony'.

There are three main senses of **goombah** in English, two of which are translations of Italian uses and one an English innovation. The earliest sense found in English is 'a friend or associate'. This is first found in the mid-1950s, and seems to have been popularized by Rocky Graziano, the boxer and (later) actor, on NBC's *The Martha Raye Show.*

The second, and most familiar, sense is 'a mafia boss; a mafioso', or broadly 'any organized crime figure'. The first known use of this sense is in Mario Puzo's 1969 novel *The Godfather,* the origin, of course, of the movie: "I don't care how many guinea Mafia goombahs come out of the woodwork."

Finally, the English-only sense is 'a stupid person', first found in the 1950s but not common until the 1980s. This sense is presumably based on stereotyped portrayals of low-level mafiosi as ignorant, loutish types.

■ ■ ■

gorge, gorgeous

Rachel Fishman writes: Etymology of "gorge" and "gorgeous." . . . Are they related words? How? Why?

■ It's a complicated question, but the short answer is that they are probably related.

Gorge is more clear, so let's look at that first. The main current sense is probably 'a deep, narrow valley', but the original sense in English was 'the throat', and this sense is still in use. The word was borrowed from Old French in the fourteenth century. The Old French word is in turn borrowed from the Late Latin word *gurga* 'throat', which is probably a variant of Latin *gurges* 'whirlpool; abyss'. (This word may be the ultimate root of English *gurgle,* but that's another complicated question.)

Gorgeous 'splendid or sumptuous in appearance; magnificent', was also borrowed from an Old French word *gorgias,* which means 'fashionable; elegant' and also 'fond of wearing jewelry'. This word is probably related to the same 'throat' word through similar words that referred to jewelry worn around the neck. The necklace was one of the prominent fashion items of the time, so it is plausible that a word for "necklace" could come to mean 'fashionable'. Not all scholars agree with the semantic connection, but it's the best we can do without resorting to that unfortunate dictionary phrase "of uncertain origin."

■ ■ ■

graduate

Roger D. Grow writes: I read an AP release the other day—dateline May 6, Gaylesville AL—which said ". . . and the staff has yet to graduate high school." Any comment?

■ The comment I expect you're trying to elicit is that this use of **graduate** is a barbarism that demonstrates the depths to which the ink-stained wretches of the AP have sunk. I'll sidestep the moral criticism, but will agree that those people who express opinions on such things almost uniformly detest this transitive use of **graduate.**

The original sense of **graduate,** which dates back to the fifteenth century, is '(of an institution) to grant a degree to'. Thus, "Brown graduated John, even though he never took a serious course in four years." When a person is the subject, therefore, one must use the passive: "She was graduated from Berkeley with a degree in philosophy."

The intransitive sense '(of people) to receive a degree', e.g., "He graduated from Harvard, the University of Chicago of the East Coast," was in use from the early nineteenth century. However, in the late nineteenth century this sense was criticized by various commentators, who insisted that only the school could do the graduating and the intransitive "He graduated from X" usage was incorrect.

Unfortunately for these commentators, the intransitive use is by far the most common, and few people object to it anymore. A 1917 book on English usage by J. Leslie Hall, a noted English scholar, states plainly: "Where did you graduate?' is, it would seem, the regular academic phrase in America, and no doubt in England." Yet there is still a lingering sense among some people that the "was graduated" formula is the only correct one (my father drilled it into me from an early age), but it's often considered old-fashioned.

The transitive use, '(of people) to receive a degree from', as in your example "the staff has yet to graduate high school," is newer still, dating from the middle of this century. As stated, most people who think about it reject this use—77 percent of the American Heritage usage panel, 85–90 percent of the Harper usage panel, almost every usage writer I've been able to check—and as a result, it's comparatively rare in edited writing. There's no compelling grammatical reason to condemn it, and some people (for example, the *Merriam-Webster Collegiate Dictionary*) regard it as standard, but given the reaction it tends to get, it would probably be prudent to avoid it.

■ ■ ■

grog

> **Brad Thompson writes:** In Australia "grog" is generically used to refer to alcohol; but historically it was more particularly applied to a rum ration—known as a "tot." My fiancee then informed me that in Germany, particularly in the north, "grog" is a term used for a hot toddy (alcoholic drink). Now, to complicate things: I also understood that "grog" referred originally to a type of dyed cloth in the eighteenth century worn by a British admiral as a shawl against the cold of the sea. Moreover, that this admiral introduced the rum ration to the sailors to maintain morale and warmth. Hence the term "grog" being applied to rum from the association with the admiral. My question is twofold: (1) was the term "grog" introduced to the Germans by RN visits to ports like Hamburg; and (2) is the etymology relating to the admiral and his clothing correct?

■ Whew! That's a lot of information. Your basic statement is pretty close, but there are a few tweaks necessary.

Grog originally referred to a mixture of rum cut with water. The admiral in question, Edward Vernon (1684–1757), had given an order in 1740 that the rum normally served to seamen be watered down—previously, they had gotten straight rum as part of their standard ration. Vernon's nickname was Old Grog, after his custom of wearing a *grogram* cloak, and **grog** was transferred from the admiral's nickname to the name of the drink he required for his men. The word is first found in the 1750s.

Grogram is a coarse fabric made from wool, silk, or a mixture of silk with wool or mohair; it's not necessarily dyed. *Grogram* is a sixteenth-century word derived from Middle French *gros grain* 'large (i.e., coarse) texture' (the English word *grosgrain* is a later and more direct borrowing from French).

Grog has a few closely related senses. After the simple 'watered-down rum', there is the sense 'a mixture of rum with water and with sugar, lemon and spices, served hot'—that is, a *toddy.* The sense 'any alcoholic liquor or beer' is first attested by the early nineteenth century. *Groggy* meaning 'drunk' is attested by the 1770s, but is now mostly archaic; the broader sense 'dazed; staggering' is attested by the early nineteenth century.

The use of **grog** in German is unquestionably a borrowing of the English term.

■ ■ ■

gross

Elizabeth Rose writes: **I've always wondered how the word "gross" attracted the baggage of "disgusting, unsavory, or unwholesome."**

■ The word **gross** is a fourteenth-century borrowing of Old French *gros* (from Late Latin *grossus*) that originally had the sense 'thick; coarse'. By the sixteenth century, the word had developed senses such as 'unrefined; uncultivated; obscene; stupid'. The current slang sense 'disgusting; unpleasant' is a direct descendant of these earlier meanings.

This adjectival use became common in the United States in the late 1950s. The verb sense *gross out* 'to disgust or revolt' first appeared in the mid-1960s, and the noun *gross-out* 'something disgusting' was in use by the late 1960s.

■ ■ ■

gubernatorial

Hadley Taylor writes: **What is the origin of the word "gubernatorial"? It's not like "governor" at all!**

■ **Gubernatorial** is now different in form from *governor,* but they did originally start off the same way. Both words go back to the same Latin root, *gubernāre* 'to steer; to govern'. The word **gubernatorial** (an American, by the way) was borrowed directly from the Latin *gubernator* 'a steersman; governor' in the eighteenth century, so it preserves the form of the Latin word. *Governor,* on the other hand, was borrowed in the thirteenth century from the Old French word *governeor.* This Old French word derives from the same Latin word, but it underwent the regular sound changes of Latin *b* to Old French *v* and Latin *u* to Old French *o*.

This two-stage borrowing process, where certain forms come directly from Latin and other forms come through Old French, is a common one in English. Such forms are called *doublets.* For example, both *quiet* and *coy* are descended from the Latin *quietus,* but *coy* went through Old French on the way, and as a result has a different form and a different meaning. Other doublets are *abbreviate* and *abridge,* and *fancy* and *fantasy.*

The Latin *gubernāre* itself was borrowed from Greek *kybernân* 'to steer', which is the ultimate root of the English word *cybernetics* and hence of all catchwords with the prefix *cyber-.*

In other words, *government* and *cyberporn* are related. Something worth keeping in mind.

■ ■ ■

hamstrung

Coleen Corbett writes: **What is the origin of "hamstrung"? It sounds like it has something to do with the hamstring muscles, but it doesn't seem to fit.**

■ **Hamstrung** is the past tense and participle of the verb *hamstring*, which means 'to rend powerless or ineffective; thwart'. The earliest example in English, by John Milton in 1641, is for this figurative sense: "So have they hamstrung the valour of the subject by seeking to effeminate us all at home."

The literal sense is the gruesome 'to cripple (someone) by cutting the hamstrings'; though not found in the historical record until slightly later, it must be the original. The sense development is paralleled by the example of *cripple* itself, which originally meant 'to make a cripple of; lame' but then developed a figurative sense 'to make nonfunctional; hinder; thwart'.

By the way, note that in technical use, the hamstrings refer only to the tendons at the back of the thigh, not to the muscles themselves. But "hamstrings" and "hamstring muscles" are often used to mean the group of muscles, all with jawbreakingly complicated names, connected to those tendons.

■ ■ ■

handicap

Richard Johnson writes: **Recently I've heard that the use of "handicapped" is no longer considered "PC" because of its derivation from "cap in hand," thus connoting begging, etc. Sounds funny to me. I've always thought that the word probably came from a "cap" or limit on being "handy." Probably neither is right. What's the real story?**

■ The word **handicap** derives from an obsolete English expression *hand i' cap*, that is, *hand in the cap*. This referred to a type of betting game in which contestants placed money in a cap and exchanged items of different value, the money being forfeited if the contestants rejected the decision of an umpire regarding the value of the exchange. The contestants indicated their acceptance of the contest by drawing their full or empty hands out of a pocket or cap. This game was described as early as the fourteenth century; the term is first attested in the seventeenth century.

The broad sense that developed from this was 'a contest (orig. a horse-race) in which advantages or disadvantages of time, weight, distance, points, etc. are given to contestants to equalize their chances of winning'. The sense that came next was 'any disadvantage that make achievement or success difficult', and hence 'a physical or mental disability'.

The so-called "PC" objection to **handicap** does not stem from an idea of begging or any other etymological sense. It is based on a rejection of the notions that, first, "handicapped" people are a special class that need charity and pity, rather than mainstream acceptance, and second, that they are not normal and should be viewed as freaks. Terms such as *physically challenged* and *differently abled* are meant to address these issues.

■ ■ ■

hanged/hung

Bruce Wright writes: What's the deal with the word "hanged"? Other than to avoid a joke like the one in "Blazing Saddles" about Cleavon Little being "hung," is there a reason for the distinction?

■ Yes, the reason is that most language commentators recommend using **hanged** for the past tense and past participle of *hang* when referring to death by hanging, and **hung** for the past tense and past participle in all other meanings. Why they recommend this is another question entirely.

The Modern English word *hang* is the result of a fusion of three verbs: two from Old English, one transitive and one intransitive (like the distinction between *lay* and *lie*), with influence from one from Old Norse. One form of the word made its past tenses by changing the vowel (like *sing-sang-sung*), and the other by adding a suffix (like *hate-hated*).

To omit many pages of confusing linguistic gibberish, I'll summarize: what happened is that the distinction between the transitive and intransitive verbs was lost, the two verbs became a single verb, and northern England and southern England had different forms. By the sixteenth century, the northern form **hung** penetrated into general English and became the dominant form used—except in the case of execution by hanging. Presumably **hanged** continued to be used here because judges would use this older form when sentencing convicts (legal language, like religious language, is usually very formal, and more resistant to change than other varieties of English).

There is, therefore, historical precedent for using the **hanged** form for hangings. However, **hung** is also found in this sense, and has been for hundreds of years; it seems to be becoming more and more frequent. In modern use, both forms are very common for this sense and must be considered standard, though as noted, **hanged** is preferred by most people who express opinions on the subject.

■ ■ ■

hands-down

Will Doak writes: A coworker used the phrase "hands-down choice" in some marketing material, and we wonder about the origin of that expression. I guessed it had to do with parliamentary procedure, and he speculated it had to do with card games. Its origin seems neither easy nor certain!

■ There are a number of plausible explanations for the phrase **hands-down**, which means, as you note, either 'easy' (a **hands-down** victory) or 'unquestionable; certain' (the **hands-down** choice for the office), or as an adverbial use of either of these ("He won **hands-down**").

The hands-down origin of the word, however, is from horse racing. A **hands-down** victory is one that is so assured that a jockey can drop his hands and relax his grip on the reins as he approaches the line.

The phrase is first found in the late nineteenth century. The two earliest examples are literal references to horse races, which makes pretty clear that this is the origin.

■ ■ ■

have

Jill Singer writes: When (and why) is it more appropriate to use the "have" or "had" auxiliary verbs rather than plain old past tense? For example, when (and why) would "I have received the book" be preferable to "I received the book"? What is the grammatical label for the "have"/"had" tense?

■ The word **have** in this use is, as you say, an *auxiliary verb*. An auxiliary verb is used with certain forms of other verbs to express distinctions usually of tense, aspect, and mood. In the sentence "I have received the book," the "have received" indicates the *present perfect tense.*

So much for definitions. In practice, the use of *perfect tenses* depends a great deal on context. In general, the perfect indicates a time in the past within which the action of the verb takes place relative to, and having relevance to, another temporal point.

In answer to your question about the present perfect, which in English is formed with **have** and the past participle, it means that the action happened in the past (relative to the present) and has relevance to the present. In "I have received the book," this means "at some point in the past, I received the book, and I probably still have the book now." The *simple past*, in contrast, doesn't imply anything else about the current situation: "I received the book" just means that "at some point in the past, I received the book, and there's nothing else to say about the book's current state."

The *past perfect* (or *pluperfect*) tense refers to actions that happened in the past relative to another point in the past and are still relevant to that other point in the past. In English it is formed with *had* (thus answering the second part of your question) and the past participle: "I had borrowed the book" means "at some point in the past, I borrowed the book, but then at a later time (still in the past), something else happened to it" (I borrowed the book but returned it, perhaps).

The *future perfect* tense refers to actions that will happen in the future relative to a time further in the future and still relevant to that time further in the future, that is, actions that will happen before some future event. In English it is formed with *will have* and the past participle: "By Sunday I will have borrowed the book" (adding context for the sake of sense) means "between now and Sunday, I will borrow the book, and I will still have it on Sunday."

■　■　■

heads-up

A colleague writes: **What's the lowdown on "heads-up"?**

■ One of the many new words entered in a recent update of the *Random House Webster's College Dictionary* is **heads-up**. Though the adjective, meaning 'alert; resourceful', has been in the dictionary for many years, what is brand new is its inclusion as a noun, with the definition: '(Chiefly Politics) a warning'. This is a very new use, first found in the 1980s. One example is from Tom Clancy's 1989 novel *Clear and Present Danger:* "The shooters got a heads-up for an important job several days ago."

Heads-up has been found in various senses in America. The most common one, familiar to anyone who's ever been on a sports field, is an interjection: 'Watch out!' As a result, the adjectival use I've mentioned, 'alert; resourceful', began to be used. This is first found in the 1930s, and it typically appears in sporting contexts: "You played a great game all year—smart, heads-up football," says Ronald Reagan in the the title role of the 1940 movie *Knute Rockne—All-American.*

The shift to a noun is a natural change, but when it happens to phrases it tends to sound like jargon (which it often is); compare the political expression *no-can-do* meaning 'an impossibility', as in "That's a no-can-do."

■ ■ ■

hebetate

Richard A. Strauss writes: **I came across the word "hebetate," and was wondering if there was any backwards relationship to the Greek goddess Hebe (who I believe was supposed to make one youthful, perhaps less or maybe more hebete)?**

■ No, they're unrelated, and the similarity of their appearance is coincidental.

Hebetate is a smashingly good word that deserves to be better known. It means 'to make dull', especially in senses of "dull" that have to do with the mental faculties. It has a number of related forms, which include *hebete* 'dull; stupid', and *hebetation* and *hebetude,* both meaning 'the state of being dull; lethargy; stupidity'.

These relatively rare words are much prized by people who go in for that sort of thing. Aside from their presence in the usual array of neat-word books, they can be found in actual use: "The robe was too big. Nevertheles, the pattern was so conservative, and the material so fine, that this seemed rather a mark of luxuriance than some deliberate hebetude on the part of the giver." (William Gaddis, *Recognitions*); and from a *real* obscure-word buff, "Aphrodite—sitting graveolent in her royal hebetation, surrounded by all her holouries . . ." (John Gardner, *Jason and Medeia; graveolent* means 'strongly odoriferous' and *holouries* are fornicators or debauchees).

Hebetate derives from Latin, ultimately from *hebet-,* the stem of *hebes* 'blunt; dull'.

The Greek goddess *Hebe* is the personification of *hēbē,* the standard Greek word for 'puberty' or 'adolescence'. She is usually presented as the cupbearer of the gods, and the daughter of Zeus and Hera. The English word *hebetic* 'pertaining to puberty' and the psychiatric term *hebephrenia* 'a form of schizophrenia characterized by puerile or silly behavior' both derive from the Greek word.

■ ■ ■

hell in a handbasket

Arthur Zura writes: **When things aren't going so well, they're "going to hell in a handbasket." As Chico Marx would say, "Why a handbasket?"**

■ Well, you have to get there *somehow,* don't you? And a *handbasket* has the advantage of alliteration, always important when it comes to this sort of phrase.

The expression *to hell* meaning 'to ruin or destruction; to an unfortunate state of affairs' is found since the early nineteenth century. The early examples are quite natural sounding today: "There's a thousand dollars gone to hell," wrote someone in 1827. ("Go to hell!" used as an exclamation is older, and is not often found in fancier forms.)

Simple but pungent expressions like this often develop elaborated variants. For example, the imprecation "kiss my ass!" can be expanded (from one direction) into "kiss my royal Irish ass!" or (from another) into "kiss my ass in Macy's window!" Similarly, the expression "go to hell" developed a number of variants describing the conveyance for reaching Pluto's realm, and these conveyances don't necessarily make sense. Carl Sandburg, writing about the 1890s, comments that "The first time I heard about a man 'going to hell in a hanging basket' I did a lot of wondering what a hanging basket is like." Whatever a "hanging basket" is, it gives us the alliteration, like such other common examples as "going to hell in a hack" (i.e., a taxicab), "handcart," and our "handbasket." Nonalliterating versions include "in a wheelbarrow," "on a poker," "in a bucket" ("But at least I'm enjoying the ride," as the Grateful Dead say), and "in a basket."

■ ■ ■

hello

Maureen Morin writes: **On CNN's Web site I found an article about a Texas county that has voted to take the "hell" out of "hello" after a three-year campaign by a flea market operator who objected to the "sinister" root of the word. People working in the county courthouse will soon be answering their telephones "Heaven-o." So, where the "hell" does "hello" come from?**

■ **Hello** doesn't come from *hell,* that's for sure, though this little anecdote is a good illustration of the point made in our CALL A SPADE A SPACE discussion that a word's true origin has little to do with whether people get upset about it or not.

Hello first appears in the middle of the nineteenth century. It is a variant of *hallo,* itself a variant of *hollo,* itself again a variant of *holla,* a sixteenth-century word. (Not everyone agrees on the precise order of these variants, to which we can add *hullo* and *hillo* too. Suffice it to say that each of these words is used as a greeting, to get attention, and so forth.)

There are two schools of thought from here. One is that *holla* is borrowed from Middle French *holà,* which comes from *ho,* the same attention getter as English *ho,* and *là* 'there', from Latin *illac,* the whole French word *holà* thus meaning something like 'ahoy there!'.

The second, and simpler, explanation, is that these words, along with similar words in other languages, are natural expressive formations that arose independently, and we should no sooner look for Latin roots of **hello** than we should try to etymologize *aaaaah!.*

■ ■ ■

Hobson's choice

> *Loren Marshall writes:* **My idiom dictionary is no help in identifying the origin of "Hobson's choice." Do we know who Hobson was? He must have had quite a problem.**

■ Hobson didn't have a problem at all; he was the man in charge. It's the choosers who had the problem.

Thomas Hobson—yes, he was a real person, and we know who he is—ran a livery stable in Cambridge, England, in the sixteenth and seventeenth centuries. A customer who wanted to rent a horse had only one real choice: to rent the horse nearest the stable door; Hobson wouldn't rent horses out of order.

As a result, we have the proverbial **Hobson's choice,** which is something that seems like a free choice but really isn't; it's the absence of a real alternative. This or nothing.

Hobson lived from about 1544 to 1631, and was apparently something of a hit in his time. Milton commemorated him in two epitaphs, and issue 509 of Addison and Steele's *Spectator* was devoted to him in 1712. The term **Hobson's choice** itself is first attested in the mid-seventeenth century.

■ ■ ■

hoist with one's own petard

> *R. Clayton writes:* **The dictionary tells me that a "petard" is an explosive device. So how is it that one can be hoisted on one's own (or anybody's) petard?**

■ Pretty easily: it's the same concept as "being blown sky-high." The literal sense of the phrase **hoist with one's own petard** is 'raised into the sky by one's own bomb'. This meaning is largely forgotten today, however; people generally remember the figurative meaning, 'caught by the very device one had contrived to hurt another'.

The phrase comes from a passage in Shakespeare's *Hamlet.* Rosencrantz and Guildenstern are sent with Hamlet to England bearing orders that Hamlet be killed. Hamlet alters the orders so that Rosencrantz and Guildenstern are killed instead. Hamlet says:

> For 'tis the sport to have the engineer
> Hoist with his own petard; and 't shall go hard
> But I will delve one yard below their mines,
> And blow them at the moon.
> (*Hamlet* 3.4.206ff, spelling modernized)

The passage clearly shows the literal sense, but it's the extended sense we know now, to the point that knowing "**hoist**" and "**petard**" won't help you decipher the phrase.

The **hoist** in the passage is not the same as our modern "hoist"; it's an older form of the word, *hoise,* with a participial ending that ends up as a -*t* (it would normally be written *hoised*). **Petard** is a word for 'bomb' that etymologically means 'farter', amusingly enough.

■ ■ ■

home in

> *KyWilliams@aol.com writes:* **I always thought focusing on something was to "hone in" on it. Lately, however, I have been hearing "home in." For example, the plane that crashed in Guam was said to "home in" on the wrong beacon. "Hone in" isn't in two dictionaries I consulted. Is it correct?**

■ No, it is not.

The correct expression is **home in**. The origin of this use comes from the world of homing pigeons. In the late nineteenth century, pigeons were said to *home,* or return back to their homes after being released at a distant point.

The verb was then applied to aviation—human aviation, that is—and from the 1920s onwards, and especially by the 1950s, **home (in)** (on) was used of planes or missiles meaning 'to proceed to (a specified target) under the guidance of an automatic system'. The figurative sense 'to approach or concentrate on (an objective)' dates from the 1950s.

The expression *hone in* is first found in the 1960s, and is a mistake for **home in** (though it's not entirely clear why such a mistake would arise). Its use is now not uncommon—it has been used by George Plimpton, George Bush, the columnist Bob Greene, and *People* magazine, among others—but the sort of people who get upset about these things will regard it as an ignorant mistake, and you should probably avoid it for that reason.

■ ■ ■

honcho

Rob Ewen writes: **The film magazine *Empire* always refers to studio bosses as "head honchos" (usually followed by a 'bless you!' sneeze wisecrack). Can you enlighten me as to the origin of this phrase?**

■ The word **honcho,** like *skosh* 'a small amount' and *hooch* 'a hut; barracks', is a slang word from Japanese that was adopted by American troops in occupied Japan after World War II and during the Korean War.

Honcho is a direct borrowing of Japanese *hanchō* 'squad or group leader', from *han* 'a squad' and *chō* 'eldest; chief'. The original sense in English, found shortly after the end of World War II, is likewise 'a boss; chief; leader; person in charge'. The other major sense is the similar 'an important or influential person; bigshot', first found in the 1950s.

Other senses include 'a fellow; hombre', known from the early 1960s, and the verb 'to be the leader of; supervise', apparently dating from the Korean War.

■ ■ ■

honeymoon

Amy Flynn writes: **My twelve-year-old daughter asked me how the word "honeymoon" came to be, and I couldn't answer her. We had fun guessing, but I promised her I'd find out from the "word expert." So, what's the story?**

■ The original sense of **honeymoon** was 'the period of pleasure immediately following a marriage', that is, before things get settled into a routine and the bride and groom get sick of each other.

Semantically, it comes from the concept of honey being sweet, and sweetness being pleasurable—*sweet* meaning 'pleasurable' has been used in English for over a thousand years. *Moon* either refers to 'a month' (i.e., roughly the period between full moons), being the amount of time everything's peachy, or, metaphorically, to the moon itself, which begins to wane again as soon as it has turned full.

The sense 'a vacation taken by a newly married couple' is an extension of this sense. The word first appears in the sixteenth century; the 'vacation' sense arose by the eighteenth century.

■ ■ ■

honi soit qui mal y pense

Ed McClelland writes: **In an old dictionary that belonged to my dad there was what he thought to be the longest word in the dictionary. I'm not sure of the spelling, but it sounded something like "hahn.ee.sot.kee.mall.ee.penz." Ever heard of it?**

■ Sure, and your representation isn't too bad. The phrase you're thinking of—it's not a single word—is **honi soit qui mal y pense,** which is the motto of the Order of the Garter. It's French for 'shamed be the person who thinks evil of it'. Supposedly, in the fourteenth century, Edward III was dancing with the Countess of Salisbury, and her garter fell off. In response to the snickers of those watching, Edward said "Honi soit qui mal y pense," and tied the garter around his own leg. The phrase then became the motto of the order, which Edward founded.

The Most Noble Order of the Garter is the oldest and most important of the orders of knighthood in the United Kingdom. Its head is the sovereign, and the garter (inscribed with the motto) thus appears on Britain's royal coat of arms. As a result, the phrase is sometimes erroneously described as "the British motto" or something similar.

The true pronunciation, which I can't represent very well in this medium, would be something like "on ee swa kee mal ee pahns."

■ ■ ■

honky

fredgm@pacbell.net writes: **"Honky." Where does this derogatory Black English term for whites come from? A black friend from the South claims it comes from REDNECKS driving around town, yelling and honking horns at blacks. That sounds a little too artificial to me. What's the real deal?**

■ **Honky** in the sense 'a white person' is almost certainly a pronunciation variant of *hunky,* an earlier derisive term meaning 'a person of Central or Eastern European ancestry'. *Hunky* was also used by blacks to mean 'a white person', thus supporting the likelihood that **honky** is just a variant, rather than an entirely unrelated word.

This *hunky,* which is first attested around 1900, is probably from *Hung(arian),* perhaps influenced by *hunk* in the sense 'a heavy-set, dull fellow'.

There are isolated Black English examples of both **honky** and *hunky* in the sense 'white person' from the mid-1940s, but **honky** does not become common until the late 1960s.

■ ■ ■

hoochie

John Sabo writes: **What exactly does the word "hootchie" mean? And where does it come from? My understanding, just from hearing it spoken, is that it's some kind of a trampy girl. So does this also tie in with Muddy Waters' song, "Hootchie-Kootchie Man"?**

■ The word **hoochie,** as it's usually spelled when one finds it written down, means 'a girl, especially one who is sexually promiscuous'.

Hoochie is of very recent origin—the earliest evidence I have is only from the early 1990s. It is mostly found in African-American English or rap music contexts, and is also found in the extended version *hoochie mama.*

The origin of **hoochie** is unclear. It seems likely to be related to *hootchy-kootchy* 'a sinuous, sexually suggestive dance resembling a belly dance, performed by a woman'; this term is itself of unknown origin. (In its early use it was often associated with a performer at the 1893 World's Fair in Chicago, but related senses are attested in 1890.) There are examples from the 1980s of *hootchy-kootchy* in the sense 'sexual intercourse', and **hoochie** probably comes from this sense; slang terms for women often have sexual meanings as well.

■ ■ ■

hooker

Ted Faber writes: **While reading Shelby Foote's *The Civil War: A Narrative, Volume II*, I came upon the delightful assertion that we get our slang term "hooker," meaning prostitute, from General "Fighting Joe" Hooker, who apparently kept quite the lively headquarters. I've checked a couple more scholarly sources for this etymology and had no luck confirming it. Can you confirm or deny?**

■ The slang term **hooker** 'a prostitute, especially a streetwalker' does not stem from the name of Major General Joseph "Fighting Joe" Hooker (1814–1879).

General Hooker was certainly known for his eccentricity; Ulysses S. Grant described him as "a dangerous man . . . not subordinate to his superiors." He was also known for the poor character of his men, who got into trouble for abuses of liquor on a fairly frequent basis. Popular stories attribute the word **hooker** to the general Hooker in several different ways; sometimes it is said that his men were especially desirous of prostitutes when on leave, and sometimes one hears that Hooker actually let his men keep prostitutes in the barracks.

However, Hooker is not responsible for the word **hooker,** simply because the word predates the Civil War by a good margin. The earliest known example of the word is found in 1845, in North Carolina: "If he comes by way of Norfolk he will find any number of pretty Hookers in the Brick row not far from French's hotel."

Another pre–Civil War example is found in the second edition of John Bartlett's *Dictionary of Americanisms* in 1859; Bartlett defines **hooker** as "A resident of the Hook, i.e. a strumpet, a sailor's trull." He goes on to make the unlikely speculation that the word is "So called from the number of houses of ill-fame frequented by sailors at the Hook (i.e., Corlear's Hook) in the city of New York."

Some historians have suggested that **hooker** was, if not coined, at least popularized during the Civil War, and that our general was indeed the cause of this popularization.

The true origin of **hooker** seems to be the earlier verb *hook* meaning 'to entice; swindle', and the agent suffix *-er*, with **hooker** thus meaning literally 'a person who entices; a swindler'.

■　■　■

hopefully

Mike Fischer writes: **Hopefully, you'll be able to clearly explain what is so wrong with stating my hopes in this manner. It "sounds" wrong to me, but I may have been swayed by critical opinion.**

■ There are two important things to remember about this use of **hopefully.** The first is that there's absolutely nothing wrong with it at all. The second is that if it sounds wrong to you, you should by all means avoid it, because so many people are convinced it *is* wrong that you're better off not getting into the mess.

The original use of **hopefully** was as an adverb meaning 'in a hopeful manner': "The beggar looked up hopefully." The newer use means 'it is hoped that; I hope; one hopes': "Hopefully, we'll get there on time." An adverb used in this way is known, variously, as a "sentence adverb," a "sentence modifier," or a "disjunct." There are very many other sentence adverbs, and few arouse any negative reaction: "Ironically, he was found guilty again," "Clearly, he's an idiot," and so forth.

Although there are examples of sentence adverbs from the seventeenth century and perhaps earlier, they do not become common until relatively recently. The sentence-adverb use of **hopefully** first seems to appear around 1900, and many examples are known from the 1930s. When it became very common, in the 1960s, there was a strong negative reaction to its use, especially among conservative writers; these objections were strongest through the 1960s and 1970s. The objections are probably the result of the sudden popularity of the use, but as mentioned, this use represents an entire class of words, most of which are considered unremarkable and a number of which have been in at least occasional use for several centuries without comment.

In short, if there are problems with **hopefully,** they are not problems restricted to this one word. If "I hope" is more accurate or more direct—which it is not, necessarily—then one is free to use it instead, but similar arguments could be made about many other words or constructions. In a few cases, some people feel that **hopefully** can be ambiguous, e.g., "Hopefully we'll go shopping tomorrow" could mean that we will go shopping in a hopeful manner or that the speaker hopes that we'll go shopping. Truly ambiguous examples, however, seem rare—my sentence is rather forced—and in any case ambiguity is more often the result of poor wording than of the use of a specific word.

Whatever can be said in defense of the sentence-adverb use of **hopefully,** the fact remains that very many people are sure that it is always wrong. If it sounds unnatural to you, you're better off avoiding it, since you won't have to defend anything that way.

■ ■ ■

horrific

Joe Kidd writes: **Is "horrific" really a word or is it just a contraction of "horrible" and "terrific"?**

■ Even if **horrific** were a contraction of *horrible* and *terrific,* it would still be a real word, but in any case **horrific** is a regular formation that's actually a few years older than *terrific.*

Horrific, which means 'causing horror', is first found in English in the 1650s (*terrific* is first found in the 1660s). It is one of many words formed from a noun and the suffix *-fic,* which means 'making, producing, or causing (the thing specified in the initial element)'. **Horrific** 'causing horror' is one example, and some others are *pacific, soporific,* and *honorific.*

The *-fic* suffix is ultimately from Latin *-ficus,* a combining form of the verb *facere* 'to make or do'. It's not always possible to determine the exact order of the development, because a word can end up with a *-fic* suffix in several ways: as a borrowing of a Latin word that ends with *-ficus,* such as *terrific,* which comes directly from Latin *terrificus* 'terrifying'; as a borrowing of a French word that ends in *-fique,* itself of course from Latin, such as **horrific,** a borrowing of French *horrifique* (we know it's from French because the first occurrence in English is in a translation of Rabelais, who uses the French equivalent); as a borrowing from another Romance language (Italian and Spanish have the suffix *-fico*), or as an English coinage *(acidific).*

Terrific is interesting in that it has undergone a semantic change. Its original meaning is 'causing terror', but it has developed the senses 'extremely great or intense' ("terrific speed," "terrific applause") and 'extremely good; wonderful' ("terrific weather"), which parallels the development of several similar words.

■ ■ ■

hose

Jerry Schwarz writes: **I just responded to a question saying that our network was "hosed" and I couldn't find an answer for him until the network was restored. I presume that "hosed" in this sense means doused by water, but what was the first thing to which that treatment was applied?**

■ It's actually not very clear what the semantic development of this sense of **hose** is; there are at least three plausible meanings that can give rise to it.

The very earliest sense of **hose** as a verb is 'to supply with hose [i.e., stockings]', which we can dismiss as irrelevant; the sense 'to water or spray with a hose' is a late-nineteenth-century use. This gave rise to a slang sense first found in World War I: 'to riddle with automatic-weapons fire; bombard heavily'. The use of **hose** meaning 'to damage or destroy' (or in your case, specifically, 'to render temporarily inoperative') could be a figurative use of this sense.

Another sense of **hose,** verb, is 'to beat with a rubber hose'. Such beatings, which could make up part of the "third degree" method of inter-rogation, were practiced in the 1920s and 1930s. Your **hose** could be a fig-urative use of *this* sense too.

Finally, there is a sense of **hose** meaning 'to copulate with', a verb use of **hose** 'the penis'. Like many words for sex, **hose** can be used in senses 'to victimize; cheat; vanquish', etc. So we could interpret your **hose** this way too, viewed as equivalent to "Our network is screwed" (or insert sex-ual verb of your choice).

There is no good way to establish exactly which strand of senses lies behind the current meaning; all three of these have been common for many years and could easily be the basis for the sense you're asking about. It's probably safe to say, though, that 'to water with a hose' is at best indirectly connected.

■ ■ ■

how come?

Maggie writes: **How come we ask "how come"? It makes no apparent sense; I've never seen its origin; we use it all the time. How come?**

■ The admittedly obscure-looking **how come?,** a colloquial Americanism for 'how is it that?' or 'why?', is based on a shortened form of an expression such as "how comes it that . . . ?" or "how did it come about (that). . . ?"

These still somewhat obscure phrases depend on a usually archaic sense of *come* meaning 'to come about; happen; occur; become', combined with an archaic word order placing "how" and "come" together at the beginning of a sentence.

Although this type of use is rare now, it was once very common. Here's a selection of examples showing this earlier use of *how* with *come* (not the same as our modern colloquial phrase), some show slightly different structures, such as the Austen quote, which is "come about" in an archaic word order: "How comes it then that he is prince of devils?" (Marlowe, *Doctor Faustus*); "How comes it that they travel?" (Shakespeare, *Hamlet*); "How comes it thus?" (Milton, *Paradise Lost*); "How comes any particular thing to be of this or that sort?" (John Locke, *An Essay Concerning Human Understanding*); "How comes it to be any concern of yours?" (Fielding, *Tom Jones*); "How comes this about; there must be some mistake" (Jane Austen, *Mansfield Park*); "How comes it that we whalemen of America now outnumber all the rest of the banded whalemen in the world?" (Melville, *Moby-Dick*); and "Then if it's so precious how comes it to be cheap?" (Henry James, *The Golden Bowl*).

The American sense is derived from uses like these, and as the original phrase "how comes it . . ." has become difficult to understand, the expression **how come** has become more and more a set phrase.

As we're familiar with it, **how come** first appears in John Bartlett's 1848 *Dictionary of Americanisms,* one of the important early books dealing with American slang and colloquial expressions. Bartlett's comments suggest that it was in widespread use when he wrote.

■　■　■

huckleberry

Warren Booth writes: **One of my favorite movies is *Tombstone*. It has an all-star cast headed up by Kurt Russell and Val Kilmer (who gives a fine performance as Doc Holliday). In the movie the phrase "I'm your huckaberry" is used several times. What does it imply?**

■ **Huckleberry** (the "huckaberry" version in the movie is a dialectal pronunciation) has had a few different senses referring to people. One is simply 'a man; fellow'—this was used very generally, the way "guy" is today. Another is 'a foolish, inept, or inconsequential person; jerk'. But the phrase *one's huckleberry* has the special meaning of 'the very person for a particular requirement; the right person'. *I'm your huckleberry* means 'I'm the right man for you'.

These senses of **huckleberry** developed around the time of the Civil War. The phrase *one's huckleberry* is found in various sources from the 1870s, 1880s, and 1890s, showing that the use in the movie, set in 1881, is historically accurate.

■ ■ ■

humongous

Scouser8@netcom.ca writes: **What can you tell me about the word "humongous"?**

■ **Humongous** is a slang word meaning 'extraordinarily large; huge; tremendous'. It is first found in the late 1960s.

The word is probably based on *huge* and *monstrous,* and has the stress pattern of *tremendous.* A partial explanation of **humongous** and its relations is that it's an "expressive coinage," which is dictionary-speak for "it sounds cool." Some similar formations are *bodacious,* a much older word blending *bold* and *audacious,* and, from the same era as **humongous,** *gigunda,* which is based on *gigantic.*

Humongous is found in several other forms, including simple spelling variants (*humungus,* etc.) and more significant alterations (*humongo,* which should be compared to *mongo* and *mondo; humongoid*).

■ ■ ■

ichor

Bob Treuber writes: **"Ichor." What is it and how would you use the word? My summer reading is Colleen McCullough's series on ancient Rome and (anachronisms aside) she uses some "interesting" words. What's your call?**

■ The mythological sense of **ichor** is 'an ethereal fluid that flows in the veins of the Greek gods instead of blood'. Using this sense of the word is pretty tough unless you're translating Homer or writing fantasy or historical fiction set in ancient Greece or Rome.

If you're set on injecting it into conversation, however, there are some options. There is a technical medical sense: 'the watery ooze from an abrasion, scar, or wound'. Perhaps you should avoid that one. There's also a technical sense in geology: 'fluid from a magma'. If you need to ask . . .

But you're safe with the figurative use 'blood' or 'any fluid (real or imaginary) held to resemble blood'. This is primarily a poetic sense. In "The Colossus," Sylvia Plath wrote: "The ichor of the spring/Proceeds clear as it ever did/From the broken throat, the marshy lip." Try having some soup on a cold winter morning and saying, "Wow, that really gets my ichor warmed up." The rhyme with "liquor" also makes it a natural for rap music, if that's your inclination. Critics will hail you.

Ichor is a direct borrowing from the Greek *īchōr*. The geological sense is from the early twentieth century; all the others have been with us since the seventeenth century.

■ ■ ■

i.e./e.g.

David Bogner writes: **Can you tell me when it is appropriate to use "e.g." and "i.e."? I have seen them both used before an example is given but I'm not sure what they stand for or if they are even synonymous.**

■ Both **i.e.** and **e.g.** are abbreviations of Latin phrases. They are not synonymous, though they are often confused.

The abbreviation **i.e.** stands for *id est,* Latin for "that is." **I.e.** is usually used to clarify or expand a previous word or statement. A made-up example: "The group performed on period instruments, i.e., ones that were made during the composer's lifetime, which have a different sound from modern instruments." The **i.e.** in this sentence explains what the expression "period instruments" means.

The abbreviation **e.g.** stands for *exemplī grātiā*, which means "for example" (literally "for the sake of example"). **E.g.** is usually used to introduce examples illustrating a previous word or statement. Another made-up example: "The group performed on a variety of period instruments, e.g., the crumhorn and the viola da gamba." Here, **e.g.** introduces examples of period instruments, but the **e.g.** does not explain the phrase itself.

The best way to keep the two abbreviations straight is to remember that **i.e.** is "that is" and **e.g.** is "for example." You should always be able to substitute the English phrases if the abbreviations are used correctly. If you're doing the writing yourself, you can always replace the abbreviation with the appropriate English translation, or rewrite the sentence to avoid any possibility of confusion.

■ ■ ■

impact

> *Gail Blaufarb writes:* **A common word usage which thoroughly annoys me is the word "impact," as in "His policies had an impact on the environment." I suspect that many people don't know whether to use "effect" or "affect," so they substitute "impact." Is this an appropriate use of the word "impact?"**

■ Yes, it is a perfectly appropriate use of the word **impact.** It is also, however, one which has generated a fair amount of criticism over the years. The use of the noun in figurative senses is now usually accepted— or at least not condemned as vigorously as it has been in previous years— but the verb **impact,** in such examples as "Poor quality will negatively impact sales" or "The decision may impact on your whole career" is still a bugbear for many people.

The noun in the sense 'influence; effect' has been used by quite a number of prominent authors over the years, including Samuel Taylor Coleridge, Bertrand Russell, Oliver Wendell Holmes, Virginia Woolf, Christopher Isherwood, Eudora Welty, and T. S. Eliot. Though this use has existed since the early nineteenth century—the Coleridge example is the first one cited in the *Oxford English Dictionary*—it did not become popular until the middle of the twentieth century, when it generated much criticism, but by now it has largely blended into common use.

The verb in the figurative sense 'to have an impact [on]' first shows up in the middle of the twentieth century, but it did not become common until around 1970. It often appears in business or political contexts. Use of this verb continues to generate extremely strong criticism, so if you're sensitive to this, you should avoid its use; substitute *affect* or *influence* instead. But there is nothing intrinsically objectionable about it, and it is rather common. It is likely that it will eventually go the way of the verb *contact*, once also the subject of intense criticism, and now usually unremarked.

■ ■ ■

in- as a prefix

Don K. Ferguson writes: **Do you have any insights, please, on why "infamous" means bad, yet another "in" word—invaluable—means good? Is there any history you can offer on why this prefix can have different connotations?**

■ The prefix **in-** has given rise to a passel of questions about the meanings of words that use it. The explanations vary—in some cases, it has to do with the fact that there are actually three different prefixes **in-**; in others, a language change has obscured the development of a current meaning.

We'll combine the first two **in-** prefixes, since they have roughly the same meaning. One comes from Old English, the other from Latin, but they are both equivalent to the English *in*. This first **in-** can have the broad meaning *in (inland, entrust)*, and can also function as a general intensive *(incantation)*. Depending on the phonetic context, it can take several different forms, including *im-, em-,* and *en-*.

The other **in-** is a Latin negative prefix, equivalent to the English *un-*. Some of its other forms are *im-, il-,* and *ir-*. This prefix is used to indicate a negative or the absence of something.

The word *infamous* uses the negative prefix. It does not mean 'not famous'; it means 'having an extremely bad reputation' and hence 'wicked'. This is because it's not an English formation of **in-** and *-famous*, but a borrowing of Latin *infāmis* 'without a reputation', formed from the sense of *fāma* in Latin meaning 'a reputation'.

The word *invaluable* also uses the negative prefix, but the explanation for the unusual sense of the word is that *valuable* is not the current meaning 'having considerable monetary or moral worth', but an obsolete meaning 'capable of being valued'. So etymologically, *invaluable* means 'not capable of being valued'; compare the semantics of *priceless*. It's the shift of the sense of *valuable* that makes it confusing.

Finally, *inflammable*, which means 'capable of being set on fire; combustible', is one that often confuses people, because the **in-** here is *not* the negative prefix. It is our first prefix, having the meaning *in*, so *inflammable* has an etymological meaning like 'into flames' (it's cognate with the English word *inflame,* which doesn't give anyone any trouble). But because of the fear that some people would mistake the prefix in *inflammable* for the negative one, the word *flammable* was coined. And that's why *flammable* and *inflammable* mean the same thing.

■ ■ ■

inamorata

Tiffany Kowalski writes: **What, may I ask, is the origin of the word "inamorata"? Seeing that it has the word "amor" in it and means a woman with whom one is in love, I always wondered where it might have come from.**

■ **Inamorata** is one of the many borrowings from Italian that English got in its Early Modern period.

Inamorata, which means 'a woman who loves or is loved; a female sweetheart or lover', and the masculine form *inamorato,* are both past participles of Italian *innamorare* 'to inflame with love'. They literally mean '(a woman/man) inflamed by love'.

The verb *innamorare* is formed from *in-* and *amore,* from Latin *amor* 'love'. It is parallel to the English word *enamor,* which is from French but has the same elements.

The masculine form *inamorato,* which is now pretty rare, is first found in the 1590s. The feminine form **inamorata** is first found in the 1650s and seems to have been rarer until recently, which is somewhat surprising given the current prevalence of this term.

■ ■ ■

indict/indite

Les Aldridge writes: **On the "Chopra Forum" (a *Random House* Web page), someone used "indict" then later decided, incorrectly, that it should be "indite". It turns out that both have the sense of "to write down, as in poetry or prose" but only 'indict' means to "charge with an offense." Both seem to come from the exact same roots. How did these homonyms aquire their slightly different connotations?**

■ This can be complicated if we try to deal with every last strand here, but bear with me and we'll try to get through it as easily as possible without too much oversimplification.

The first word to consider is **indite.** The main sense of this word is 'to compose or write (a speech, poem, etc.)'. Another main sense is 'to dictate', but this is now obsolete. **Indite** is found in various spellings, but we'll ignore those that don't cross the path of **indict**, and just say that it comes from Old French *enditer,* which in turn comes from an unattested Vulgar Latin form *indictāre,* the frequentative (a form that indicates habitual action) of Latin *indīcere* 'to say; proclaim'. The base of the frequentative form is the base of English *dictate* and related words. The spelling of **indite** with *in-* instead of *en-* reflects the spelling of the Latin original.

Let's turn to **indict,** which broadly means 'to accuse of a wrongdoing' (we'll ignore definitional subtleties as irrelevant to our purpose now). This word was originally spelled *endite* or **indite** or in various other ways that don't have the -c- in them, which is the problem. These early forms of **indict** (we'll spell it that way to avoid confusion) are also borrowed from Old French *enditer,* but with the different meaning 'to accuse'. The spelling **indict**—with the -c-, that is—was adopted in the late sixteenth century (the spelling is first attested in the derived form *indictment*), a consciously altered spelling under the influence of Medieval Latin *indictāre.*

To put things simply, **indict** is a spelling variant of **indite**. Before the spellings diverged, it would have been appropriate to call them different senses of the same word. Both are influenced by Latin forms, but **indict** is thoroughly Latinized, while **indite** has a Latinized prefix but keeps the French root. Both words, by the way, are pronounced identically.

■　■　■

inept/inapt

Marty Breslow writes: **Inapt and inept: The definitions of these words seem to be the same. Is there any reason we have both of them? "Inept" seems to apply to the actor and "inapt" to the action.**

■　The words **inapt** and **inept,** though related and having some semantic overlap, are not synonymous. Let's look at this historically and see how the two words developed.

The original root for these words is the Latin adjective *aptus,* which means 'fastened' and hence 'prepared; suitable', and derives from the verb *apere* 'to fasten; attach'. This Latin *aptus* gives us the English word *apt,* which has various meanings including 'disposed; prone', 'likely', and 'suitable'. Still in Latin, however, the negative of *aptus* is *ineptus,* formed from the negative prefix *in-* and *-eptus,* the combining form of *aptus* (the change from *a* to *e* is regular under these conditions).

In Latin, *ineptus* meant 'having no sense of propriety; lacking in judgment; foolish; silly'. It was usually used of people, but also of things. The English word **inept** is a direct borrowing of the Latin word. It has several meanings, including 'lacking skill or aptitude', 'awkward or incompetent', 'inappropriate or out of place, usually to an absurd level' and 'foolish; absurd' (e.g., "an inept remark"). The main connotation of **inept** is that of active incompetence or absurdity; describing someone or something as **inept** is an actively negative statement.

Inapt is an English coinage, based on the negative prefix *in-* and the existing English word *apt* (both of which, of course, are derived from Latin). It has two main senses: 'not apt or fitting; inappropriate; unsuitable', and 'without aptitude; unskillful'. The first sense is fairly distinct from **inept;** the second sense can be similar. The important difference, though, is in the connotation: **inapt** is much less strong than **inept; inapt** means 'not appropriate' or 'without aptitude', but not 'absurdly bad'. **Inapt,** therefore, is also negative, but not actively so.

Inept is first found in English in the early sixteenth century; **inapt**, in the early seventeenth century.

■ ■ ■

infra dig

> *Sam Pratt writes:* How did the latinate (?) expression "infra dig" come into the language? My family used it pretty often, but it wasn't until high school that I realized it wasn't "in for dig." It also seems to have a lot of possible connotations, indicating anything from mild distastefulness to run-of-the-mill tackiness to outright offensiveness.

■ **Infra dig,** which, contrary to expectations, is not a form of bibliographic reference, is indeed of Latin origin. It is a colloquial shortening of the Latin phrase *infrā dignitātem,* or 'below (one's) dignity', and is used in English in that sense; 'undignified' is a shorter way of saying the same thing. Example from Saul Bellow: "Doing the floors on his knees didn't bother him.. . . It never occurred to him that it was infra dig."

Like "undignified" itself, its interpretation depends entirely on one's own sense of dignity: the very proper could use it for mildly distasteful things, while the shameless could reserve it for things of extreme offensiveness. This makes the expression admirably useful for all sorts of condescension.

The shortened **infra dig** is first found in English in the 1820s, from the pen of Sir Walter Scott; the essayist William Hazlitt used the full form slightly earlier in the 1820s. The expression was first regarded as an abbreviation and written *infra dig.;* like *per cent.,* it eventually dropped the period and was considered an expression in its own right.

■ ■ ■

in like Flynn

> *Chip Hartford writes:* I say the phrase "in like Flynn" is a reference to Errol Flynn. My boyfriend insists that the phrase is "in like flint," but offers no explanation of what it refers to. We both understand what the expression means but can't agree on the actual wording. What do you say?

■ The phrase **in like Flynn** does refer to Errol Flynn, the Australian-born movie actor noted for swashbuckling romantic roles *(Captain Blood, The Adventures of Robin Hood)* and for, um, a colorful private life.

The phrase means 'quickly or emphatically in' (in any sense of the word "in"); usually, in other words, 'in circumstances of assured success'. The allusion is usually assumed to be to Flynn's celebrated sexual exploits, the most notorious of which resulted in a charge of statutory rape for an affair with a teenage girl. Flynn's drinking, drug taking, and sexual libertinism were notable even by the standards of Hollywood at the time. The earliest example of the phrase, however, in a glossary of air force terms from World War II, claims that the allusion is to the ease with which Flynn accomplished his cinematic feats.

The appearance of this phrase in the form *in like flint* refers to the 1967 movie *In Like Flint,* starring James Coburn, a sequel to *Our Man Flint.* The title of this spy film spoof alludes to the phrase **in like Flynn,** which was quite well established by the late 1960s.

■ ■ ■

inveigle

Suzanne Whalen writes: **A new word for me is "inveigle." Would you give me two different examples of it used in a sentence so I can put the word to use myself? What is the origin?**

■ The word **inveigle** has two closely related senses that have to do with accomplishing something through artful talk. The first is 'to entice or lure through artful talk or inducements', and the second is 'to obtain by beguiling talk or methods'.

A good example of the first, personal sense may be found in Milton's great poem *Comus,* from 1634: "Yet they have many baits, and guileful spells/To inveigle and invite the unwary sense." A more recent example, from that children's favorite *Anne of Green Gables:* "Matthew was there, having been inveigled into the party only goodness and Anne knew how." And for a very up-to-date citation, let's jump to 1996 and a *New York Times* article about a chess match between Garry Kasparov and the IBM chess computer Deep Blue: "Deep Blue had tried to inveigle Kasparov into grabbing several pawn offers, but the champion was not fooled."

The second sense, 'to obtain by beguiling talk or methods', is more recent and is considerably less common. An invented example is, "He managed to inveigle a free ticket from the usher."

Inveigle is first attested in the late fifteenth century, and is a variant of *envegle,* from Old French *avogler* 'to blind', ultimately from Latin *ab oculis* 'with eyes taken away'.

■ ■ ■

irregardless

Lynn Duffield writes: **Should I let it bother me when people use the word "irregardless"? I don't feel that "regardless" deserves a prefix, but people use it anyway, regardless of what I say. To me the word is redundant.**

■ To most people the word is redundant. **Irregardless** is one of the few words eliciting uniform condemnation across the spectrum of usage writers.

Irregardless, which has the same meaning as *regardless,* is an Americanism first recorded in the early twentieth century. It combines the negative prefix *ir-* (a form of IN-), probably taken from *irrespective,* and *regardless,* which already has a negative meaning through the suffix *-less.* It is thus, in theory, redundant, and like many theoretically redundant words it has been criticized by usage commentators. Its use may stem from a desire to add emphasis to *regardless.*

A common response is to deny the fact that **irregardless** is even a word. A year ago, after a prominent book editor used it, the *New York Times* called it a "non-word"; a recent usage book claims that "this isn't a word" and "there is no such word." One is tempted to ask, "If it's not a word, what is it? A ham sandwich?"

What is clear is that this ham sandwich, while occasionally found in the speech of educated people, and very rarely in edited prose, is so widely condemned that it cannot be considered Standard English.

In sum, yes, you should let it bother you.

■ ■ ■

isograms

Yolanda Patterson writes: **There is a contest going on in my office and I cannot figure out the answer; can you *please* help me. The question is this: What word has 15 letters and none of the letters repeat themselves?**

■ I normally don't answer "contest"-type questions, but since this seems to be an office-only affair, and since we haven't tackled any word-game issues lately, we'll give it a shot.

Words that don't repeat any letters are known as **isograms.** (There are also more specific types of **isograms,** such as **isograms** that do repeat a specified letter, but these are beyond the scope of your question.) The longest **isogram** in English that is common—by "common" I mean that it appears in most small dictionaries, and people who aren't word nuts know it—is *ambidextrously,* which has fourteen letters.

There are two fifteen-letter isograms; the one usually cited as the longest **isogram** in English is *dermatoglyphics,* which refers to the ridged patterns on the fingertips (fingerprints, in other words), palms, and soles of the feet. I assume that this is the answer you are charged with finding. The other fifteen-letter isogram is the adjective *uncopyrightable,* which appeared in dictionaries only recently and thus never made it into the canonical list of **isograms**. A theoretical nominalization of this word could be pluralized to *uncopyrightables,* making a sixteen-letter **isogram**, but this has never been found and does not appear in dictionaries.

Finally, the mother of all **isograms** is *subdermatoglyphic* 'of or pertaining to the layer of skin beneath the fingertips'. This seventeen-letter **isogram** is actually attested in a dermatologists' journal, but it was placed there at the suggestion of a word buff, who asked a doctor to use it in print in order to claim it as the longest **isogram**.

I'll leave you with the interesting fact that the English word having the most different letters only has sixteen different letters—in other words, being able to repeat letters doesn't actually give you many more. (There are four words with sixteen different letters, including *pseudolamellibranchiata;* suffice it to say that the others aren't any more interesting.)

You can send my share of the prize to me care of Random House, thank you.

■　■　■

jawbone

Gail Griffin writes: **Hey there! I am seeking the origin of the term "jawboning" (in use today to an appalling degree in relation to Alan Greenspan and the markets). (A coworker suggests perhaps it has to do with an ape beating another ape to death with a human bone in *2001*!) Any thoughts?**

■ Yes, that your coworker has a vivid imagination.

Jawbone, which in its literal meaning 'the bone of a jaw, especially a mandible' goes back to the fifteenth century, also has a number of senses referring to the faculty of speech. These parallel other uses of words for the mouth (or related body parts) that refer to speech: *mouth (off)* 'to speak, especially abusively', *lip* 'impudent or disrespectful speech', *chin-wag* 'to speak or gossip', and *bump one's gums* 'to chat' are a few examples.

Jaw by itself has been used as a noun and verb meaning 'talk' and 'to talk' since the middle of the eighteenth century. **Jawbone,** which can be viewed as an elaboration of this, has had a variety of speech-related meanings as well. As a noun, **jawbone** has meant 'credit in a store' and 'talk'; we have a *jawbone wager* 'a bet made orally as a pastime (rather than a real bet)', and **jawbone** as an adjective meaning 'authorized orally; (hence, of a military command) temporary or acting'. These various senses date from the Civil War to World War I. The sense 'to talk', which is the direct source of your sense, comes a bit later, but since *jaw* 'to talk' is from the eighteenth century, the idea was certainly there.

The specific sense of **jawbone** you're asking about is 'to admonish or persuade, especially by urging voluntary compliance upon rather than by exerting one's authority'. The interpretation of this is somewhat up for grabs—if the president says, "I think it would be a good idea for you to make some changes," and the implication is "because if you don't, I'm going to regulate your industry out of existence," this may not be everyone's idea of "voluntary compliance," but the point is, it's not the same as the president introducing regulatory legislation directly.

This **jawbone** is found in three parts of speech—as a verb, as cited above; as an adjective, meaning 'persuasive but noncompulsory' (e.g., "the jawbone approach to market stabilization"), and as a noun, meaning 'the practice of persuasion rather than compulsion as a method of accomplishing political goals'. These senses are all first found in the late 1950s to mid-1960s. The movie *2001: A Space Odyssey* was released in 1968.

■ ■ ■

Jesus H. Christ

Daniel Gordon writes: What does the *H* stand for in "Jesus H. Christ!"?

■ "Haploid" is the joking answer if you're a techie, but the real answer is probably that it comes from the Greek monogram for *Jesus*, "IHS" or "IHC." The *H* is the capital form of the Greek letter eta, but was reinterpreted as being the Latin letter *H* (that is, "aitch"). (In the "IHC" variant, the *C* is the Byzantine Greek form of sigma, the *S* letter.)

The *IHS* or *IHC* monogram was (and still is) used on religious articles as an emblem, and people unfamiliar with the Greek assumed that the *H* was a part of the name "Jesus" or of "Jesus Christ." (A similar mistake was made many centuries earlier; a common spelling of *Jesus* in Medieval Latin was "Ihesus.")

The use of **Jesus H. Christ** as a profane oath dates back at least to the late nineteenth century, but was probably around earlier. Mark Twain wrote in his autobiography that even in his childhood the oath was considered old.

■　■　■

jitney

Charles Knapp writes: What is the origin of "jitney," for a bus on a regular route?

■ **Jitney** was originally a slang word for a nickel, or five cents. The word then came to be used for a bus that carried passengers along a regular route, since the fare for these rides was five cents. Buses like this continued to be called **jitneys** long after the fares rose.

The word's first known appearance is in 1903, in the 'nickel' sense. The 'bus' sense is first attested in 1914, but seems to have become popular very quickly, since we have a number of pre-1920 examples of the term.

The ultimate origin of the word is unknown.

■　■　■

Jones

Brendan Pimper writes: I was reading something about English last names, and how they typically came from the family profession (Miller, Carpenter, Smith, etc.). We'll ignore my last name for now, thank you. For some reason, "Smith" always brings up a free-association link to "Jones" for me. Did "Jones" once mean something? I know it has a meaning today of "craving," such as "I am jonesing for a cigarette" or "I've got the love jones." I think that this meaning is more modern, though, and I don't see how it could become a surname. Got any clues?

■ Names derived from a family job, called "occupational names" by onomasticians (that's the fancy way to say 'specialists in proper names'), are certainly common, but they are only one form of family name (as "last names" or "surnames" are properly called). Another very common derivation is the "patronymic" family name, that is, one derived from a male ancestor's given name. Patronymic family names include Henry, Raymond, Williams(on) (and virtually every name ending in "-son" or "-sen"), and MacDonald (and virtually every name beginning with "Mac" or "O' ").

The family name **Jones** is simply a patronymic for the given name "John." Though Jones is by far the most common patronymic based on John, there are many others, in many languages. **Jones** is especially common in Wales.

The use of **jones** in the sense 'crave' is a rather recent development. The first meaning was 'a craving for heroin', attested in the early 1960s; the sense 'a craving of any kind' developed by 1970. This parallels the history of *yen,* which now means 'a desire or craving', but originally referred specifically to 'a craving for opium'. The verbal use 'to crave' arose by the mid-1970s.

Though it seems likely that this word is based on the family name **Jones,** the semantic development is unknown.

■ ■ ■

juggernaut

yoden@ibm.net writes: What does the word "juggernaut" mean? Where does it come from?

■ The usual sense of **juggernaut** is 'any large, overpowering, or destructive force or object that crushes everything in its path'. Some recent examples: "Mr. Versace started his own house just as the Milan fashion juggernaut was getting under way" (*New York Times*); "Apparently, contrary to popular belief, the Barnes & Noble juggernaut does not inevitably flatten any bookstore in its path" (also *New York Times*).

Another sense is 'anything requiring blind devotion or cruel sacrifice'. A sense common in England is 'a heavy truck', but this is not found in America.

The word **juggernaut** comes from Hindi *jagannāth* 'lord of the world', from Sanskrit; the elements are *jagat* 'world' and *nātha* 'lord'.

In Hindu mythology, **juggernaut** was originally an epithet of the god Krishna. Specifically, it refers to an idol of Krishna, at Puri in Orissa, India, annually drawn on a large cart; devotees of Krishna are said to have formerly thrown themselves under the wheels of the cart to be crushed to death.

■ ■ ■

jury-rig

Holly Duthie writes: **What about "jury-rig"? How did rigging a jury lead to fixing something with Band-Aids and bubble gum?**

■ It didn't; despite the fact that rigging a jury and **jury-rig** use the same words, their resemblance is coincidental.

Jury-rig is based on one word, "jury," which is a nautical sense meaning 'makeshift; temporary' and another word "rig," referring to a ship's sails and masts. The first known example of this "jury" is the compound *jury-mast,* 'a temporary mast put up to replace one that has been broken or lost', attested since the early seventeenth century. A **jury-rig,** then, is 'a temporary or makeshift rigging', and the verb is used figuratively in the sense 'to assemble or arrange hastily in a makeshift manner'. The origin of this word "jury" is not certain, but some scholars identify it with *iuwere,* a late Middle English word meaning 'help; aid', borrowed from the Old French *ajurie.*

The expression *to rig a jury* is based on a different "jury" and a different "rig." The "jury" in question is the standard sense 'group of people sworn to render a verdict under the law', which is from an Old French word meaning 'to swear' that's unrelated to the previous "jury" we've discussed. The "rig" means 'to manipulate fraudulently or underhandedly', and is probably from an earlier noun 'a prank; swindle', ultimately of unknown origin. This "rig" may be related to the nautical sense, but this is unclear. It is first found in the mid-nineteenth century.

■ ■ ■

kangaroo court

Motekaitis Ramunas writes: **We all use the term "kangaroo court" at times, but what is its origin?**

■ I don't know. **Kangaroo court** has gotten a great deal of attention from word buffs, but none of the proposed theories seems certain.

The expression **kangaroo court** is first found in the American West in the 1850s; there's no evidence tying it directly to Australia, where kangaroos are from.

The original sense is 'an unauthorized or irregularly conducted proceeding (as one in frontier areas or among criminals in prison), especially one where principles of justice are ignored or travestied'. The common current sense is 'an actual court or legal proceeding that is flagrantly unfair'. There's also a verb *to kangaroo* meaning 'to convict in a prisoner's kangaroo court' or 'to convict unjustly in an actual court'.

One etymology is that **kangaroo court** alludes to the kangaroo as something eccentric or unusual. There are stories from the midnineteenth century of the kangaroo seeming to defy "laws of nature," so this should be considered at least plausible.

Less likely explanations are that a **kangaroo court** would always result in a conviction, and Australia was known as a penal colony; that **kangaroo courts** tried claim jumpers, with the "jump" connection being exploited for a pun; or, least likely of all, that kangaroos, like juries, would sit staring stupidly for long periods of time before jumping to a decision.

■　■　■

kaput

Margot Liggett writes: **Please explain the origin of the word "kaput," which is commonly used to mean "finished," "dead," or "over." I can't think of any words it could be related to or where it may have come from.**

■ The word **kaput,** used in various related senses having the general meaning 'done for; ruined; broken; etc.', is a borrowing from German, where it had the same sense. The German word is borrowed from the French *capot,* which meant 'without tricks (in the card game piquet)', that is, 'having a score of zero'. The semantics are similar to *bust,* which can mean both 'ruined' and 'over the limit and hence losing the hand (in the card game blackjack)', except that of course the blackjack sense is a development of the 'ruined' sense, while **kaput** is the other way around.

Kaput is first attested in an isolated example in the 1890s, which probably represents a use of the German word in an English passage; it doesn't become widely used in English until World War I.

■ ■ ■

keister

Tim Cavanaugh writes: **I must be getting old, because nobody seems to understand what the word "keyster" means anymore. Since I can't find it in the dictionary, I don't even know how to spell it, so I can't help. Is it "keyster" or "keister" or "keester" or "kiester"? All I know is that it's a slang word for buttocks, and it's only used by oldsters. Can you fill me in on at least the spelling, and possibly the history of this colorful term?**

■ You are not alone in a search for the spelling this word: Over the years, it's been recorded as *keister, kiester, keyster,* and *keester*—every form you suggest has been used in print. However, the most common spelling, and the one given as a preferred form by those dictionaries that include it, is **keister.**

Though there is some disagreement over the etymology, the most likely explanation is that it is a borrowing of German *Kiste* 'a box; case; chest', which also means 'the rump; buttocks' in German slang. Interestingly, the earliest use of the word in English slang is 'a traveling bag; suitcase', corresponding to the standard German sense. The 'suitcase' sense is first found in the 1880s, and is well attested by the 1910s or 1920s. Derived senses, used mainly in criminal circles, include 'a safe' and 'a jail; lockup'.

The usual current sense 'the buttocks' and occasionally 'the rectum or anus' is first found around 1930. While the word is somewhat old-fashioned, it is still in use. Like many words referring to the buttocks (especially *ass*), it has developed various subsenses, including 'copulation' (e.g., "I'd like to get some keister") and 'one's body; self' (e.g., "Get your keister out of here"). But the most interesting development, to my mind, is a rather gruesome verb use among prisoners: 'to hide (contraband) in the rectum', as in "I keistered that knife and brought it in here." This verb is first recorded in the 1980s, though there are examples of expressions like *keister plant* 'an act of concealing narcotics in the rectum' in prison memoirs from the 1940s. Here's hoping you never encounter this one personally.

■ ■ ■

kismet

Liz Fowler writes: **Whence comes the word "kismet," and what is its proper use?**

The word **kismet** means 'fate' or 'destiny', and comes from Turkish, a language underrepresented in these pages. In Turkish it means 'portion' or 'lot', and is a borrowing from Persian *qismat,* which itself is a borrowing from Arabic *qismah,* akin to *qasama* 'to divide'.

In English, **kismet** is used, for all intents and purposes, as a synonym for 'fate', albeit a rather cool-sounding one. From Rudyard Kipling: "It is my Kismet. No man can escape his Kismet" (*Kim,* 1901). From F. Scott Fitzgerald, as a heading: "KISMET Within two weeks Amory and Rosalind were deeply and passionately in love" (*This Side of Paradise,* 1920).

The best-known use of the word in English may be as the title of a 1953 Broadway musical, which featured "Stranger in Paradise," among other songs.

■ ■ ■

kit and caboodle

Brendan Pimper writes: **"The whole-kit-and-caboodle" (spelling stolen from the "Seuss" pages at your very own Random House Web site) is a phrase whose origin puzzles many of us here at work. Can you enlighten us?**

■ Of course. That's my job.

Kit and caboodle is simply a set phrase made up of two words that are both rare when used independently of each other. *Kit* is the same word as the one meaning 'a set of items for a specific purpose' (as in "tool kit"), but in this phrase is used broadly to mean 'a group of persons or things'. **Caboodle** is the word "boodle" (from Dutch *boedel* 'property' meaning 'a lot; pack; crowd; large quantity', with a variant of the intensive prefix "ker-" (as in *kerplunk* or *gazillion*—the prefix appears in many forms). The entire phrase *the whole kit and caboodle,* as it usually appears, is therefore redundant.

As discussed elsewhere (see FLOTSAM AND JETSAM), this use of a set phrase whose elements are individually unfamiliar (and are often synonyms) has many parallels in English.

Caboodle is first found in the mid-nineteenth century and is now rarely found alone. The phrase **kit and caboodle** is first found later in the nineteenth century. Both are Americanisms.

■ ■ ■

kitty-corner

Larry Zirlin writes: **Would you say that "kitty corner" from "cater-corner" meaning "placed at the diagonal" is an example of** FOLK ETYMOLOGY, **like "piggyback" and "bridegroom"? Do you think it's somehow mixed up with "caterwaul," which translates as "cat wailing?"**

■ Yes, **kitty-corner** 'on a diagonal line; in a diagonal position' is an excellent example of a folk etymology. FOLK ETYMOLOGY, also discussed under PIGGYBACK and WHEELBARROW, is the process of altering an uncommon word or element to conform it to one that's better known.

The original form, as you say, was *catercorner,* which is still the usual term. The "cater" element in this term is from the English dialect word *cater,* meaning 'diagonally', which is from an obsolete word meaning 'four', which ultimately goes back to *quattuor,* the Latin word for 'four'. This "cater" also turns up, in modified form, in the word *catawampus* 'crooked; askew'. Here it combines with our familiar word "corner." Since the "catercorner" form is obscure, it developed many variants, including **kitty-corner,** *catty-corner,* and others.

Catercorner is not related to *caterwaul,* the elements of which do mean 'cat wailing': the assumption that the "cater" in "catercorner" means 'cat' is exactly what gives rise to the folk etymology of "kitty-corner" in the first place. The existence of a word where "cater" actually **does** mean 'cat' (actually 'tomcat' in Middle Dutch, the source of English *cater-* in *caterwaul*) is a coincidence—one which may strengthen the folk etymology, but a coincidence nonetheless.

■ ■ ■

klick

Mike James writes: **Somewhere I've gotten into the habit of using "click" to mean both "kilometre" or "kilometre per hour," depending on the context. Can you tell me where this comes from?**

■ I can tell you where the word comes from geographically, but not why it comes from there.

Click, or in its more frequent spelling **klick,** is a military slang term that was used in the Vietnam War to mean 'a kilometer'. It's in common use, especially in the military, but it is still often associated with Vietnam. There are several less common subsenses, such as 'kilometers per hour' and '1,000 yards [rather than meters]'.

The word is first found in the early 1960s among American soldiers in Vietnam, though later recollections claim that it was in use in the 1950s by American soldiers in Germany. Its origin is unknown. The most likely possibility is simply that it's a shortening and alteration of *kilometer*, since both words have the "k" and "l" sounds in the same order. (The earliest evidence for the word spells it "click," but since *click* is an existing word, the 'kilometer' word may have been conformed to that spelling.) The shortening of words is a common feature of military lingo. But there's no firm evidence for this appealing story; most dictionaries that include the word give the etymology only as "origin unknown."

■ ■ ■

lame duck

willie6@mail.idt.net writes: **Where does the term "lame duck" come from?**

■ Ultimately, the origin comes from the idea that a **lame duck** is unable to move or accomplish anything at all; all the senses, viewed very broadly, mean 'ineffectual'.

The earliest sense, which first appears in the eighteenth century in England, is 'a person bankrupted by financial or stock speculation; a person not able to meet his or her debts'. Aside from the image of a **lame duck** as something that's floundering about, there are several other ducks to consider: a *dead duck* ('useless or powerless'), a *queer duck* ('peculiar'), and a *sitting duck* ('helpless target'). And among other animal figures, we have the well-known *bulls* and *bears* of the stock market. Probably more relevant is *dove,* a British slang term meaning 'sucker', and *rook,* which means 'a swindler' or 'to swindle', after a European type of crow. These terms must have helped to give rise to the phrase **lame duck.**

The broader sense, 'any person or thing that is incapacitated or ineffectual' turns up—first in England, but the sense is found in America too—by the early nineteenth century. Finally we get to the usual sense in America: 'an elected official or legislative body whose term of office is nearing an end, especially a legislator still in office after losing a bid for re-election'. It is difficult to tell exactly when this specific sense arose. There is a quotation from 1863 that may attest this sense, but it is not clear; the first clear example shows up in 1910, after which point the word is well documented.

The political sense is the most common sense in America; in Britain the financial sense is dominant.

■ ■ ■

larrup

Stacey Abbott writes: **My grandfather has often been known to make up words or terms and we've always assumed that the word "larapin" was one such example. However, my brother drove through Illinois where he saw the word on a billboard. Larapin, as my grandfather uses it, means 'something exceptional'. He usually uses it in relation to food. "It's larapin good pie," for example, or just "Mmm, larapin!" He told us it was a word his family used and they did move to Arkansas from Illinois after the Civil War. Is it possible that this is a regional term? Has anyone else ever heard of it? What language might it have derived from?**

■ This one wasn't invented by your grandfather. The verb **larrup**, as it's usually spelled, is a fairly common regionalism. The meaning of the base form is 'to strike; thrash', and is in use across the country. While this sense is found primarily in rural language, it can't be placed in any specific part of the country.

The derivative *larruping* 'extremely; exceptionally', is usually found in the construction *larruping good*. This is usually used in reference to food, as your grandfather used it; so *larruping* by itself often means 'delicious'. The form *tad-larruping* is also seen. According to the records of the *Dictionary of American Regional English,* this culinary sense of *larruping* is found chiefly in the West Midlands (which includes Arkansas and and most of Illinois), Texas, and Oklahoma.

Larrup is first found in the United States in the early nineteenth century. Its etymology is uncertain, although it may come from a Dutch word *larpen,* which means 'to thresh'.

■ ■ ■

latchkey children

Walter Bode writes: **What is the origin of the phrase "latchkey children"? The word "latch" would suggest it's old, maybe from the '30s. Was it always a term of opprobrium?**

■ To start, the word **latchkey** is first attested in the 1820s, then meaning a key to open a latch on a door. As locks developed and spring locks became the standard, the word also developed an encompassing sense 'a key for releasing a latch or a spring lock on a door'. In modern times latches are rather rare, but the word continues to be used to refer to a key for any outside door, regardless of mechanism.

Latchkey is found in combination with other words, in reference to people who use a **latchkey**, since the turn of the century. An example from 1902, referring to lodgers: "At the beginning of the latchkey life everything looks delightful." Another construction was "latchkey voters."

The special formation **latchkey child** (or *kid*) is first found in 1944. Here it means not just 'a child who uses a latchkey' but specifically 'a child who spends part of the day alone and unsupervised, as when the parents are at work'. This sense seems to have become common in World War II, when the need for women to work in the war industry led to a large number of children being left alone after school. Even at the time it was considered a distinct social phenomenon; the 1944 example is from an NBC documentary examining the problem and considering what could be done about it. Thus, to the extent that the existence of **latchkey children** was regarded as something to be avoided, the term has apparently always been opprobrious.

■　■　■

lay on, Macduff

Heath Row writes: In Neil Gaiman's BBC miniseries *Neverwhere*, a character says, "Lead on, Macduff." Later on, another character says (and I paraphrase), "It's actually, 'Lay on, Macduff,' but I hadn't the heart to correct him." I've always seen or heard it as "Lead on, Macduff." Which is it? Why?

■ Which? **Lay on, Macduff.** Why: Because that's what Shakespeare wrote.

This catchphrase is a famous quote from the last scene of *Macbeth*, when Macbeth and his nemesis Macduff are in battle together. Macduff gives Macbeth the opportunity to yield, but Macbeth refuses, saying "I will not yield,/To kiss the ground before young Malcolm's feet,/ . . . I will try to the last. Before my body/I throw my warlike shield. Lay on, Macduff;/And damned be him that first cries, 'Hold, enough!'" (*Macbeth* 5.8), immediately after which Macbeth is slain.

In this use, *lay on* means 'to attack'. Some other examples: "He came at us . . . and laid us on with a great quarter-staff" (John Vanbrugh, 1698); "I will lay on for Tusculum,/And lay thou on for Rome!" (Macaulay, 1843). This is not, granted, a terribly common use, and so the expression has been "corrected" to the more sensible-seeming *lead on, Macduff!* in the broad meaning 'let's go!' or the like. This alteration of famous quotes is common; another classic example is "Music has charms to soothe a savage breast," from William Congreve, often cited as "Music hath charms to soothe the savage beast."

The *lead on, Macduff* variation is found at least as early as the 1910s.

■　■　■

less/fewer

Monica writes: **Is the word "less" in "10 items or less" at the supermarket acceptable if one argues that "less" refers to an uncountable noun such as "quantity" instead of "items"?**

■ Let's just go back a bit to review the history of the **less/fewer** debate before we look at this particular question.

A traditional rule of English usage holds that **less** should be used only of uncountable things, that is, things that can be measured but not counted as discrete units. Thus "less electricity," "less than a quart," "less doubt." **Fewer,** on the other hand, should be used only of things that can be counted: "fewer people," "fewer cars."

According to this rule, **less** should modify plural nouns only when they suggest combination into a unit, group, or aggregation. Thus "less than three miles" (with "three miles" being a single distance, not three individual miles), "less than $50" (fifty dollars as a sum of money, not fifty one-dollar bills).

In actual usage, **fewer** almost always adheres to the traditional rule; the "problem" is that **less** is often used with countable things. (It is worth mentioning here that the traditional rule has little basis in reality; **less** has been used with countables since the ninth century, and such use is easily found in the works of major writers throughout the history of English literature. Why the rule was adopted with such intensity is an interesting question, but for our purposes beside the point.)

It seems that there are two constructions in which **less** is often used with countable things: *less than* (including "no less than") and *or less.* Thus, "less than two hundred people" and "fifty words or less" are very common constructions, and many people regard these as acceptable.

To return to your original question, then, it seems quite clear to me that "item" is a countable thing no matter how you look at it. Not only is it conceptually countable, but in the scenario you mention, ten items would be permissible for a place on the express line, but eleven would not, period. (Of course, how one determines an "item" is up to the supermarket—a bag of four onions could be considered one bag or four individual onions. Either way, however, you are asked to conform to a specific number, not a general quantity.) So if you're strictly adhering to the traditional rule, you'd have to say that the sign "10 items or less" is not acceptable, and it should properly read "10 items or fewer." Since, as mentioned, the "or less" construction is common even with countables, and the "rule" is not based on much anyway, I myself wouldn't worry about correcting the supermarket.

■ ■ ■

letch

Kent M. Phillips writes: **My friend recently called me a "letch" because I turned on the Howard Stern Show on E! She said that this was not a bad thing. I've looked in all my resources and cannot find the origin of this word. Can you tell me the origin of this word please?**

■ The noun **letch** has two main meanings: one is 'a lecherous desire', as in "I had a letch for that schoolgirl," and another is 'a lecher', as in "You letch!" (Note that for all uses of these words—*letch, lecher, lecherous, lechery*—the main sense refers to sexual indulgence; the figurative sense, 'a perverse but non-sexual desire or craving,' is presumably what we're discussing here, although that's a question for you, your friend, and Howard Stern to explore.)

Letch is almost certainly simply a back formation from *lecher,* which is a much older word. I say "almost" because "lecher" is spelled without the *t* and "letch" almost always has it, so some etymologists prefer to hedge their bets by saying "perhaps" or "probably."

Lecher, which dates back to the twelfth century or so, is a borrowing from an Old French word *lecheor* which meant 'a libertine or glutton', and derives from the verb *lechier* 'to lick'. This verb is borrowed from a Germanic language and is cognate with the English verb *lick.* The derived forms *lecherous* and *lechery* are also early, dating to the thirteenth or fourteenth centuries. **Letch,** however, is first attested in the late eighteenth century, in the third edition of Captain Francis Grose's *Classical Dictionary of the Vulgar Tongue.*

■ ■ ■

libertine

Ron Vocelka writes: **In your article on** IN LIKE FLYNN **you mentioned libertinism. The only other place I recall hearing this word was in the musical *The Music Man* where Prof. Harold Hill refers to "libertine" women. Obviously this is no compliment. Please enlighten me.**

■ This sense of **libertine** is 'a person who is morally or sexually unrestrained; a dissolute man; profligate; rake'. A good early example from our favorite poet: Laertes gives his sister Ophelia a long speech about how she should spurn Hamlet's advances; Ophelia replies in kind, saying "Do not, as some ungracious pastors do,/Show me the steep and thorny way to heaven,/Whiles, like a puffed and reckless libertine,/Himself the primrose path of dalliance treads" (*Hamlet* 1.3).

The earliest sense of **libertine** is the historical sense 'a person freed from slavery in ancient Rome'. For our purposes, the earliest relevant meaning is 'a freethinker in religious matters', that is, 'a person whose religious opinions differ from established belief'. This usually disparaging description is a late-sixteenth-century sense probably borrowed from the Middle French *libertin*. Our sense 'a morally or sexually unrestrained person' is an outgrowth of this.

Libertine is rather common from the late sixteenth century onwards. It is usually at least mildly disparaging, since it describes someone whose behavior is considered unconventional in an immoral manner. Its application to women is rather rare (due, no doubt, to social rather than linguistic reasons), but does occur: "The sportiveness of innocence, so pleasing to refined libertines of both sexes, is widely different in its essence from this superior gracefulness" (Mary Wollstonecraft, *A Vindication of the Rights of Woman*).

Libertine ultimately comes from a Latin adjective meaning 'of or pertaining to a freeman', and is related to our English word *liberty*.

As for *libertinism*, I'm sorry to say that I did not coin the word; it has been around since the early seventeenth century.

■ ■ ■

-lived

> *Mike Forester writes:* **The mispronunciation of "short-lived" by practically everyone, esp. nitwits on TV, is one of my longest-lived pet peeves. It has a long *i*, of course, because it's an adjectival form of "life," not of "live." It's always seemed obvious to me: He had a short temper; he was short-tempered. He had a short life; he was short-lived. Care to join my campaign to stamp out "short-livd"?**

■ Well, no, because it's almost certainly a losing battle.

Etymologically, you are correct. The **-lived** in *short-lived* (or *long-lived*, for that matter) comes from the noun *life* + the adjectival ending *-ed*. The *f* turns to a *v* the same way it happens in the *leaf/leaves* pair. The form **-lived** should therefore be pronounced with a vowel rhyming with "eye." The problem is that *lived*, the past tense of the verb "to live," is tremendously more common, so people often pronounce the **-lived** adjective as if it were the verb *lived*.'

Confusion between verb forms in *-ed* and adjectives in *-ed* is not that unusual. In the expression "shelled peanuts," most people interpret "shelled" as being from the verb "to shell," meaning 'to remove the shell'. Sometimes, though, people mistake "shelled" for being the noun "shell" + *-ed*, so that "shelled peanuts" means 'peanuts in the shell'. In your example, the confusion is amplified by the rarity of the adjective form **-lived.**

Changes in pronunciation based on analogy are also common: to take a famous example, *zoology*, which etymologically should be pronounced "zoh-AHL-uh-gee," is often pronounced with the first syllable rhyming with *zoo*, which is a more frequently used word.

Pronouncing "short-" or "long-lived" to rhyme with "give" has been noticed and objected to for some time. It's even warned against in H. W. Fowler's 1926 *Modern English Usage*, considered *the* handbook for this sort of thing. Nowadays, it seems as if this pronunciation is rapidly becoming the only one. An informal survey of recent college graduates showed not only that they all pronounced it to rhyme with "give" but that they all thought the pronunciation rhyming with "eye" was pretentious. So I'm afraid that there seems little likelihood that you will ever succeed in stamping out the "short *i*" variant.

■   ■   ■

lobby

gbs@panix.com writes: **Does "lobbyist" come from "lobby" or vice versa? Are they related to the verb "to lob"? And where does "lobby" come from (as a lunch partner wanted to know as we left the building Tuesday)?**

■ Let's take your questions in reverse order, since that'll take care of the historical development too. The first appearance of **lobby** meaning roughly 'an entrance hall' is (of course) in Shakespeare: "How in our voiding lobby hast thou stood/And duly waited for my coming forth?" (*Henry VI, Part II;* Shakespeare is using "voiding lobby" here to mean a lobby that people pass through as they void, or leave, a room). The very first use came earlier in the sixteenth century and appears to refer to some sort of cloister in a monastery; there's only one example and it's not very clear. The word is borrowed from the Medieval Latin *lobia,* which meant 'a covered way', and came from a Germanic word related to English *lodge.*

The word developed a more specific sense in the seventeenth century, when it was used to refer to an anteroom of the House of Commons; in one of these anterooms, the public could meet with the members of Parliament and talk with them. This specific sense was itself generalized to mean the anteroom of any legislative assembly.

The verb **lobby** arose in the early nineteenth century meaning 'to visit a lobby in order to influence members', and that's where we get the political use. The noun *lobbyist* developed later in the nineteenth century from this verb. Both the verb and the noun were American developments.

The verb *to lob* is completely unrelated; it comes from a noun meaning 'a dangling object'.

■   ■   ■

lock and load

Herschel Purvis writes: **The sound bites from Pat Buchanan were driving me crazy during the Republican primary. What does "lock and load" refer to and why was he using it?**

■ **Lock and load** is a metaphor of military origin. Its current, mainstream use is in the sense 'to prepare oneself for imminent action or confrontation'. In other words, "Get ready!"

The reference is to the loading of ammunition in a gun. The version of the command to chamber a round that's most familiar to World War II veterans seems to be *load and lock,* that is, load the ammunition and lock the weapon in firing position. More recently, the more popular version—and the only one used in this metaphorical sense—is reversed to **lock and load,** that is, **lock** the weapon in the safety position and then **load** the ammunition.

This expression has been in use since World War II. It seems to have spread beyond the military only in the last several years.

■ ■ ■

long in the tooth

Coleen Corbett writes: **I was watching the HBO movie *Truman* and heard the expression "long in the tooth." What exactly does it mean (longwinded?), and what's the origin?**

■ **Long in the tooth** means 'elderly; old', and by extension 'past one's prime; over the hill'.

The expression derives from horses, of all things. As horses age, their gums recess, which is the origin of the practice of examining a horse's teeth to determine its age (and therefore value), a sort of early version of kicking the tires. (Horse traders, like their used-car counterparts, are not to be trusted.) An old horse's gums will have recessed so much that the roots of the teeth are visible, thus making the teeth appear longer—hence **long in the tooth** to mean 'old', and hence the parallel figurative senses of 'old' such as 'past one's prime'.

Long in the tooth is first found in England in the nineteenth century, though it's likely that it was in use much earlier but never got recorded.

■ ■ ■

luck, Lucifer

E. J. Howard writes: **My mother-in-law claims that the word "luck" comes from Lucifer. Is there any truth in that?**

■ None whatsoever. (Of course, as demonstrated at HELLO and CALL A SPADE A SPADE, erroneous ideas about word origins can still carry emotional weight.)

The word **luck** was borrowed from Middle Dutch or Low German; it is cognate with forms in several other Germanic languages. It seems to have been first popularized as a gambling term, not surprisingly. The ultimate origin is uncertain.

Lucifer is from Old English, where the word meant both 'the morning star' and 'Satan'. The Old English word is from Latin; its etymological meaning is 'light-bearing', derived from the stem of *lux* 'light' (cf. Modern English *lucid*) and *ferre* 'to bear; carry'. The use of **Lucifer** as an epithet for Satan comes from a passage in Isaiah 14:12, which actually refers to Nebuchadnezzar, the king of Babylon, who was compared to the morning star; early Christian writers took this passage to be alluding to the fall of the archangel who was hurled from heaven because of his wickedness.

■ ■ ■

lukewarm

syene@acsworld.net writes: **Just wondering about the expression "luke" warm, as in "I like my coffee luke warm."**

■ **Lukewarm,** meaning 'moderately warm; tepid', is another of those words that is either rather simple or somewhat complicated to explain, depending on how thorough one prefers one's etymological analysis.

The simple explanation is that **lukewarm,** which first appears in English in the late fourteenth century, is formed from Middle English **luke,** which itself means 'lukewarm; tepid', and **warm.**

Once we get to **luke** it begins to get a bit hairy. This word is often connected to *lew,* or in Old English *hlēowe* 'tepid', but the alteration with the added -*k*- cannot be readily explained. However, there are various forms equivalent to **luke** in other Germanic languages, such as Low German *lūk* and Modern Dutch *leuk,* both also meaning 'lukewarm; tepid'.

Skipping the mumbo-jumbo, it thus seems likely that these words stem from an original Indo-European base meaning 'warm', which developed one way into the **luke** forms and another way into the *lew* forms. Related words probably include *calorie, cauldron,* and *scald,* all from Latin roots.

■ ■ ■

Mac

Jim Bookout writes: **I am interested in the origins of the "Mc" that is prevalent in Irish names.**

■ The prefix **Mac** (also spelled *Mc* or less commonly *M'* or *M^c*) is extremely common in family names of Irish or Scottish Gaelic origin. **Mac** is the Irish and Scottish Gaelic word for "son," and is thus equivalent to the element *-son* in family names of English origin. It also appears, especially in Scottish names, before the names of saints or before occupational names (e.g., McWhirter, from a Scottish Gaelic word for 'harpist'). **Mac** always appears before a name, like *Fitz-* in "Fitzgerald," which is from Anglo-French *fi(t)z* 'son'. In Gaelic **Mac** is usually written as a separate word; *Macdonald,* for example, is an Anglicized version of *Mac Dhomhnuill.*

Mac is related to words for "son" in other Celtic languages also, notably Welsh and Cornish *mab,* which in Old Welsh was *map* (the relationship between the "k" sound in Irish and Scottish Gaelic and the "p/b" sound in Welsh is a regular feature of these languages). *Map* gave rise to the Welsh prefix *Ap,* which is equivalent to **Mac** but is less common; one example is the family name *Price,* a reduction of *Ap Rhys* 'son of Rhys'.

The use of hereditary family names arose in Ireland much earlier than in most countries. These names, with **Mac** or Ó (which means 'grandson or descendant of'), were often shared by the members of a clan or a group living in the same region even if they did not have a common ancestor.

■ ■ ■

mad money

Susan M. King writes: **Yesterday I said I would bring my "mad money." A friend asked what was mad, me or the money. How should I answer her?**

■ By telling her that you had no idea, until you asked this terrific knowledgeable guy who runs a Web site who told you: *you* are mad.

The original sense of **mad money** is 'money carried by a woman in case she wants to return home from a date without her escort', especially if the reason for this is the escort's unwanted sexual advances. So it's the woman being **mad** at the escort.

This sense dates from the early 1920s—the same general period when middle-class women began going on unchaperoned dates, to any reasonable extent—and reflects a time when the woman would be under the man's control thoughout the date, so that going home alone would be a notable act.

The usual current sense of **mad money** is 'money that may be used for unplanned or impetuous purchases; extra spending money'. This sense, which dates from the 1950s, suggests that the money is to be used for "mad" or irrational needs, so once again, you're the **mad** one.

■ ■ ■

make love

gabriel@esa.org writes: **I have been reading a collection of F. Scott Fitzgerald short stories and I've noticed that he frequently uses the phrase "making love." His use of this phrase, though, does not seem to have the same meaning as today. It seems that he is using it to refer to mainly flirting, courting, and, perhaps, kissing. Today, this phrase applies almost exclusively to sex. When and how did this phrase change meanings?**

■ The original sense of the phrase **make love** is 'to court; woo'. This sense is quite old and well established; it goes back to the late sixteenth century, and was used by John Lyly, Shakespeare (a number of times), Joseph Addison, Laurence Sterne, and Jane Austen, among other notables. When seen through the lens of modern usage, these examples can seem strange; Jane Austen in particular seems much more lively than we'd normally expect.

The shifts in meaning to 'to engage in amorous caressing; neck; pet' or 'to engage in sexual intercourse' are natural extensions; the word **love** by itself has had explicitly sexual senses for many centuries (for example, from a fourteenth-century religious tract, with spelling modernized, "A youngling that had obliged himself to the devil for the love of a wench"). It is thus difficult to tell exactly when the shift in **make love** occurred, since even the older examples are often ambiguous. But the 'sexual intercourse' interpretation was certainly in use by the 1940s, and it was the dominant sense by the 1960s at latest.

The expression **make love** is probably a translation of the French *faire l'amour* or the equivalent Italian *far l'amore*. While the 'court; woo' sense is still well known from its frequent uses in older literature, it must be considered archaic today.

■ ■ ■

manifest

Pam Rider writes: **Is there a past tense to the verb "manifest" (as in "something was manifested")? I think not, but am wavering. Please clarify the usage.**

■ There certainly is. **Manifest** can be a bit confusing because it is often used in the passive, but it functions like any other verb.

The usual sense of the verb **manifest** is 'to make clear or evident to the eye or the understanding'. Though this main meaning can be divided into ever smaller subdefinitions—the *Oxford English Dictionary* gives seven numbered senses with several additional lettered subsenses—it still covers most meanings one would be likely to encounter. An example from Shakespeare: "Thy life did manifest thou lov'dst me not" (*Henry IV, Part II*, 4.5.104). Another example from Shakespeare, because we like him so much: "For Coriolanus neither to care whether they love or hate him manifests the true knowledge he has in their disposition" (*Coriolanus* 2.2). And, to show a passive use and give our friend Bill S. a quotational hat trick:

> I have a letter from her
> Of such contents as you will wonder at,
> The mirth whereof so larded with my matter
> That neither singly can be manifested
> Without the show of both.
> (*The Merry Wives of Windsor* 4.6)

Just to be clear on the subject, here's an unequivocal example of a past tense: "He manifested the greatest eagerness to be upon deck to watch for the sledge which had before appeared" (Mary Shelley, *Frankenstein*).

■ ■ ■

marlinespike

Mike James writes: **My officemate and I were recently discussing the word "marlinespike." We've seen it used as a name for a pointed tool used for untying knots. It also seems that "marlinespike seamanship" refers to knot tying. Can you sort out what it means and from where it comes?**

■ The **marlinespike,** also spelled *marlinspike* and found in hyphenated and open forms, is, as you say, a long, pointed iron tool used in separating the strands of a rope in splicing, marling, etc. The phrase *marlinespike seamanship* refers to the art of using a **marlinespike.**

Wilfred Granville, in his *Dictionary of Sailors' Slang* (1950), defines it as the "Art of knotting and splicing, and general rope work in which the marline spike, a pointed tool for unravelling, is used."

The word **marlinespike** is first attested in the early seventeenth century. The original form was apparently *marling spike,* with *marling* being the gerund of the verb *marl* 'to tie; wind a rope with cord', of Germanic origin. (*Spike* is, of course, the standard word 'a nail-like fastener'.) The *marling* was then reinterpreted as *marline* 'a light cord wrapped around the end of a rope to keep it from fraying', from *marl* (as discussed above) and *line.* There's a late-fifteenth-century example of *marling iron,* which gives credence to this explanation.

The game fish *marlin,* which has a long, spearlike upper jaw, is a clipping of **marlinespike,** and **marlinespike** was also a nineteenth-century slang term for a type of tropical bird with long, pointed tail feathers. The expression *look marlinespikes* was a nineteenth-century nautical version of *look daggers* 'to glare'.

■ ■ ■

maroon

> *Don Willmott writes:* **In Bugs Bunny cartoons, the "wascally wabbit" sometimes refers to stupid people as "maroons," as in "What a maroon!" I'm wondering if this put-down has a racist genesis and what, if anything, it has to do with being "marooned" on a desert island.**

■ It is neither racist nor related to **maroon** 'to abandon' (though this word does originally refer to fugitive slaves), except through their identical pronunciation.

The word **maroon** 'a foolish or obnoxious person' is simply a jocular mispronunciation of *moron.* It is probably reinforced by the existence of **maroon** 'abandon' and **maroon** 'brownish red color' (which are themselves unrelated, by the way, giving us three different unrelated **maroon**s).

Our **maroon** is first found in the 1940s, and was not coined by Bugs Bunny (though his use of it surely did a great deal to popularize the term). It is part of a number of words from that general period which represent jocular mispronunciations of common words. Some other examples are *anyhoo, fox paw* (for *faux pas*), *martooni,* and *nertz.*

■ ■ ■

marshmallow

Coral Jones writes: **I am seeking the origin of the word "marshmallow."**

■ **Marshmallow** is one of those words that seems as if it should have a really interesting etymology, but is in truth rather mundane.

A *mallow* is a type of shrub. It is a member of the mallow family, which also includes hibiscus, okra, cotton, and some other plants. A *marsh mallow,* as you are probably about to guess, is a variety of mallow that lives in marshy places. *Althaea officinalis,* if you're keeping track.

Marshmallow is a confection made from the root of the marsh mallow (or, more often nowadays, from a bunch of unpleasant artificial sweeteners, flavorings, and thickeners), just as a dish made from the root of the carrot plant is called—carrot. And that's the story.

The plant name is really old, first found in an Old English medical book written around 1000 c.e., when it was spelled *merscmealwe.* The confection was developed by the late nineteenth century, by which point the spelling had changed to its modern form, luckily for the marketing departments of candy companies, who'd probably have a lot of trouble trying to convince people to toast merscmealwes over the campfire.

■ ■ ■

maven

James R. Jansen writes: **Maven . . . "An expert"? I couldn't find it in Internet Roget's or two dictionaries.**

■ . . . Thus exemplifying why an up-to-date dictionary is a good thing to have.

The word **maven** does indeed mean 'an expert; knowledgeable or skilled person; connoisseur' or occasionally 'a person interested in (a specified subject)'. **Maven** is often used in combination with a word indicating the subject of expertise. It is occasionally spelled *mavin.*

Maven is first found in English in the early 1950s, but it remained rare until about 1964, when it was popularized by a series of television commercials for Vita Herring, featuring "the beloved herring maven" as a spokesman. The word was further popularized, especially among journalists, in the 1980s by William Safire, who used it often and referred to himself as "the language maven"; two of his books were titled *Quoth the Maven* (alluding to Poe's poem "The Raven") and *Language Maven Strikes Again.*

Maven is a borrowing from Yiddish, and Yiddish borrowed it from Hebrew, all in pretty much the same meaning.

■ ■ ■

mediocre

Jeremy St. John Smythe writes: **What's with the word "mediocre"? It's supposed to mean moderately good, but it's always used to mean pretty bad. And where does the "ocre" part come from?**

■ You've hit upon one of my big pet peeves here. Yes, **mediocre** technically means 'of ordinary or moderate quality', but it usually appears in disparaging contexts. The generous interpretation is that the word usually describes something one had expected to be good, so calling it **mediocre** is actually an insult. So we should probably read it as meaning 'of moderate to low (but not extremely low) quality'—in other words, not completely dreadful, but worse than one would like.

Mediocre is borrowed through French from the Latin *mediocris* 'in a middle state', literally 'at a middle height'. The first element is *medius* 'middle', and the second element is *ocris,* the Old Latin word for 'a rugged mountain', distantly related to the English word *edge.* **Mediocre** first appears in English in the late sixteenth century.

■ ■ ■

metanalysis

John Lowville writes: **Would you please further explain your definition of "metanalysis"—"a shift in the division between words in a phrase; misdivision"? An example would help.**

■ **Metanalysis** is a technical term in linguistics that was coined in 1914 by Otto Jespersen, a Danish linguist who was one of the great grammarians of English.

Metanalysis can be broadly defined as 'a reinterpretation of the division between words or syntactic units', as the *Oxford English Dictionary* does. A usual example in English is the shift of the letter *n* based on a misunderstanding of the previous indefinite article *a/an.* So—and I'll be oversimplifying some of the changes here—the word *adder* was originally *nadder,* but the phrase "a nadder" was reinterpreted as "an adder." Likewise, *apron* was originally *napron.*

In the other direction, *newt* 'type of salamander' was originally *ewt,* but "an ewt" was taken as "a newt." And *a nickname* was originally *an ekename* (*eke* is an archaic term for 'also').

Metanalysis is also used to refer to syntactic interpretations. Jespersen gave the following example: "It is good for a man/not to touch a woman," which could be apprehended as "It is good/for a man not to touch a woman."

Sometimes **metanalysis** is given an especially broad range, and it is applied to any process of counteretymological regularization—as when the plural of *Walkman* becomes *Walkmans* instead of *Walkmen,* or when the nonce past tense of *sing-song* is *sing-songed* instead of *sang-song.* But it's likely that by the time you encounter the word used in such a restricted way, you'll already be a linguist, and won't need my help anymore.

■ ■ ■

middle-aged

Sherney Alexander writes: **I have often heard people use "middle-aged" to refer to others. Can you tell where the term "middle age" comes from, and at what age is a person considered old?**

■ A great advantage of imprecise terms is, to be precise, their imprecision. One of my favorite definitions, from the eminently respectable *Chambers Twentieth Century Dictionary,* is "**middle-aged** adj. between youth and old age, variously reckoned to suit the reckoner." Though this seems uncharacteristically flip for a dictionary, it really is quite a useful way of looking at things. The danger of specifying things is that if you describe *middle age* as being, say, the years between 40 and 60, someone who's 61 will shout at you, "I'm not old!"

With that in mind, however, the usual ages now included in "middle age" or "middle-aged" are 40 to 60, or 45 to 65.

The term *middle age* is first found in the fourteenth century, where we also see the now obsolete expressions *middle eld* and *middle life.* With the shorter lifespans in that era, it is likely that a **middle-aged** person in the fourteenth century would be considerably younger than a person considered **middle-aged** today.

While we're here, we should mention the capitalized term *Middle Ages.* The Middle Ages can be loosely defined as the time in European history between classical antiquity and the Renaissance, or roughly from the late fifth century to the fifteenth century, but again, this is a fluid range. Sometimes the Middle Ages are held to begin around 1000 C.E., with the earlier period being the *Dark Ages,* and the end of the Middle Ages can be variously reckoned as 1350, 1400, 1450, or 1500. It's also worth noting the curiosity that English is one of the few languages to interpret "Middle Ages" as a plural; the equivalents in most other languages, as Medieval Latin *medium aevum,* French *moyen âge,* German *Mittelalter,* and Italian *il Medioevo* are all singular.

■ ■ ■

mojo

Brendan Pimper writes: **I've seen it in popular music for years. Old Flat-Top has got mojo filter. I got my mojo working. I could even stretch and bring up Mojo Nixon. Now it's showing up in the "digital culture": there's a game called "Bad Mojo," and "Mojo" was used in *Wired* magazine this month. What is it?!? Contextual clues aren't enough. I've got a feeling that it's a reference to cannabis, but I can't find it in a dictionary locally.**

■ **Mojo** is, in a word, magic. The word first appears in the 1920s, in blues songs and collections of folklore among African-Americans, and has been popular especially in blues ever since. It has a number of shades of meaning: **mojo** can be 'the ability to cast a magic or voodoo spell'; 'such a spell itself'; 'a magical charm or amulet'; 'magic (in the broad sense)'; or even simply 'power or ability (in any form)'. *To have one's mojo working,* thus, can mean 'to be lucky' without any suggestion of magic.

Mojo has been used occasionally since the 1930s to refer to drugs, usually heroin or cocaine, but this is not a very common sense. It's likely that the examples you think are talking about cannabis are actually vague uses of one of the 'magic' senses.

The exact etymology of **mojo** is uncertain, but it's probably of African origin. It's usually connected with *moco,* a word in Gullah (a creole spoken by blacks in coastal Georgia and South Carolina) that means 'witchcraft; magic', and *moco'o* a word in Fulani (an African language, also called Fula(h)) that means 'medicine man'.

■ ■ ■

mook

Kristina Merlo writes: **What does it mean (really) to call someone a "mook"? Harvey Keitel was confused about it in *Mean Streets,* and I remain so. . . .**

■ It's usually difficult to say what people *really* mean by terms such as **mook,** because they're usually used as very vague terms of insult. The definition we use in the *Random House Historical Dictionary of American Slang,* Volume II, is 'an ineffectual, foolish, or contemptible person'. I know, this covers a lot of ground, but it's necessary.

Most of the time, examples of **mook** are found in phrases like "What a mook!" or "You mook!," which doesn't help us very much. There are occasional attempts to clarify the meaning; for example, in a discussion about the desirability of certain frequenters of chic restaurants: "Mooks spend money and can keep you in the black, but they don't make for a very attractive social environment. . . . By Mooks I mean not only outer-borough types and out-and-out greaseballs, but Wall Streeters, unattractive and socially useless Eurotrash, advertising execs and Upper East Siders." (*New York Press*, 1995). Unfortunately, even something this specific ends up confusing the issue, for it is clear that **mook** just means 'any disliked person'.

So, in sum, there's no way to be very precise about it.

The discussion of **mook** in *Mean Streets*, in 1973, was the most prominent example of the word in its most recent history. The earliest known example comes from S. J. Perelman in 1930, but between that and *Mean Streets*, there's only a single use in a student newspaper in 1958 and the adjectival "mooky-lookin' blond guy" in the musical *Hair.*

The origin of **mook** is uncertain, but it's probably a variant of the earlier *moke.* This word is from the nineteenth century, and originally meant 'a donkey or mule', but its main use in the United States was as a contemptuous term for a black person, a sense very common in the late nineteenth century, but apparently obsolete after the 1910s. *Moke* was also used to mean 'a contemptible person', like **mook.** *Moke* is itself of unknown origin, but it seems likely that the later **mook** is derived from it.

■   ■   ■

moot

> ***Jim Griffin writes:*** **You may have covered this previously, but the discussion of** STEMWINDER **brought to mind my recent discovery that the word "moot" means "debatable as a point of argument." But in many contexts that I have seen the word, it seems to suggest that it means a point that is accepted and/or settled. For instance the fact that the sun will rise tomorrow is a moot point (hopefully). But is it? What does "moot" mean anyway?**

■ The shift in meaning of the word **moot** is one that has vexed several critics in recent years. What has happened is that a technical sense of the word has become common in the mainstream, and the distinction between the technical sense and the original sense has become confused. Let's look at this one in historical order.

Moot goes back to Old English, where it was a noun meaning 'an assembly of the people for making judicial or political decisions'; this sense is now only found in historical or archaic uses. (J. R. R. Tolkien had "ent-moots," or meetings of "ents," treelike creatures now primarily cherished by crossword puzzle enthusiasts.) From there we got the sense 'a discussion or argument', which by the sixteenth century developed a specific meaning in the legal profession of 'a discussion of a hypothetical legal point as an exercise'.

The meanings we're examining both derive from here. One meaning, which picks up the "discussion" aspect, is 'able to be argued at a moot', that is, 'open to discussion; debatable; arguable'. This has always been the more common meaning. Another meaning, which picks up the "hypothetical" side, has until recently been strictly a legal sense: 'able to be argued *only* at a moot, but without significance in the real world', that is, 'hypothetical; purely academic' and hence 'irrelevant'. The use of this sense, which is now about as common as the original, is what's causing the grief.

Your example of the sun rising is an excellent one. Let's say we have a contract that says, in part, "When the sun rises on June 21, you will pay me one million dollars." This could easily be discussed, for example: on the morning of June 21, the sun won't actually rise. The earth will have turned on its axis, so from the viewpoint of a stationary observer, it will *look* as if the sun is rising, but it'll actually be standing still. Therefore the contract is void. This is indeed a **moot** argument, since everyone knows the sun will rise; everything else is playing with words. (And knowing how to keep track of this sort of argument is why lawyers get paid more than lexicographers.)

■   ■   ■

mother lode

Coleen Corbett writes: **OK, I've been wondering about the term "mother lode." Why is it "lode" not "load" and what does my mother have to do with it?**

■   OK, it's *lode* because the phrase is a figurative use of the mining term *lode,* which means 'a vein of metal ore'. *Lode* was indeed the original spelling of *load,* meaning 'burden' and earlier 'course, way'; the two spellings became differentiated in meaning in the sixteenth century. It's *mother* because *mother* is being used in the sense 'bearing a relation like that of a mother, as in being the origin or source'.

The original sense of **mother lode** is 'the main lode of a particular region'; this sense goes back to the mining days of the late nineteenth century. The figurative sense, which is the more common one now that mining is a relatively rare topic for discussion, is 'an abundant source or supply'. As in, "New York is the mother lode of neurotic writers." This sense developed by the middle of this century.

■   ■   ■

moxie

Abrupt NYC writes: Now, how about the origin of "moxie," which you seem to have?

■ Thank you. **Moxie** has several closely related senses, including 'vigor; pep', 'courage; guts', 'know-how; savvy', and others. All of these senses are figurative uses derived from **Moxie,** the trademark name of a popular soft drink marketed especially in New England. **Moxie** is thus a sort of "Pepsi spirit" of the 1930s, if you will.

The generic **moxie** is first found in 1930 in a short story by Damon Runyon. The soft drink **Moxie** was trademarked in 1924, and was probably modeled on a yet earlier **Moxie,** a patent medicine developed around 1880. Finally, **moxie** is a word for the berry of the wintergreen bush; it is not known whether the patent medicine contained this berry. The name of the berry probably derives from an Algonquian language.

■ ■ ■

myself

Mike Raimondi writes: Can you discuss usage of "myself"? It seems like every e-mail or vendor correspondence I get has a phrase such as "Please contact myself if you have any questions."

■ There are a number of uses of **myself** that are considered standard and raise no concern. One is **myself** as a reflexive form of *me,* as a direct object ("I excused myself from the table"), an indirect object ("I bought myself a new suit"), and after a preposition ("I'll pay for myself"). A second is **myself** as an intensive of *I* or *me* ("I myself wouldn't say that"). A third is use in absolute constructions ("A writer myself, I understand his concern"). A fourth is as a noun meaning 'my customary self' ("I wasn't myself when I said that").

It is the use of **myself** (and the less frequent use of other pronouns in -*self*) as an emphatic substitution for *I* or *me* (or equivalent forms of the other pronouns) that many people object to. This use is fairly common in speech or informal writing, in various grammatical constructions: as direct object ("Please contact myself," in your example), as object of preposition ("The letter was addressed to myself"), as part of a compound subject ("My fiancé and myself will be in London next week"), after *as, like,* or *than* ("Writers like myself are always broke").

Constructions like these have been part of the English language for over four hundred years, and may be found in the works of a very large number of well-respected writers. *Merriam-Webster's Dictionary of English Usage,* which has an especially full treatment of this issue, gives examples from Samuel Johnson, T. S. Eliot, E. M. Forster, W. H. Auden, Lord Byron, Jane Austen, Robert Frost, Henry James, William Blake, Lewis Carroll, and the King James Bible, among many others.

There is no sound grammatical reason for objecting to these uses, especially given the weight of historical precedent we find for them. Some commentators consider them fully standard. However, many people consider them incorrect, or at least awkward or informal (or, conversely, pretentious), and it's probably best to avoid them unless you're sure of what you're doing.

■　■　■

nasty

David R. Smith writes: I read somewhere that the word "nasty" was originally a reference to the work of the cartoonist Thomas Nast. Is that true?

■ No, definitely not, but this story seems to be a rather widespread one.

Nasty, though of obscure origin, had been in the language hundreds of years before the birth of Thomas Nast, the German-born American cartoonist who worked in the late nineteenth century. **Nasty** is first recorded in the fourteenth century in the sense 'disgustingly dirty; filthy'.

It developed a number of related opprobrious senses over the next few hundred years, including 'offensive to taste or smell; nauseating', 'morally indecent or obscene', 'objectionable or unpleasant' (in a broad way), 'difficult to deal with or experience' ("a nasty cut"), and '(of people) vicious or spiteful; ill-tempered'. It is this last meaning that people occasionally associate with Thomas Nast, after his highly critical editorial cartoons, which helped bring down Boss Tweed in New York, but this meaning is clearly attested in the early nineteenth century, before Nast was born. It's also worth mentioning that **nasty** was considered somewhat offensive in nineteenth-century America, and was not used in polite conversation.

The origin of **nasty** is unclear, though there are two main suggestions. One is that it is an alteration of Old French *nastre* 'bad', which is a shortening of *villenastre* 'bad; ignoble', formed from the root of the English word *villain* and the pejorative suffix *-astre* as in the English *poetaster.* The other suggestion is that it's of Scandinavian origin, based on a dialectal Swedish word *nasket* 'dirty; filthy' (early English forms of **nasty** include *naxty* and *naskie*). It is also possible that these two forms influenced each other.

In any case, there's no doubt that **nasty** predates Thomas Nast by about five hundred years, showing that Nast's **nasty** style is a linguistic coincidence.

■　■　■

nee

Elena Gonzalez writes: **I have a question about the use of "nee," as in: Cynthia Smith nee Reynolds. Recently, including today in the *Washington Post,* I saw this expression used when referring to a married woman. I'm assuming it's the same construction seen in Spanish: "Elena Diaz de Gonzalez" which implies Diaz is my maiden name. Am I correct? Where does the "nee" come from?**

■ Yes, you are correct. The word **nee**, also spelled **née,** is usually used in English to introduce the maiden name of a married woman. Your name would thus be "Elena Gonzalez, nee Diaz" using this construction.

Nee is from French (where it is spelled *née*), and it is the feminine form of *né,* the past participle of *naître* 'to be born', ultimately from Latin *natus,* the source of English *native.* It is first found in English sources in the mid-eighteenth century.

In actual usage, **nee** does not mean simply 'born', but something like 'formerly called'. One sees it in all sorts of extended senses—introducing the original name of a person using a pseudonym, even introducing an original name of anything (e.g., "the Acura SLX (nee Isuzu Trooper)"— *New York Times,* 1996).

Along these lines, recent years have seen the introduction of the masculine form *né* in English, used similarly but of men: "NWA's main man is Easy-E (*né* Eric Wright), considered the Pavarotti of the rap world" (*Daily Telegraph,* 1990).

There is a minor usage controversy regarding the use of **nee** with full names. Since the word literally means 'born', some usage writers hold that it can only be used with women's family names, not their given names. "The type *Mrs John Jones,* née Ann Smith (i.e. with the Christian name added after *née*) is not always acceptable," notes one usage book, the point being that the woman in question was not *born* "Ann Smith," but was born a Smith and given the name "Ann" after she was born. This complaint strikes me at being unbelievably pedantic, but it's also probably becoming irrelevant, since fewer and fewer women choose to be identified by their husband's full name today. Some people, feeling that it suggests an outdated world of society gossip, advise omitting the word altogether and substituting "born" or "formerly known as" in any context.

■ ■ ■

nerd

David M. Martin writes: **We are all now accustomed to using the term "nerd" to represent an intelligent but socially inept person, but where did the word originate?**

■ The most probable suggestion is that **nerd** was suggested by "the nerd," the name of an imaginary creature in the children's book *If I Ran the Zoo,* by Dr. Seuss (Theodore Seuss Geisel), 1904–1991, in the passage "I'll sail to Ka-Troo / And Bring Back an It-Kutch, a Preep and a Proo, a Nerkle, a Nerd, and a Seersucker, too!" The book was published in 1950, and the word **nerd** is first recorded in 1951, making this etymology plausible. However, it could just be chance; after all, "preep," "proo," and "nerkle" never made it into the language. So another suggestion is that it is a expressive formation of obscure origin, like *dweeb.* Yet another holds that it represents *knurd,* which is *drunk* spelled backwards. A final, and even less likely, suggestion is that it is a euphemistic alteration of *turd.*

The original sense of the word was simply 'a dull, unattractive, or offensive person; jerk; square'. This sense first became popular as student slang in the 1960s, when it was frequently spelled *nurd.* The subsense 'an intelligent but socially inept person; a person slavishly devoted to a (specified) nonsocial activity' ("a computer nerd") seems to have arisen in the late 1970s.

■ ■ ■

nickel

Don Willmott writes: **I saw your writeup on PUMPERNICKEL, and I was wondering whether "nickel" as in the type of coin is related to this. Where does it come from? Is it simply because nickels are made of nickel?**

■ I was hoping someone would ask this, because **nickel** is itself an interesting word that I didn't have space to discuss at *pumpernickel.*

The first thing to say is that yes, the word **nickel** referring to a U.S. five-cent coin is so called because it is made largely of **nickel.** But the five-cent **nickel** is not the only coin that has been made of **nickel,** or called a **nickel.** The original **nickel** was a one-cent piece issued from 1857 to 1864; a three-cent **nickel** was minted from 1866 to 1883; and the now familiar five-cent **nickel** (having various designs) since 1883.

With that out of the way, let's turn to **nickel** itself. **Nickel** is a metallic element whose atomic number is 28. The word is borrowed from Swedish, where it is a clipping of *kopparnickel,* from German *Kupfernickel,* the word for niccolite, the copper-colored metallic mineral **nickel** arsenide.

Kupfernickel is from *Kupfer* 'copper' and *Nickel* 'demon, devil', which as we've seen is a nickname of *Nicholas*. The mineral niccolite is literally called "copper demon," because although it looks like copper (which is relatively valuable) it yields none. A worthy English comparison is *fool's gold*, for iron (or sometimes copper) pyrite, both of which resemble gold and can lead the prospector astray.

The word **nickel** is first found in English in the mid-eighteenth century.

■ ■ ■

nosopoetic

David M. Sampson writes: "Nosopoetic." I ran across this word on the Net the other day along with its supposed definition which is "to cause disease" or something like that. I attempted to find it in my dictionary without luck. I searched on the net and found it used on two very obscure personal Web sites. Can you help with a more official definition and maybe a little background?

■ It's hard to give too much background, because the word is so ridiculously obscure. **Nosopoetic** means 'producing or causing disease', and derives from Greek elements meaning 'disease' and 'making' (the last element is from the same word as *poet*, which etymologically means 'maker'). The *noso-* prefix is found in several other words, including *nosography* 'the systematic description of diseases' and *nosology* 'the branch of medicine dealing with the systematic classification of diseases', but even it isn't very common.

Nosopoetic occurs in an essay by John Arbuthnot, the Scottish physician and writer who coined the phrase *John Bull* and was a friend of Pope and Swift. In *On Air* (1733), Arbuthnot wrote: "I shall make a few Observations upon the Qualities of the Air, so far as they are Nosopoetick, that is, have a Power of producing Diseases." The *Oxford English Dictionary* also cites a nineteenth-century example from a literary magazine, which also refers to air, but that's pretty much the formal record on **nosopoetic.**

The word appears in a small number of huge dictionaries, but in very few other places; it's even omitted from obscure-word havens such as *Mrs. Byrne's Dictionary.* However, one does come across it occasionally as an example of an obscure word, which is no doubt why you've found it on the Net. Peter Bowlers' delightful *The Superior Person's Book of Words* lets us know that " 'Ah, how perfectly nosopoetic!' is the proper exclamation for you to employ when the wealthy Pimplewickers, of whose possessions you are already insanely jealous, proudly show off to you their new fishpond/seaside cottage/sunken garden," etc. etc.

■ ■ ■

not worth the candle

Don Young writes: **I have had no luck finding the origin of the phrase "not worth the candle." I can guess at the origin, and have a general understanding of current usage, but I'm hoping you can provide some better insight.**

■ **Not worth the candle** is an old expression that now means 'not worth the trouble or effort involved'. It was originally used literally, in cases where doing something (playing a game, for example) was not even worth the expense of supplying the light. The expression is now only figurative, candles today being mainly a decorative touch.

The expression is first found in English in the late seventeenth century. It is apparently of French origin; Randle Cotgrave's French-English dictionary in 1611 has an entry for the expression *Le jeu ne vaut pas la chandelle,* ("the game is not worth the candle"), which Cotgrave rendered in English as "it will not quit cost."

■ ■ ■

o'clock

Ben Arbogast writes: The word "o'clock" is sure awkward. Just try saying "Your appointment is at 6:30 P.M. o'clock," as a recent invitation attested. Any history for this word?

■ **O'clock** may be somewhat awkward, but not nearly as awkward as what it's replacing.

The original form of this expression—now the usual way of expressing time—was *of the clock.* This form is quite old—it's found in Chaucer in the late fourteenth century, and consistently thereafter. Today this full form is obsolete, but in Victorian England it was still sometimes found as the most formal way of designating time.

Various shorter substitutes are found over the years for *of the clock.* In the fifteenth century both *of clock* and *a clock* were in use; in the sixteenth and seventeenth centuries both *at clock* and simply *clock* ("three clock") are found.

Our standard form **o'clock** is first attested in the early eighteenth century; the use of *o'* as an abbreviation for *of* is found since the Middle Ages and still used in such other set expressions as *Jack o' lantern* and *will-o'-the-wisp.*

During most of its history, these forms were usually used with names of whole numbers only—*three o'clock,* not *three thirty o'clock.* Indication of day or night was done by specifying *six o'clock at night.* The style you cite—*6:30 P.M. o'clock*—is a very formal style found in invitations and other rigid contexts. In most cases one would simply say *6:30 P.M.,* but in formal situations the expression of time is felt to be incomplete without both P.M. and the **o'clock.** While this is indeed awkward, it is rare; and it can be pretentious when used in informal ways. And very formal invitations have enough awkward elements to them that we probably shouldn't worry too much about how the time is stated.

■ ■ ■

Odd's bodkins

Dave Varon writes: I work with a guy named Botkin, to whom we refer from time to time as Odds Bodkin. What is an odd bodkin, and in what context is the expression used?

■ **Odd's bodkins** is a mild profane oath, which literally means 'God's dear body!' It's now archaic, but was used as an exclamation like *God damn!* or a host of others.

The usual form of the second word is *bodikin,* which is a diminutive of *body* (the diminutive suffix *-kin* is found in such other words as *lambkin*). The expression occurs in Shakespeare (*Hamlet:* "Odds bodikins, man," with a variant reading from the Quarto of "bodkin"), Fielding, and Smollett, among others. Expressions like this were very common in the sixteenth and seventeenth centuries; some other examples are *'sblood* (God's blood), *'snails* (God's nails), *zounds* (God's wounds), and *gadzooks* (God's hooks, i.e., the nails of the Cross).

The word is unrelated to *bodkin* 'a small dagger or pointed instrument', which itself occurs in *Hamlet,* in the "To be or not to be" speech ("When he himself might his quietus make / With a bare bodkin"). This word dates back to the fourteenth century, and is of uncertain origin.

■ ■ ■

ollie ollie oxen free

> **Dave Schreiber** writes: **What's the meaning and origin of the phrase "ollie ollie oxen free"? I occasionally hear references to it as a phrase spoken by children, but I never used it or heard it when I was growing up (I was born in 1971 and grew up in San Jose, California).**

■ **Ollie ollie oxen free** is one of about a bajillion variants (I know—I counted) of a phrase used in various children's games. As we have seen, children's language and folklore hasn't been as thoroughly studied as one would like, but in this case, researchers have tracked down a huge number of forms.

The phrase is used in a variety of children's chasing games, especially hide-and-(go-)seek. The rough form of this game is that a player (called "it") gives other players a chance to hide, and then tries to find them. When "it" finds the first hider, he calls out some phrase indicating that the other players are "safe" to return "home," at which point the person "it" found will succeed him as "it."

The original form of the phrase was something like *all in free* or *all's out come in free,* both standing for something like *all who are out can come in free.* These phrases got modified to *all-ee all-ee (all) in free* or *all-ee all-ee out(s) in free;* the *-ee* is added, and the *all* is repeated, for audibility and rhythm.

From here the number of variants takes off, and we start seeing FOLK ETYMOLOGIES in various forms. The most common of these has *oxen* replacing *out(s) in,* giving *all-ee all-ee oxen free;* with the *all-ee* reinterpreted as the name *Ollie,* we arrive at your phrase, which, according to the *Dic-*

tionary of American Regional English, is especially common in California. Norwegian settlement areas have *Ole Ole Olsen's free.* For the *out(s) in* phrase, we also see *ocean, oxford, ax in, awk in,* and even *oops all in.*

This multiplicity of examples demonstrates the unsurprising fact that young children often have little idea what phrases like this mean, and transmute them into variants that involve more familiar terms, losing the original meaning in the process. It's difficult to determine early dates for these expressions—most of them weren't collected until the 1950s and later—but based on recollections of the games, it seems that they were in common use by the 1920s, and probably earlier (*home free* is found in print in the 1890s, and the game hide-and-seek is at least four centuries old).

■ ■ ■

one-off

Gary Knapp writes: **Recently we appear to be doing things on a "one-off" basis or someone is always getting a "one-off" deal. This appears to have various usages along the lines of unique, exceptional, or ad hoc. What *does* it mean and where did it come from?**

■ **One-off** as an adjective means 'done, occurring, or made only once', and as a noun (much less common) 'something that occurs, is done, or is made only once'. Depending on context, it can be interpreted as meaning 'unique' or 'exceptional', as you suggest; good synonyms are "singular," "unique," or "one-shot."

The word stems from the British use of *off* in commerce to indicate a quantity of items produced at one time: "Please supply 500 off." A **one-off,** then, was an item produced only once, and the current usage is a figurative application of this technical sense.

One-off is chiefly a Briticism, first found in the 1930s; it has been increasingly common in America in recent years.

■ ■ ■

onomatopoeia

Kathleen Kuzmick writes: **I discovered your address from your home page (which is very helpful BTW; I bookmarked it) while I was frantically searching for a word. What is the term used for words which sound like the sound they give? As in, "I'm going to *pop* if I don't figure this out soon."**

■ The word you're seeking is that perpetual spelling bee fave, *onomatopoeic.* **Onomatopoeia** is the rhetorical term for 'the formation of a word, such as "cuckoo," "boom," or "hiss," by imitation of a sound made by or associated with its referent'. It's also used to mean 'the use of imitative and naturally suggestive words', so this entire passage from Tennyson can be described as **onomatopoeia**: "The moan of doves in immemorial elms, / And murmuring of innumerable bees."

Onomatopoeia is derived through Latin from Greek *onomatopoiía*, which means 'the making of words'. Its elements are forms of *ónoma* 'name', an English cognate of which is *onomastics* 'the study of proper names', and *poieín* 'to make', related to *poet*.

Onomatopoeia is, like many rhetorical terms, first recorded in the sixteenth century. The form *onomatopoetic* is also found, but this is comparatively rare and is sometimes considered an error.

■ ■ ■

opprobrium

Ogden Copeland writes: **You used the word "opprobrium" in your explanation of the origin of the word** ROOK. **What does it mean?**

■ The word **opprobrium** is one of those useful words that sounds fancy but expresses insult, and 'insult' is pretty close to what it means. The main sense of **opprobrium** is 'reproach or scorn; (specifically) the disgrace or reproach attached to shameful conduct'.

Opprobrium is a direct borrowing from Latin, and is first attested in the mid-seventeenth century (which means that no, Shakespeare never used it; substitute "contumely" if you need a Shakespearean equivalent). The earliest related form in English is the adjective *opprobrious*, meaning '(of words or a speaker) conveying or expressing reproach or disgrace; abusive' or 'disgraceful; shameful'. This is first attested in the late fourteenth century, and lo!, our friend Bill S. did use the adverbial form: "Think you, my lord, this little prating York/Was not incensed by his subtle mother/To taunt and scorn you thus opprobriously?" (*Richard III,* 3.1.151).

Some other examples that should clarify the use of these words: "Shall the rest, . . . /Accept this dark opprobrious Den of shame . . . ?" (Milton, *Paradise Lost*); "He called the poor cripple by several vile and opprobrious names, and was absolutely proceeding to beat him" (Fielding, *Tom Jones*); "This form of government can be rescued from the opprobrium under which it has so long labored, and be recommended to the esteem and adoption of mankind" (*The Federalist Papers*); "Multitudes of drivers might howl in his ear, and passengers might load him with opprobrium" (Stephen Crane, *Maggie*).

Opprobrium is derived from the Latin prefix *op-*, a variant of *ob-* 'to; towards; against; over', as in "object" and "obligate," and the root *probrum* 'infamy; disgrace'.

orientate/orient

Craig Klampe writes: **I'm confused about "orient" and "orientate" and "orientation." If I give an orientation, am I orientating or orienting?**

■ You are doing either, for **orient** and **orientate** have the same meaning in nontechnical senses.

These two verbs, drawn from the same base (French *orienter* 'to place facing the east', originally used of the placement of churches) have developed the same extended sense 'to familiarize with or adjust to new surroundings or circumstances'. The shorter form arose in the eighteenth century, the longer in the nineteenth. **Orientate** is sometimes criticized, but it is fully standard and has been used by a variety of major authors, including W. H. Auden, Margaret Mead, Tennessee Williams, and Aldous Huxley. It is probably more common in England, while **orient** seems to be the preferred form in the United States.

Robert Burchfield, for many years the chief editor of the *Oxford English Dictionary,* has written, "I have decided to use the shorter form myself in all contexts, but the saving is not great. And one can have no fundamental quarrel with anyone who decides to use the longer of the two words."

■ ■ ■

outsource

Jeanne McGough writes: **Is "outsource" to be used only as a noun, or is a verb form also acceptable?**

■ The verb **outsource** is a relatively new word that's perfectly acceptable. In fact, it's the only acceptable form; while a noun is plausible—"We'll get it from an outsource"—I've never encountered this use.

Outsource is a business term that means 'to buy (goods or services) from a source outside a company or division'. At first, it was used mainly to describe subcontracting components or other manufacturing work from a nonunion or foreign supplier. The usual form was the verbal noun *outsourcing.* In more recent years, it has broadened to refer to purchasing any sort of work from an outside source: one can still outsource brake pads, say, but one can also outsource one's Web page design, or publicity, or a maintenance contract.

Outsource is first attested in the late 1970s; it became widely used in the mid-1980s.

■ ■ ■

pandemonium

Brendan Pimper writes: **Our illustrious local newscaster com-mitted the most atrocious pun by referring to the pandemoni-um at the zoo surrounding the arrival of some pandas recently. Surely these words cannot be related? One source tells me that "pandemonium" is one of the levels of hell where all the demons live (pan + demon).**

■ They're definitely not related; it wouldn't be nearly as funny if they were. The whole point of puns is to juxtapose similar-sounding words, or different meanings of the same word, and in this case if *panda* and **pandemonium** were really related, the effect would be lost.

Pandemonium was coined by John Milton in *Paradise Lost* (1667), from Greek elements *pan-* 'all' and *daímon* 'demon'. In Milton the word referred to the capital of Hell: "A solemn council forthwith to be held/At Pandaemonium, the high capital/Of Satan and his peers." By transference, **Pandemonium** is used to refer to Hell itself as well. These senses, usual-ly with an initial capital, are found outside of Milton: ". . . as exquisite and divine a retreat as Pandemonium appeared to the demons of hell after their sufferings in the lake of fire"—Mary Shelley, *Frankenstein*, for example.

The figurative sense meaning 'wild uproar or tumult; a place of such disturbance', usually lowercase, is first found in the late eighteenth centu-ry. Example from our great American humorist "Mark Twain": "A great multitude of natives from the several islands had kept the palace grounds well crowded and had made the place a pandemonium every night with their howlings and wailings, beating of tom-toms and dancing" (*Roughing It*, 1872).

Panda is ultimately of uncertain origin. It first appears in French in the early nineteenth century. It is often stated to be a name for the animal in a language of Nepal, and while this seems likely, an exact source has not been found.

■ ■ ■

Pandora's box

Shirley Hirsch writes: **I have been searching the Internet for information on the meaning and the origin of "Pandora's Box" and came across your page. Would you please help me out?**

■ Glad to. The allusion is to the Greek myth of Pandora, found in a particularly full form in the *Works and Days* of Hesiod, the early Greek poet. The story is that after the Titan Prometheus stole fire from the gods to give to the human race, Zeus, the supreme deity, determined to punish Prometheus and humanity. He caused Pandora, the first mortal woman, to be created. (Zeus also had Prometheus chained to a rock where an eagle would swoop down every day to tear out Prometheus's liver, which would regenerate, since Prometheus was immortal; this is not relevant to our story, and I include it only for the gore value.) Hephaestus, the smith, formed her out of clay, and all the gods gave her many gifts (*Pandora* means 'all-endowed'). Pandora was sent to Epimetheus, Prometheus's brother—Prometheus knew not to accept a gift from Zeus. While on earth she opened a jar the gods had given her that had all the sorrows and evils of the world contained within, and all escaped into the world to torment humanity. Only hope (in Greek, *elpís*) remained in the jar to counterbalance these.

There are other versions of the story, but the basic idea is that **Pandora's box** contained all the evils of mankind. The usual use now is in the figurative sense 'a source of extensive but usually unforeseen troubles or difficulties'. A recent example from the *New York Times*: "The return of professional figure skaters to Olympic competition has exposed a Pandora's box of problems that the sport's antiquated system of categorizing and judging skaters cannot handle."

Pandora's box is first found in this figurative sense in English in the late sixteenth century.

■   ■   ■

per se

Brenda Stine writes: **What is the definition and correct usage of "per se"?**

■ The Latin phrase **per se** means 'by, of, for, or in itself or oneself; as such; considered alone; intrinsically'. It is usually used after the person or thing it modifies.

A few examples, from various years: "They say he is a very man per se and stands alone" (Shakespeare, *Troilus and Cressida*); "Those subjects who believe themselves bound to acquiesce to a foreign authority . . . do not per se constitute a City, but are the subjects of that foreign power" (Thomas Hobbes, *De Cive*); "The extracts from other books, though always sufficiently pertinent, are rarely very entertaining *per se,* and the author's own text consists mainly of enumerations and catalogues" (Henry James, *English Writers*); "Partisanship per se does not preclude political action" (*Christian Science Monitor*). Note that the phrase is sometimes given in italics, on the grounds that it is a foreign phrase, but by now it is usually considered to be fully Anglicized and is printed in roman type.

Per se is a Latin translation of Greek *kath' autó.* It is first found in English in the sixteenth century.

■   ■   ■

peruse

Fred Ridder writes: I am wondering whether I am alone in thinking that one of the most misused words in English is "peruse." I am continually astonished at how pervasive is its incorrect use to mean a casual or cursory reading rather than its defined meaning of a detailed, in-depth examination.

■ Let's look first at the question of whether others have commented on the use of **peruse** in the sense 'to read casually'. You are definitely not alone; many usage books make some (usually negative) comment on this meaning. The Evans and Evans *Dictionary of Contemporary Usage*, for example, says that "*Peruse* is often used loosely for *read* but such use is ostentatious and improper." The more recent *Harper Dictionary of Contemporary Usage* (second edition) doesn't even bother to send the question to its usage panel, but merely notes that "Too often *peruse* is used loosely as a synonym for 'read.' Its precise meaning is 'to read very carefully . . .' " And American Heritage, which did bother to send the question to its usage panel, reports that 66 percent of its members find the 'read casually' sense unacceptable.

In fact, when examining the history of **peruse** in English, what becomes clear is that there has never been a meaning that could be considered "precise." Most of the time, it means simply 'to read'—which is how Johnson defined it in his great dictionary in 1755—and any additional discrimination of the sense is provided by context.

There are many uses that do suggest a 'read carefully' meaning. A few examples: "Hold, take this book, peruse it thoroughly" (Marlowe, *Dr. Faustus*); "He that will carefully peruse the history of mankind . . ." (Locke, *An Essay Concerning Human Understanding*); "I have carefully perused them three times: the style is very plain and simple . . ." (Swift, *Gulliver's Travels*); "Which we hope will be very attentively perused by young people of both sexes . . ." (Fielding, *Tom Jones*); ". . . the evening paper, which she perused daily from the first line to the last" (Henry James, *Washington Square*).

We should observe that in most of these examples, the "careful" connotation is provided by the context; we could substitute "read" (rather than "read carefully") without changing anything. For **peruse** to have a core meaning, rather than just a suggestion, of "read carefully," there would have to be examples such as "He didn't have time to peruse the paper, so he read it hastily," and we don't really have many of these.

Here are a few uses that suggest a 'read cursorily' meaning: "Those quotations which to careless or unskilful perusers appear only to repeat the same sense, will often exhibit, to a more accurate examiner, diversities of signification" (Samuel Johnson, preface to the *Dictionary*); "Advertisements are now so numerous that they are very negligently perused" (Samuel Johnson, *The Idler*); "The paper was right easy to peruse" (Byron, *Don Juan*); "He then perused the letter in haste" (Sir Walter Scott, *Ivanhoe*); ". . . leisurely perused the next document . . ." (Dickens, *Martin Chuzzlewit*); "the unlearned peruser of their opinions" (Hawthorne, *House of the Seven Gables*). Again, the nature of the "reading" is made clear by a modifier overtly present in the context.

In the overwhelming majority of cases, however, it is impossible to derive a meaning other than 'to read; read through or over'; there's nothing more one can conclude from looking at the citations. Some examples from a very long list: "Madam, please you peruse this Letter" (Shakespeare, *Two Gentlemen of Verona*); "I confess I have perused them all, and can discover nothing" (Sir Thomas Browne, *Religio Medici*); "I have perused several books of travels with great delight in my younger days" (Swift, *Gulliver's Travels*); "And yet, when in calm retirement we peruse the combats described by Homer or Tasso . . ." (Gibbon, *Decline and Fall of the Roman Empire*); "And now I looked upon the living scene;/Familiarly perused it" (Wordsworth, *Prelude*); "While she broke the seal and perused the document, I went on taking my coffee" (Charlotte Bronte, *Jane Eyre*); "Mr. Ruskin, of whose writings he has perused, I suspect, an infinitesimally small number of pages" (Henry James, *American Writers*); "some illustrated paper, which he perused till, raising his eyes, he saw that her face was troubled" (Hardy, *Jude the Obscure*).

Conclusion: **peruse** is very often used in the sense 'to read carefully', but this is not and has never been the "precise" or "only" use of the word. The usual sense is 'to read; to read through or over', and this sense cannot be regarded as an error, despite the comments of Evans and Evans and Harper quoted above. The sense 'to read casually; glance over' is less common—though you yourself call it "pervasive"—but also should not be regarded as an error. However, considering the fact that many people object to this sense, and that **peruse** is primarily a literary word, it would be prudent to avoid this sense in one's own writing. See also SCAN.

■ ▨ ▨

pettifogger

Don Young writes: **On a local radio news broadcast this morning, there was an item about an accused party who called the prosecuting attorney "a common pettifogger," with the connotation that he (the pettifogger) had resorted to trickery in the case. It's a nice little word, reminding me of Charles Dickens, but I wonder about its history. Can you shed any light?**

■ **Pettifogger** has more than a connotation of trickery; the deceit is the integral meaning of the word. The most common sense is 'a lawyer who engages in deceitful practices'. Other senses derived from this include 'any person who practices chicanery', and 'a person who quibbles over trifles'. The verb *to pettifog* is a back formation from **pettifogger.**

Though it does have a splendidly Dickensian ring, **pettifogger** is much older than the Victorian age. The word is first attested in the late sixteenth century. It is formed from *petty,* in its usual sense of 'trivial; inconsequential; minor', and *fogger,* an obsolete English word with the same meaning as **pettifogger.**

The origin of *fogger* itself is uncertain. The verb *fog* meaning 'to obscure; bewilder' is not attested until the late seventeenth century, making it unlikely that this *fogger* is an agential form of it. One theory is that it is a variant of *Fugger,* the name of an important banking family in the fifteenth and sixteenth centuries in Bavaria; words taken from the name *Fugger* had senses in various German dialects of 'monopolist', 'usurer', and hence 'huckster'. Another theory is that *fogger* derives from a Middle Low German or Dutch word *voger, voeger* respectively, meaning 'a person who arranges things'. There is no way to be certain what the exact origin is.

■ ■ ■

phat

William Larry Wood writes: **"Phat": My students used this to describe a computer game that I downloaded for them to write a review. One black student was quite alarmed that I did not know or use "phat." Since that time I noticed a movie called *Phat Beach* featuring a famous rapper. Do you have a list of meanings and can you tell me when the word came into common usage?**

■ Ah, the **phat** question. **Phat** is hard to define accurately, since it has so many approbatory meanings that it's hard to narrow down. But 'wonderful; excellent; exciting; stylish; attractive; satisfactory' should handle the basics. You can substitute *cool* and cover most of the same ground. **Phat** is currently in rather wide use among high school students.

The most interesting thing about this word is just how much older it is than people generally think. In recent usage, **phat** derives from the rap music scene, where it seems to have become popular in the mid-1980s. But in fact it is somewhat older; there are examples of **phat**—in the same spelling—going back to the early 1960s, when it appears in a listing of "Negro argot" in *Time* magazine, included alongside such other "general adjectives of approval" as *mellow, cool,* and *boss.* Although there are occasional examples after that, the word didn't reach mainstream attention until the early 1990s.

There have been several suggestions that **phat** is an acronym, usually for *p*retty *h*ips *a*nd *t*highs, used to describe attractive women, but in reality **phat** is a jocular spelling of *fat,* which has had similar senses since the turn of the century. In fact, the question we're actually discussing here is the history of the spelling of **phat**.

Phat Beach is a 1996 movie starring the musician Coolio, who plays himself.

■ ■ ■

piebald

Michael Abrams writes: Do you have any idea where the word "piebald" comes from? I get the "bald" part, but what's "pie" have to do with it?

■ There are a few different *pie*s in English, and the one in **piebald** is not the same *pie* as the one you eat.

The *pie* in **piebald,** which means 'having patches of two colors, especially black and white', comes from *magpie,* the bird. (Actually, that's not really true. *Magpie* comes from this *pie,* which is earlier, but in current use *pie* is obsolete and *magpie* is the only name of the bird. The *mag* element is from the given name *Mag,* a nickname of *Margaret.* This *pie* is derived from Latin *pīca,* via Old French.)

The magpie is noted for its black-and-white plumage (and its noisy habits, but that's not relevant here), and *pie* has been broadened to apply to combined dark-and-light colorings for many centuries. The fourteenth-century word *pied* 'having dark-and-light coloring' is a derivative, and one that puzzled me throughout childhood—what the heck is a Pied Piper anyway?, I wondered. ("His queer long coat from heel to head/Was half of yellow and half of red," as Browning put it.)

Bald is used in the figurative sense 'streaked with white'. It also appears in the word *skewbald.*

This *pie* is first found in the mid-thirteenth century. (The *pie* that means 'a filled pastry crust' is from the early fourteenth century; it's of unknown origin, but is usually assumed to be unrelated to the magpie word.) **Piebald** is from the late sixteenth century.

■ ■ ■

phony

Don Willmott writes: I was rereading "The Catcher in the Rye" this weekend and was struck again by Holden Caulfield's hatred of "phonies." That got me thinking: how did "phony" become a synonym for "fake"?

■ Probably through English criminal slang, originally from an Irish word. The word **phony** first appears in America in the 1890s. It had various related meanings that arose at about the same time: 'fraudulent or fake'; 'insincere'; 'worthless'; and as a noun 'a counterfeit or fake'; 'an insincere person; fraud', Holden's sense; and 'cheap or worthless jewelry'.

The generally accepted explanation hinges on an eighteenth-century swindle known chiefly as the *fawney rig,* in which a swindler would pretend to find a gold ring—actually a gilt brass ring—and sell it to a victim for less than its supposed, but much more than its actual, value. The word *fawney* denotes the ring itself, and derives from the Irish *fáinne* 'a ring', which, you might be interested to know, may ultimately be related to the word *anus. Fawney* was reinterpreted to mean 'false; fake' in this context, in reference to the bogus ring, and the other senses naturally developed from this 'fake' sense.

The existence of the 'cheap or worthless jewelry' senses lends credence to this theory. The respelling of *fawney* to **phony** could be influenced by *phone* 'a telephone', an 1880s Americanism; even in the late nineteenth century there was an established belief that one could easily conceal one's identity while using a telephone.

■ ■ ■

piggyback

Brendan Pimper writes: "Piggy-back"? I'll admit to being a city boy, but I don't recall any pictures of pigs used as beasts of burden in *National Geographic.* Yesterday my daughter (nearly four years old) explained what "piggy-back" meant, and I got to wondering about origins. Could you explain?

■ I can put some theories out there, but it's probably not possible to give a definitive explanation. One thing seems clear, though: the connection to pigs is accidental.

Piggyback, the main sense of which is '(of something carried, esp. a person) carried on the back or shoulders', dates back to the sixteenth century, but is found in many different forms. The earliest forms vary widely: *pickback, a pickback, a pick pack, on pick pack,* and *pick-a-pack* were all in use before 1700. The usual assumption is that the *pick* word is a dialectal word for 'to throw' that is related to the standard word "pitch." The second element is probably *back,* in reference to where the burden is carried. It could also be *pack,* which was the more common form in the seventeenth century. So the compound could refer to "a pack pitched (onto one's back)," or "(a burden) pitched on one's back."

The alteration to **piggyback** is an illustration of FOLK ETYMOLOGY. FOLK ETYMOLOGY, which we have discussed elsewhere, is the process of altering an uncommon word or element to conform it to one that's better known. *Pickback,* which had become obscure, was changed in the eighteenth century to *pig back;* this was in turn changed (perhaps influenced by the *pick-a-back* form) to the familiar **piggyback** in the nineteenth century. So while *pickback* definitely doesn't make any sense, **piggyback** at least seems as if it could. Since the word had so many variant forms even in its early history, the one thing we can conclude for sure is that people interpreted it in many different ways as soon as it appeared, and this same reanalysis is the source of our current word.

■   ■   ■

pig Latin

Rob Ewen writes: **"Ixnay on the ottenray!" Please help a confused Brit! This phrase is spoken by Marty Feldman in Mel Brooks's *Young Frankenstein.* I realise that it is a method of speaking in code, i.e., take the first letter of a word, carry it to the end and place an "ay" after the whole thing, but how and where did it originate?**

■ The line "ixnay on the ottenray" is an example of **pig Latin,** a common "private language" in America. There are various forms of **pig Latin,** but in the standard version, the initial consonant or consonant cluster of a word is moved to the end, and the sound "ay" is added. If the word begins with a vowel, the "ay" sound (or a "way" sound) is simply added to the end: "it's" becomes "itsay" or "itsway." The phrase "speak pig Latin" would thus be rendered "eakspay igpay atinlay." In the *Young Frankenstein* example, the words "on the" are left untouched, but "ixnay" is **pig Latin** for "nix," (i.e., 'no') and "ottenray" is "rotten." I don't know the context of the quote, so I can't explain what "nix on the rotten!" means.

Pig Latin has been used since the early part of this century. It resembles a number of other methods of altering the language. A common British form is "back slang," where words are spelled backwards and then pronounced; one well-known word is *yob* or *yobbo*, back slang for "boy." Another type is "eggy-peggy," where a "g" sound is inserted in the middle of syllables, so "Put that book down" becomes "Pugut thagat begook dowgun." Forms of private languages are found in many different languages. **Pig Latin** never really caught on in Britain, but is fairly widespread in America. (Conversely, rhyming slang is widespread in Britain and Australia, but has never been popular in the United States.)

Pig Latin is primarily used by children, but it is occasionally used for jocular effect by adults, as in the example you cite. There are also a few words in **pig Latin** that have become established independently, including *ixnay* and *amscray* 'scram'.

■ ■ ■

plurals of compounds

Connie Aronson writes: **I recently asked a friend if she knew of any official rule in grammar when it comes to the plural of certain compound titles. Examples of such titles are "mothers-in-law" or "notaries public." My father-in-law recently showed me a catalog advertising "jack-in-the-boxes," which he felt was incorrect. Consequently, he asked me if I knew of the rule. Can you help?**

■ I can try, but this type of formation cannot be covered by one simple rule. I'll also point out that there's no government body responsible for the English language, and thus no "official" rule of grammar to cover anything. There are, however, some common standards.

In general, nouns form plurals by adding some sort of *-s* to the end of the word. There may be other additions (*-es*) or variations in the end of the word (*leaf/leaves*), but these don't need to concern us now. A small number of words form plurals by a vowel change in the stem (*foot/feet*); and words borrowed from other languages often form plurals according to the rules of the original languages (*datum/data, concerto/concerti,* and so on); and there are a few other possibilities (invariant plurals, such as *deer/deer*; plurals in *-en* such as *child/children*) that are also beyond the requirements of this discussion.

Compounds that are written as a single word usually form plurals the way the final element does: *hairbrush/hairbrushes; gentleman/gentlemen.* Compounds ending in *-ful* usually form plurals by adding an *-s* to the end (*tablespoonfuls*), but occasionally plurals are formed by adding the *-s* before the suffix (*cupsful*), with the compound being considered a noun plus a separate adjective.

When the compound is hyphenated or open, and consists of a noun followed by some qualifier (an adjective, a prepositional phrase, or an adverb), the plural is usually formed by making the noun plural and leaving the other elements alone: *father-in-law/fathers-in-law; notary public/notaries public; passer-by/passers-by* (which is often written as a single word but keeps the *passersby* plural form). The rationale is that the "in law" describes the type of father, in effect, so the plural is based on *father*; and *heir apparent* is a type of heir, so the plural is *heirs apparent*.

Compounds of verb and an adverb form plurals by adding a final *-s: knock-out/knock-outs.*

Other compounds, which, despite consisting of several words, are conceptually one thing—that is, they are not simply nouns with following modifiers—form plurals at the end. A *jack-in-the-box* is not a type of jack; it is a singular toy, and so the plural is usually *jack-in-the-boxes*. A *gin and tonic* is a single cocktail, not a type of gin, so the plural is *gin and tonics*. Similarly, the plurals of *forget-me-not, ne'er-do-well,* and *will-o'-the-wisp* are *forget-me-nots, ne'er-do-wells,* and *will-o'-the-wisps,* respectively.

These guidelines can only be regarded as suggestions, because in actual usage there is a great deal of variety. The recent trend is to form all plurals of compounds at the end; thus such forms as *notary publics, court martials, son-in-laws,* and the like are increasingly common. Conversely, one also sees *wills-o'-the-wisp* and *jacks-in-the-box.* These suggestions, then, should get you through most of the questions you'll be likely to face, but to be absolutely sure, you'll have to consult a dictionary. Ours, of course.

■ ■ ■

(the) proof of the pudding

Cevza M. Zerkel writes: **Last night distinguished *New Yorker* writer Ken Auletta, on the *Newshour* on PBS was heard to utter "the proof is in the pudding." Surely this meaningless distortion of the axiom "the proof of the pudding is in the eating" must be quashed (and he should know better). Agreed?**

■ Well, "quashed" is a rather strong word. The variant *the proof is in the pudding* is fairly well established; and since many people don't know what the full form of **the proof of the pudding** means to begin with, we should start worrying about that.

Proof in the full version of this proverb is used in the now largely archaic sense 'test'. **Pudding** originally referred to a type of sausage, then to any food in a casing or crust. The proverb "the proof of the pudding is in the eating" means something like 'don't judge something superficially, judge by the true result'. **Proof** does not mean 'a demonstration of truthfulness', the usual current meaning.

It is true that the shortened version, *the proof is in the pudding*, doesn't mean much on its own but proverbs often shift their meanings and their forms, so the shortening shouldn't be regarded as that unusual. The shortened form is well attested; at Random House in the last ten years we've collected examples from a variety of sources, including the *New York Times* and a senator's speech, as well as your example from an unquestionably distinguished writer.

The first known use of the proverb is around 1300; it was attested in America in the late eighteenth century, and is considered one of the most common English proverbs.

■ ■ ■

P.U.

Matthew Daly writes: **When something smells really bad, we often use the term "P.U." to show how unpleasent a smell is to us. Example: "I guess Molly worked out during lunch . . . P.U.!" I am interested in finding out how the term "P.U." came into being. Any ideas?**

■ The interjection **P.U.** to indicate disgust, especially of a smell, does not stand for anything humorous. Rather, it is a lettered spelling of a disyllabic pronunciation of a very old interjection that exists in a number of different spellings.

Since about 1600, there have been a number of interjections indicating (variously) disgust, relief, exhaustion, surprise, and the like, all representing something like the whistling sound you get by blowing a puff of air out of closed lips. The most common form is probably *phew,* but *pew, phoo, pfew, peugh,* and *fogh* have all been recorded in writing.

The spelling **P.U.** shows a emphatic, two-syllable pronunciation (*pee you*) of the *pew* form of this interjection. Other words can be given emphasis in a similar way: *kee-rist!* for *Christ,* or *bee-yoo-ti-ful* for *beautiful* are two examples. The difference with **P.U.** is that it has the advantage of sounding like two named English letters, which is why it's spelled out that way, instead of something like *pee-yew.* A similar but not entirely comparable example is the slang expression *on the q.t.* 'secretly'; 'stealthily', where *q.t.* (pronounced as individual letters) represents *quiet.*

Expressions like **P.U.** are hard to track down in their early years. The disyllabic pronunciation of a *phew*-like interjection is probably very old; certainly the spelling existed by the 1950s, if not earlier.

■ ■ ■

pumpernickel

Gerald Bonanno writes: **Do you have any information on the origin of the word "pumpernickel"? Some years ago a friend offered a theory that the word originated as a French phrase during the reign of Napoleon. He believes that as Napoleon's army pushed north into Russia, the wheat used to make bread for the troops gradually gave way to rye which was more hardy in the northern climate and was not well liked by the soldiers due to the coarse dark consistency of the bread. He also says that the French cavalry frequently referred to their horses by the affectionate term "Nicole," much the same as Americans used to refer to their cars as "Betsy." The French troops therefore, being forced to eat rye bread, would exclaim that the bread was not good for them and was only good for their horse or "bon pour Nicole." This sounds cute but is there any basis in fact?**

■ You are right to regard this story with skepticism; it is completely untrue. But the remarkable thing about the word **pumpernickel** is that its etymology is almost as interesting as this ridiculous story (which is, to give your friend the benefit of the doubt, both amusing and fairly widespread; it is also found with the punchline *pain pour Nicole* 'bread for Nicole').

Pumpernickel 'a coarse, dark, slightly sour bread made of unbolted rye', is from German, as one might expect. The word was originally used in German as an insulting term for anyone considered disagreeable. Its elements are *pumpern* 'to break wind', and *Nickel* 'a goblin; devil; rascal', originally a nickname from *Nicholas*. **Pumpernickel,** in other words, literally means 'farting bastard'.

Presumably the word was applied to the bread in reference to its supposed indigestibility.

Pumpernickel is first found in English in the mid-eighteenth century, about a decade before Napoleon was born.

■ ■ ■

punctuation within quotations

Robin E. Bauer writes: **I'd appreciate it if you could set me straight on quotation marks when the words in quotes are at the end of a sentence. Example:**

Jane and Joe are, as the proverb has it, like "two peas in a pod".

or should it be:

Jane and Joe are, as the proverb has it, like "two peas in a pod."

Is the period inside or outside the quotation mark?

■ This is a style question that depends largely on what standard you adopt. In normal American usage, periods and commas appear inside quotation marks, regardless of how this fits the sense. Thus, the correct version of your sentence would be as follows:

Jane and Joe are, as the proverb has it, like "two peas in a pod."

Colons and semicolons appear outside the quotes:

We were like "two peas in a pod": our taste in music was identical, and we liked the same movies too.

Exclamation points, question marks, and dashes appear inside or outside depending on whether or not they refer to the quoted material:

He asked me, "Do you have the time?"

But:

Can you believe she had the gall to say, "I've never seen you before in my life"?

"I don't believe you could have—" he began.

But:

Spare me your "consideration"!

British style differs from American in that British style uses single quotation marks for a first reference, and then double quotes within the single quotes:

'Where are we going?' she asked.

She told me, 'I heard him shout "Help!" but no one listened.'

American usage has double quotes for a first reference and single quotes thereafter:

She told me, "You should remember the proverb: 'a rolling stone gathers no moss.' "

(Note also that the period, or comma, is placed within both quotation marks.)

British usage also places periods and commas outside quotation marks if the period or comma does not refer to the quoted text. Thus,

He called me 'arrogant', but I think he was only joking.

Some readers may wonder why I often use single quotes with punctuation outside for defining words: *cool* 'exciting'. This is a standard linguistic practice that takes precedence over the usual style rules.

pupil

Brynn Sandler writes: **I am curious about the word "pupil." Where did it originate, and how did it evolve to mean both a student and the black spot in the iris of someone's eye?**

■ **Pupil** is an interesting example of a Latin word that evolved in two different ways.

The Latin word where everything starts is *pupus,* which means 'a boy', and its feminine form *pupa,* which means both 'a girl' and 'a doll'. The diminutives of these forms are *pupillus* (masculine) and *pupilla* (feminine), which meant 'a male/female orphan; ward'; the feminine form also meant 'a little doll'.

This word *pupillus/a* came into English (by way of Middle French) as *pupille* in the sense 'a minor ward; a young person under another's supervision' in the fourteenth century, and by the sixteenth century it had made the natural jump to the sense 'a student', picking up the **pupil** spelling en route.

Going back to Latin, the word *pupilla* in the sense 'a little doll' was also used to mean 'the pupil of the eye', in reference to the tiny reflections of oneself one sees in another person's pupil. This semantic shift is also found in Greek, where the word *korē* also meant 'girl', 'doll', and 'pupil'; the sense development of the Latin word is either parallel to, or borrowed from, this Greek development. This sense of Latin *pupilla* came into English the same way as the 'ward' sense, and arrived in English in the same form—*pupille* and then **pupil**—but with a totally different meaning.

■ ■ ■

purple

Brad Thompson writes: **Where is the usage of "purple," as in overflowery "purple prose," derived from?**

■ **Purple** in the sense 'marked by ornate rhetoric or elaborate literary devices' is a literary allusion. In the *Ars Poetica* or "Art of Poetry," the Roman poet Horace combines astute literary criticism with practical advice on writing poetry. Early in the poem, he writes:

> *Inceptis gravibus plerumque et magna professis*
> *Purpureus, late qui splendeat, unus et alter*
> *Adsuitur pannus.*

In other words, "With serious works and ones of great import, some purple patch or other is frequently stitched on, to show up far and wide."

The reference is to a piece of **purple** cloth sewn onto a plain fabric; purple was the color of the emperor and later of royalty, since it was derived from an expensive dye.

The *Ars Poetica* was an extremely important work and was used in the Elizabethan era and later as a model for writing. The phrase *purple patch* was used as a conscious allusion to Horace, meaning 'an overly ornate passage in a literary work', and **purple** itself was then extracted as an adjective meaning 'ornate'.

The word **purple** itself is borrowed from Latin *purpura* 'purple dye', originally 'a kind of shellfish yielding purple dye', from Greek *porphyra* (the source of English *porphyry*).

The change in the second syllable from *r* to *l* is an example of the process of *dissimilation,* where a sound changes to become different from a neighboring sound. Another example of *r* to *l* dissimilation is *marble,* from Old French *marbre.*

■ ■ ■

push the envelope

Bob Sutton writes: **From where do we get the expression "pushing the envelope"?**

■ From aviation jargon, where **envelope** means 'the known limits of safe performance'. Test pilots often have to take aircraft beyond these limits—flying a plane faster or higher than had been done before—to establish exactly what the planes could do. This was known, by the 1960s, as **pushing the envelope.**

The phrase was popularized in the mainstream by Tom Wolfe's best-selling novel *The Right Stuff* (1979). Figurative use of the phrase, meaning 'to stretch the boundaries', dates from the late 1980s. It is similar to other figurative expressions involving boundaries or limits, such as BEYOND THE PALE, discussed elswhere, or *moving the goalposts.*

■ ■ ■

red herring

Rob Ewen writes: **How did a false clue in a detective story come to be called a "red herring"?**

■ This question has come up several times recently, and I'm not sure why. But the answer is not that complicated. A **red herring** is an old term for a smoked herring. (This is a literal use—the process of curing a herring with smoke turns the fish a reddish color.) By the seventeenth century, there is evidence that smoked herrings were used as a training aid for hunting dogs: pulling the fish along a trail would obscure an original scent, and the dogs needed to be able to ignore this diversion. A red herring was thus something used to throw the hounds off the trail.

By the late nineteenth century, the expression "draw a red herring across the trail" was used figuratively to mean 'to divert attention from the real issue or problem', and **red herring** itself was used independently to mean 'something intended to divert attention from the real issue', and hence 'a false or misleading clue'.

I might add that the term **red herring** has been widely used in American politics over the past fifty years, perhaps more extensively than in reference to detective stories. A favorite political ploy during an election campaign is to charge one's opponents with "dragging red herrings into the campaign," i.e., dodging the real issues or problems. It's possible that the frequent questions about this phrase have come up recently because of its overuse by politicians.

■ ■ ■

red-letter day

Louis Mancuso writes: **Do you know the origin and meaning of the term "red-letter day"? The term is currently used as a title on the Pet Shop Boys' latest album, and is frequently used by television newsreaders in reference to a particularly favorable occurrence.**

■ **Red-letter** means simply 'memorable or important, especially in a happy or favorable way'.

The expression comes from the long-established practice of using red ink to indicate holy days in ecclesiastical calendars. A **red-letter day**—

literally a day written in red letters—was a holy day, or church festival, and thus came to mean 'any memorable or happy day'.

Red letter meaning 'a red letter that indicates a holy day on a calendar' dates at least to the fifteenth century; the expression **red-letter day** is first found in the early 1700s.

■ ■ ■

redneck

> **Chris Bonneu writes:** No, not that you are one, but just where did the term "redneck" originate?

■ In the South, as you will probably not be surprised to learn.

The term **redneck** first meant 'an uneducated white farm laborer in the South'. It comes from the literal notion of one's neck being colored red by sunburn from working in the fields all day (and not, as some have suggested, from the alleged habit of southerners of wearing red bandannas around the neck).

In its earliest use, recorded especially in Arkansas and Mississippi, **redneck** was used chiefly by other Southerners as a disparaging term for lower-class people. More recently it has been applied by Northerners to Southerners in general. The most recent extended sense is 'a bigot or reactionary', that is, a person whose views resemble those attributed to the Southern working class.

Redneck is first attested in 1830, but seems to have been very rare before the twentieth century.

■ ■ ■

roger wilco

> **Judy Pineda writes:** I've always wondered how "Roger Wilco" came to be used in radio transmissions, especially on airplanes. Was there a person with that name?

■ No, Mr. Wilco isn't a real person. In fact, the combination **roger wilco** was never even intended to sound like a name. It's just chance that both **roger** and **wilco**, which have separate meanings, get used often enough together that they seem like a set phrase, and since **roger** is a given name the whole thing sounds like a name.

Roger is a word used in one prominent radio alphabet to stand for the letter *R*. These alphabets use words to represent letters; such alphabets are known as "radio alphabets" or "phonetic alphabets," among other names, and are used for many different languages. The alphabet in which

Roger stands for *R* begins "Able Baker Charlie Dog . . . ," and was the official radio alphabet of the U.S. Navy before 1954. Another familiar alphabet, the NATO phonetic alphabet, which is used by the International Civil Aviation Organization and the Federal Aviation Administration, begins "Alpha Bravo Charlie Delta"; this alphabet uses *Romeo* for *R*.

The *R* that **Roger** represents stands for *received,* indicating that a radio message has been received and understood. The use of radio alphabet terms to stand for other words is common in the military; **roger** is a well-known example, and another example is *Charlie* referring to Viet Cong troops, which comes from *Victor Charlie*, a radio alphabet spelling of *VC* for *Viet Cong.*

Wilco is not from a radio alphabet; it's a military abbreviation for "will comply," indicating that a message that has been received will be complied with. It's necessary to acknowledge receipt of a message with **Roger** before indicating compliance with **wilco**, hence the frequent combination **Roger, wilco.**

Both **Roger** in this sense and **wilco** appear for the first time during World War II.

■ ■ ■

rook

***Gary Knapp writes:* What is the origin of "getting rooked"? It's usually used now in the sense of cheated or unjustly excluded—even "gypped." Does it come from chess? birds?**

■ Birds. The **rook** is a type of crow common in Europe. (This is off the subject, I know, but I just want to share my favorite **rook**-related quote: "Light thickens, and the crow/Makes wing to th' rooky wood." —Shakespeare, *Macbeth*, 3.2.51. Sorry.) Like the crow, the **rook** has a reputation for being a not especially pleasant bird—it steals things, it makes a lot of noise—and the word **rook** became used as a term of opprobrium by around 1500 in England. Compare the use of *ass* 'a stubborn or foolish person', taken from the name of the animal.

By the late sixteenth century, another sense had developed, picking up the idea of crows' thievery: 'a cheat or a swindler, especially at cards or dice'. This word underwent a functional shift to a verb, meaning 'to cheat or swindle'. The verb, which also appears in the late sixteenth century, originally referred to cheating at cards or dice, but then broadened to refer to cheating or swindling by any means.

The word **rook** that means 'a bird of the crow family' comes from an Old English word that stems from a Germanic root; cognates are found in several of the Germanic languages. It is unrelated to the word **rook** meaning 'a chess piece that can move any number of unobstructed squares horizontally or vertically', which comes from Persian, by way of Arabic and Middle French.

■ ■ ■

rubber

> *Don Willmott writes:* When I was a kid, I used to watch *The Hollywood Squares,* and Peter Marshall would always refer to the tie-breaking round as "the rubber match." I'd sit there and think, "Huh?" In later years, I found out that it was a term relating to cards (bridge specifically?). But why rubber?

■ I don't want to be forced to repeat this answer, but: no one knows. **Rubber** meaning '(in various games) a series of three (or sometimes five) games', and hence 'a deciding game played in a contest when the score is tied' first appears in the late sixteenth century referring to the game of bowls (that is, lawn bowling).

The word **rubber** meaning 'a highly elastic solid substance made from the milky juice of various plants' is a different story: it is formed from the verb *to rub* with the agentive suffix *-er,* with a few semantic twists before it gets to the current sense. The original meaning, from the mid-sixteenth century, is 'a tool used for rubbing in order to polish or make clean'. The more specific sense that concerns us is 'a piece of rubber used to erase pencil marks', which appears in the late eighteenth century.

Though it seems backward, **rubber** in the sense 'an elastic substance', which is first attested around 1800, actually derives from the use of this substance as an eraser. This is an impressive example of the process called *generalization,* where a word is generalized from a specific application. Other examples, not quite as striking, are *pigeon,* which originally meant 'a young dove', and then came to mean 'any bird, regardless of age, of the family Columbidae'; and *virtue,* which originally meant 'manly excellence; valor', and then came to mean 'moral excellence'.

This is all a long way of saying that the word **rubber** you're asking about is two hundred years older than the word rubber meaning 'an elastic substance'. The origin of the 'series of three games' sense is unknown; it could be related to the other word **rubber** (which, at the time, meant only 'a tool for rubbing'), but the connection, if any, is obscure.

■ ■ ■

rule of thumb

> *Tim Olsen writes:* I have heard that the origin of the phrase "rule of thumb" comes from an old law that stated a husband could not beat his wife with a stick larger than the diameter of his thumb. The date of this law is unknown.

■ The date is 1782.

Absolutely amazing, isn't it? This is the sort of explanation that sounds like the worst sort of FOLK ETYMOLOGY, or after-the-fact explanation. In fact it *is* a FOLK ETYMOLOGY, but one that is based on a fact.

It seems that in 1782 a well-respected English judge named Francis Buller made a public statement that a man had the right to beat his wife as long as the stick was no thicker than his **thumb**. There was a public outcry, with satirical cartoons in newspapers, and the story still appeared in biographies of Buller written almost a century later. Several legal rulings and books in the late eighteenth and nineteenth centuries mention the practice as something some people believe is true. There are also earlier precedents for the supposed right of a man to beat his wife.

This "rule" is probably not related to the phrase **rule of thumb,** however. For one thing, the phrase is first attested in the late seventeenth century, a hundred years before the thumb-stick-beating practice is first known. (Of course, it's possible that it was a well-known, but unrecorded, practice before Buller.) Another problem is that the phrase **rule of thumb** is never found in connection with the beating practice until the 1970s. Finally, there is no semantic link between the **rule of thumb,** which means 'a general method based on experience or practice as opposed to scientific calculation; a rough or practical method' and the idea of beating one's wife with a thin stick.

The precise origin of **rule of thumb** is not certain, but it seems likely to refer to the **thumb** as a rough measuring device for length (*rule* meaning 'ruler' rather than 'regulation'), which is a common practice. The linkage of the phrase to the wife-beating rule appears to be based on a misinterpretation of a 1976 National Organization for Women report, which mentioned the phrase and the practice but did not imply a connection.

■ ■ ■

sally forth

Dee Christoff writes: **I have a question of etymology. "Sallies forth." What objects are capable of "sallying forth?" And, how does this terminology relate to the cartoon strip/character of the same name (Sally Forth)?**

■ In standard use, only a person or group can **sally forth**. The original sense of **sally** is '(of troops) to rush forth from a besieged place against the enemy'. The main figurative sense is the broadened use 'to set out, as on an excursion; venture'. This sense is usually, but not necessarily, used with **forth**. The word can be used of any sort of object, meaning 'to rush or burst out', but this is chiefly a poetic use.

    Sally first appears in English in the middle of the sixteenth century. It is a borrowing from the Middle French word *saillir* 'to rush forward', which is itself a borrowing from Latin *salīre* 'to leap'.

    The cartoon character *Sally Forth* is named after this English expression, based on the pun between the word **sally** we've been discussing and the female given name *Sally,* which is a familiar form of "Sarah" and is not related to our "rush forth" word.

■ ■ ■

Santa Claus

Brendan Pimper writes: **'Round these parts, the words "San" and "Santa" often begin the names of cities. It didn't take too long before I figured out that "San" was the masculine form of "Saint," and "Santa" the feminine form. So how did manly Kris Kringle/Father Christmas/St. Nicholas end up being "Santa Claus"? Different language?**

■ Yes, **Santa Claus** is a borrowing from Dutch, not Spanish. The source was a dialectal Dutch form *Sante Klaas* (the standard form was *Sinterklaas*), made up of *sint* 'saint', *heer*, a form of a Dutch word meaning 'Mr.' or 'Sir', and *Klaas*, a short form of 'Nicholas'. In short, "Santa Claus" is Dutch for "St. Nicholas."

    One of the stories about St. Nicholas is that he gave dowries to three poor women by throwing bags of gold into their open windows; the legend that he gives gifts to children stems from this. The original day of this event was Nicholas's own holiday, St. Nicholas's Day (December 6); this was later shifted to Christmas Eve.

Both the folklore of **Santa Claus** and the custom of this gift giving on Christmas Eve were essentially invented at the turn of the nineteenth century in New York. Several prominent and wealthy New Yorkers, including Washington Irving and Clement Moore, created most of the legend, claiming that it was part of New York's ancient Dutch heritage. It was Moore's famous poem "A Visit from St. Nicholas" (" 'Twas the night before Christmas, and all through the house . . .") that gave us most of the now familiar Christmas ritual, which had the effect not only of grounding the holiday in a fake historical tradition but also of keeping the riotous lower classes quietly at home; in addition, it ensured a commercial windfall for the merchants of the day. The story of the creation of this Christmas tradition is excellently told in *The Battle for Christmas,* by Steven Nissenbaum, which I would recommend even if it weren't published by Random House.

■　■　■

sawbuck

Ariel Kaminer writes: **How did "sawbuck" come to refer to a $10 bill?**

■ Originally, a **sawbuck** (or, more commonly, *sawhorse*) referred to a movable frame used to support wood while it is being sawed. **Sawbuck** is probably a borrowing from the Dutch word *zaagbok,* literally "saw-trestle."

Also originally, a $10 bill had the roman numeral X '10' printed on it. Most U.S. paper currency had values in roman numerals; even in the early nineteenth century bills were called "Vs," "Xs," "Cs," and so forth. The "C" for a $100 bill is the origin of the current term "C-note." A $10 bill, already called an "X," started being called a **sawbuck** because of the resemblance of the letter X to the crossed legs of the sawhorse.

The popularity of **sawbuck** was strengthened by the introduction of the word BUCK 'a dollar', which arose slightly later.

Sawbuck is first found in 1850 in the once common expression "double sawbuck," meaning a $20 bill or $20. Another, recent variant is *sawski.* **Sawbuck** itself, like "dime," is also used to refer to a ten-year prison sentence.

■　■　■

scan

Mary Beth Protomastro writes: **Your excellent write-up on** PERUSE **brought to mind another word: "scan." The** *Random House Webster's College Dictionary* **says "scan" can mean either "scrutinize" or "glance at"—which are opposite meanings! How did those meanings develop, and which one is more common today?**

■ Very good question, which I couldn't address at PERUSE. Let us look at this interesting note on *peruse* by Frank Vizetelly, the conservative pronunciation expert and apparently the first person who actively objected to the 'read casually' sense of *peruse* I discussed elsewhere:

> Peruse should not be used when the simple *read* is meant. The former implies to read with care and attention and is almost synonymous with *scan*, which is to examine with critical care and in detail.

The reaction of most people today to this passage would be "Huh?," a reaction I confirmed by asking a bunch. Everyone seems to think that **scan** means 'to read hastily; glance at', and the fact that **scan** used to mean 'to read carefully' was considered surprising. The 'read hastily' sense of **scan** is by far the more common in current use.

Scan first appears in English in the late fourteenth century, where it meant 'to analyze (verse) for its prosodic or metrical structure', a sense that is still current. It is a borrowing from Latin, where it literally meant 'to climb'.

The sense 'to examine closely' is found by the mid-sixteenth century, and was for a long time the main sense (when, of course, it can be discerned from the sense 'to read or examine'): "Aloof with hermit-eye I scan/The present works of present man" (Coleridge, "Ode to Tranquility"); [after a long discussion of God] "It is not impious thus to scan the attributes of the Almighty" (Mary Wollstonecraft, *A Vindication of the Rights of Woman*); "Man scans with scrupulous care, the character and pedigree of his horses" (Darwin, *The Descent of Man*); "But did you deeply scan him in his more secret confidential hours" (Melville, *Moby-Dick*).

The development of the sense 'to read hastily; glance at' is hard to pinpoint but had certainly occurred by the 1920s.

What is notable about this sense is not its existence—after all, words develop contradictory senses all the time, *peruse* being a case in point—but that hardly anyone cares about it. A few usage critics make negative comments about it, but most simply point it out. The *Harper Dictionary of Contemporary Usage,* which blasted the "loose" use of PERUSE, merely cautions against the confusion of the contradictory senses of **scan.** While 66 percent of the 1993 American Heritage usage panel disapproved of the 'read casually' sense of PERUSE, in 1969 (the last time they bothered asking), a whopping 85 percent thought that this sense of **scan** was fine, at least in informal use.

Both PERUSE and **scan** once meant 'to read carefully' and then developed a sense 'to read casually', but in one case the change was harshly criticized while in the other it passed largely unscathed. This disparity demonstrates that questions of usage are very complicated, and can rarely be answered by simple appeals to the history of a word. As for **scan,** it is unlikely that you will be criticized for either sense, but be sure to make clear through the context what sense you are using.

■ ■ ■

scapegoat

Jennifer Hindman writes: **Would you please discuss the etymology of the word "scapegoat"?**

■ **Scapegoat** is a biblical reference, to Leviticus 16. The scapegoat was a goat let loose in the wilderness on the Day of Atonement after the high priest symbolically laid the sins of the people on its head. The usual sense now, 'a person or group made to bear the blame for others or to suffer in their place', is a figurative use of the biblical meaning.

The word was coined by William Tyndale, an English religious reformer, in his influential translation of the Bible in 1530. Tyndale formed **scapegoat** from *scape,* an obsolete form of *escape,* and *goat,* with the word thus meaning 'the goat that departs'. Tyndale used this word to translate the Hebrew word *'azāzēl,* which he read as *'ezāzēl,* or 'the goat that departs'. The actual Hebrew word, however, does not mean 'the goat that departs'; it is a proper name of uncertain derivation.

This same mistranslation occurs in the Vulgate, the fourth-century Latin translation of the Bible, and in several other translations.

The first appearance of the word in its original sense was in 1530 in Tyndale's Bible. The figurative sense is first found in the early nineteenth century, and the verb, meaning 'to make a scapegoat of; blame for' is first found as a psychological term in the 1940s.

■ ■ ■

scarlet

John Benz Fentner, Jr. writes: **The recent question about Prof. Harold Hill's use of 'LIBERTINE' reminded me of his other use: "Libertine men and scarlet women and ragtime, shameless music . . ." So why "scarlet" in conjunction with less than reputable women? It must predate Hawthorne's Letter.**

■ It does indeed.

A common assumption is that **scarlet** in senses referring to moral offenses stems from the color of a person blushing, and there do exist examples of **scarlet** in descriptions of reddened faces: ". . . Change the complexion of her maid-pale peace/To scarlet indignation" (Shakespeare, *Richard II* 3.3), for one.

However, while this association may support the 'immoral' sense, the actual reference is to the use of the word **scarlet** in biblical passages condeming immorality, especially of a sexual nature: "Come now, and let us reason together, saith the Lord: though your sins be as scarlet, they shall be as white as snow; though they be red like crimson, they shall be as wool" (*Isaiah* 1:18). (Note also, in this passage, the even better established association of *white* with moral purity.) An even more striking example is the description of the Whore of Babylon: "I saw a woman sit upon a scarlet colored beast, full of names of blasphemy. . . . And the woman was arrayed in purple and scarlet color . . . having a golden cup in her hand full of abominations and filthiness of her fornication" (*Revelations* 17:1–6).

The sense '(of an offense or offender) heinous; severe; immoral' is an allusion to these passages, and is first found in the seventeenth century. Example from 1656: "The Final cause [of earthquakes], is a sign of an Angry God, justly provoked by the Scarlet crimes of a sinful People." The use of a scarlet *A* as a badge that adulterers were compelled to wear, as described in Hawthorne's novel, also derives from this. (The actual phrase *scarlet letter,* used figuratively to mean 'a mark of guilt (of any sort)', derives from Hawthorne's title itself.)

■   ■   ■

schadenfreude

Jeff Tyzzer writes: I came across the word *Schadenfreude* in the current issue of the e-zine *Slate*. What does it mean?

■ **Schadenfreude** is a word so wonderfully useful that if it didn't exist, it would have to be invented, as the saying goes. It means 'the malicious pleasure one feels at someone else's misfortune'. (As Gore Vidal has noted, "It is not enough to succeed. Others must fail.")

Schadenfreude is a borrowing from German, where it is a combination of *Schaden* 'harm' and *Freude* 'joy'. It has been in used in English since the late nineteenth century, though English writers noted the word's use in German earlier that century.

Whether the word appears in roman or italic type depends on whether it is thought to be a German word used in English, or an English word that has been borrowed from German. There is no easy way to judge this. *Kindergarten* and *waltz* are both German borrowings that are always considered to be English, while words like **Schadenfreude** or *Realpolitik* are often considered to be German words used in English. (Nouns in German are capitalized.)

The latest development of this word, which I especially enjoy and encourage people to use as often as possible, is *schadenfreudian*, punning on **Schadenfreude** and the name of Sigmund *Freud.* So far I've only seen it in a few smirky intellectual-type magazines, but it deserves to be more widespread.

■　■　■

schm-

Stanley Newman writes: **"Fancy-schmancy": The rhyming second word with *"schm-"* in front is used in a mocking way for many words, right? I saw a new usage in this week's *People* magazine: *"gravity-schmavity"* (for a Wonderbra ad!). Where did *"schm-"* come from?**

■ The element **schm-** (also **shm-**) is added to the initial part of a word to form what linguists call a "reduplicated rhyming compound" jocularly expressing disparagement or derision of the word. It is a borrowing from Yiddish, where it was used long before it was introduced into English (e.g., Yiddith *latkes-schmatkes* 'pancakes-schmancakes'), and linguists have traced it back to German of the Middle Ages. In English the **schm-** sound has been reinforced by a number of words borrowed from Yiddith, where the sound is quite common, as in *schmaltz* 'sentimentality', *schmatte* 'a rag or cheap garment', *schmooze* 'to chat or gossip intimately', *schmuck* 'a jerk', and others.

This usage is well established in English, going back at least to the 1920s. Your first example, *fancy-schmancy,* itself goes back to 1935. Although the early examples are primarily from Jewish writers, its current use is widespread, as is demonstrated by the widely promoted Wonderbra ad you mention.

■　■　■

scimitar

Barb Richardson writes: **We do know that the word "cimeters" refers to weapons . . . what kind? It is in no dictionary we have. Thanks.**

■ You have the misfortune to have chosen a weapon found in many, many different spellings. The usual one is **scimitar,** and that describes a type of curved, single-edged sword that is wider near the end, used especially by Arabs and Turks.

People whose business it is to collect such things have found about forty different spellings of the word over the centuries, and of the other variants your *cimeter* (which happens also to be the earliest form of the word) was the most common, and was still in use in the nineteenth century. Edward Gibbon, in his *Decline and Fall of the Roman Empire*, used the "cimeter" spelling, and Spenser also spelled it with an initial *c*.

Scimitar was borrowed in the mid-sixteenth century from French *cimeterre* and Italian *scimitarra* (the source of the usual spelling). Its ultimate origin is uncertain, though Persian *shimsheer* 'a type of sword' has been suggested.

■　■　■

scot-free

> *Steve Casale writes:* **What is the origin of the term "going scot-free" or "getting off scot-free"? Does it have something to do with Scots or Scotland?**

■ No, **scot-free** is unrelated to Scotland. (It is also unrelated to *Scot,* a dialectal word used as a name for a horse; I mention this obscurity only because this word appears in Chaucer, and someone once assured me that this word is the origin of **scot-free.** She was wrong.)

Scot-free actually comes from *scot,* meaning 'an assessment or tax'. This word is a borrowing from Old Norse, perhaps from *scot* 'contribution' or a related word *scattr* 'tax; treasure'. It also seems to be related to Old English *gescot* 'shot', and there is also the possibility of the influence of Old French *escot,* which was itself borrowed from a Germanic source. *Scot* is first found in this sense in the early thirteenth century.

Scot-free originally meant 'free from payment of scot', a sense that is now almost totally obsolete, except in historical contexts. By extension, it came to mean 'free from obligation, harm, punishment, or restraint'. (Yes, the idea that a tax is a punishment is a very old one.) Since the word *scot* on its own is now rare, most people probably interpret *scot* to be some sort of intensive of *free.*

Scot-free, like *scot* itself, is first found in the thirteenth century. The broader use of the word is attested in the sixteenth century.

■　■　■

scuttlebutt

> *Valerie Stecher writes:* **I know that "scuttlebutt" is slang for "gossip" but where did this word come from?**

■ A **scuttlebutt** was originally a nautical term for a container of water, or a drinking fountain, for use by the crew. Just as modern corporate wonks hang around the water cooler to chat and gossip, seamen of old would gather around the **scuttlebutt** to pass the time, and the **scuttlebutt** became known as the place to go for gossip. (Amazing how little things change, isn't it?)

By 1901 there was a miscellany column called "Scuttle Butt" in a military newspaper. (In 1996, the "chat room" section of Random House's internal computer network came to be known as the "Water Cooler.") Though this column never explicitly used the word **scuttlebutt** in the sense 'gossip', the word did appear in the phrase "scuttlebutt gossip." Roughly by World War I, **scuttlebutt** was being used on its own to mean 'gossip; rumor'—a development that has yet to occur with "water cooler."

Scuttlebutt, in its literal sense, first appears at the turn of the nineteenth century. It is formed from *scuttle* 'to cut a hole in' (*scuttling* a ship means to sink it deliberately by cutting holes or opening hatchways below the water level), and *butt* 'a large cask'.

■ ■ ■

sea change

R. Clayton writes: **The dictionary definition of "sea change" ("a change brought about by the sea") doesn't seem to match its current use as indicating a complete change from what's held in the past ("It's a sea change—yes, the network really is the computer." John Doerr in *The Red Herring*). What's the current meaning of sea change and from where did it come?**

■ The usual sense of **sea change** is 'a major transformation or alteration'. The phrase is an allusion to a passage in Shakespeare's *The Tempest:*

> Full fathom five thy father lies;
> Of his bones are coral made;
> Those are pearls that were his eyes:
> Nothing of him that doth fade
> But doth suffer a sea-change
> Into something rich and strange.
> (*The Tempest,* 1.2, spelling modernized)

Here the sense is literally 'a change brought about by the sea', but the transferred meaning 'a major change' is the one most people are familiar with. This shift from an obscure literal sense to a more common popular meaning is frequent in phrases quoted from Shakespeare; compare HOIST WITH ONE'S OWN PETARD, which literally means 'raised into the sky by one's own bomb' but is used to mean 'caught by the very device one has contrived to hurt another'.

■ ■ ■

send-up

Jerry writes: **Request the meaning of "send-up." I get the impression it means "spoof."**

■ Your impression is correct. A **send-up** is 'a burlesque; parody; satire; spoof'.

A few examples: "[Mel] Brooks had just shown a clip from *High Anxiety,* his next comedy. . . . The film is half homage to Alfred Hitchcock, half send-up of famous Hitchcock scenes" (Roger Ebert); "*Gulliver's Travels* is a send-up of the eighteenth-century vogue for travel writers" (Gene Lyons); "Even Hollywood, sniffing the winds of change, managed *M*A*S*H,* a send-up of the war effort" (John Lahr).

The expression **send-up** is first found in the late 1950s in British English. It is a nominalization of the verb phrase *to send up* 'to burlesque; satirize; parody', a Briticism from around 1930.

■ ■ ■

serial comma

Tammy Trinker writes: **When writing a "list" sentence in which several different points are listed, and the last item in the sentence is preceded by the word "and," should a comma be used in front of the word "and" or is it not necessary? It is a minor point, but as I have minutes to begin next week, I am most curious of the proper grammatical structure.**

■ A comma after the next-to-last item in a list, when the next-to-last item and the last item are separated by a conjunction, is known as a *series comma* or a **serial comma** (or, in England, as the *Oxford comma*). An example is, "We visited London, Paris, and Milan." Without the **serial comma** the sentence would be "We visited London, Paris and Milan." Sometimes the omission of the comma can make a sentence ambiguous: "He ordered coffee, bread and butter and a muffin." This could mean that "bread and butter" is one item ordered together, or that "butter and a muffin" were ordered together; one can't tell from context. The debate about whether or not to use it is a stylistic issue, not a grammatical one, but it's a noisy debate nonetheless.

Some writers, chiefly journalists, think that the **serial comma** should be avoided unless the sentence is ambiguous, on the grounds that the conjunction makes the preceding comma superfluous. Most, however, recommend using the serial comma in all cases, since the inclusion of the comma is always clear and doesn't force the writer to evaluate every sentence for possible ambiguity.

Most newspaper style books—for example, those of the Associated Press and the *New York Times*—recommend omitting the **serial comma**, and many newspapers and newsmagazines don't use it. Most book publishers do use the serial comma, and most nonnewspaper-related style guides recommend using it.

I myself strongly recommend using the **serial comma**, and find its absence distracting.

I should also point out that if a sentence is complex, and has lists which themselves contain commas or clauses, a semicolon should be used instead of a comma: "He ran out of the office; went to the gym, doing only half of his normal workout; took a cab home to pick up the dogs; and made it to the train station with two minutes to spare."

■ ■ ■

shiftless

Stacy Abbott writes: **Where does the meaning of "shiftless" come from? Shiftless means without resources. "Shift" has many meanings, but none seem to mean resources. Is there any relation to the woman's garment once called a "shift"?**

■ There are two main meanings of **shiftless:** 'lacking in resourcefulness; inefficient' and 'lacking in incentive; lazy'. There's also an earlier meaning 'helpless; lacking in cunning' that is now obsolete.

The key to the question is found in your statement that "*shift* has many meanings." Indeed it does, and one related group of senses is 'an expedient; ingenious device; artifice; resource' and hence 'resourcefulness'. Our obligatory Shakespearean example: "I'll find a thousand shifts to get away" (*King John*). While these senses are rare or obsolete today—the specific sense 'resourcefulness' seems always to have been rare—they are the basis for the word **shiftless**.

The garment known as a *shift* was originally a loose undergarment for either sex, and now either refers to a straight, loose dress or a woman's chemise. It apparently derives from *shift* 'change', after the idea of changing clothes.

Shiftless is first found in the sixteenth century. *Shift* itself derives from the Old English *sciftan* 'to arrange; divide', of Germanic origin.

■ ■ ■

sic

Margot Liggott writes: **Where does the word "sicced" as in "I sicced my dog on him" come from? Are there any other meanings besides the one which applies to dogs?**

■ **Sic** in this sense is originally a dialectal pronunciation of *seek*. It is first attested in the middle of the nineteenth century.

This word **sic** has only three meanings, and they're closely related. The first is 'to attack', usually used as an imperative ("Sic 'em!") to a dog. The second is 'to incite (a dog) to attack' ("I sicced my dog on him"). The third sense is the figurative use of *sic* to mean 'to cause to pursue', as in "I sicced my lawyer on him."

Though these are the only meanings of this word **sic,** there are two other unrelated **sic**s. One is a Scottish adjective meaning 'such', which you'd normally only encounter when reading Scottish literature. It's a variant of "such."

The other is the Latin word **sic,** which means 'thus'. It is almost always used within brackets to indicate that a previous word or phrase that seems erroneous or unexpected has been written intentionally or is exactly quoting the way something was written. Examples: "I bought the new book by bell hooks [sic]," where the "sic" indicates that the use of lowercase letters for a person's name is not accidental (in this case because bell hooks prefers to spell her name that way), or "The magazine wrote an article about 'the countdown to the next millenium' [sic]," where the **sic** indicates that the magazine, not the person writing, misspelled "millennium."

■ ■ ■

simoleon

Don Willmott writes: **Recently you held forth on SAWBUCKS. Very edifying. Now, I have another money-related question. I read this today on the Web: "A team of Netly News accountants, surveying the huge amount of somolians the tobacco industry has funneled into magazine ads during the past five decades, has determined that tobacco money alone could make the entire Web economically viable." What's the deal with "somolians" as a synonym for "dollars"?**

■ The deal is, someone doesn't know how to spell. The slang word **simoleon** 'a dollar' is found in all major college dictionaries, spelled that way. It's usually considered somewhat old-fashioned, but is still in use.

The word's origin is uncertain. The most widely accepted theory suggests that it's a blend of *simon,* an obsolete slang term for a dollar, and *napoleon,* a gold coin of France that was worth 20 francs.

Simoleon is first found in the very late nineteenth century and is an Americanism through and through.

■ ■ ■

sinister

Adam Davies writes: A word question on my mind: Relationship between "sinistral" and "sinister." Left-handed equals evil?

■ Well, without wanting to offend any left-handers out there, that's a little close to the origin. But the old line that **sinister** means 'evil' because lefties were more likely to mess things up is only a small part of the story.

In Latin, the word meant 'on the left side', and another meaning was 'unfavorable; harmful'. But it wasn't because of clumsiness, but rather because of the direction people faced when interpreting omens: the east was considered the fortunate direction, and in the Greek practice, people faced north while prophesying, so the left side was the unlucky one. In the Roman practice, people faced south, so the left side was lucky: the word **sinister** in Latin thus could mean both 'lucky' and 'unlucky', according to the different traditions, but the Greek interpretation predominated, perhaps through the suggestion of left-handedness being clumsy. But the "left-handed = evil" statement is not really true, since it's not handedness that's the main point.

The early senses in English were 'false; dishonest' and later 'unlucky'; these both appeared in the early fifteenth century. The sense 'evil' shows up later in the fifteenth century, and the sense 'threatening; ominous', as in the expression "a sinister glare" does not arise until the eighteenth century.

■ ■ ■

skell

Jim Johnson writes: I've heard the word "skell" several times recently, and I can't tell what it means. I think it's something like "criminal." Can you help?

Skell is a recent slang term meaning 'a slovenly person, especially one living in the streets; a homeless person; derelict'. Example: " 'Wolfman Jack' is a skell, living underground at the Hoyt-Schermerhorn station in Brooklyn . . . 'Skells' are not merely down and out. Many are insane, chucked out of New York hospitals." (Paul Theroux, *New York Times*, 1982).

The origin of **skell** is uncertain. The strangest suggestion I've heard is that it's from the Latin *scelus*, meaning 'a wicked deed; crime; wickedness', which is plausible semantically but otherwise ridiculous. There is a long-established Scots and English word *skelm* (also spelled *skellum* and a few other ways), of Dutch origin, which means 'scoundrel', but it's effectively obsolete (except in South Africa), and the *-m*'s presence is pesky.

In my opinion, it's most likely that **skell** represents a clipping of the standard word *skeleton.*

Skell is first found in the mid 1950s. It is associated chiefly with New York City.

■ ■ ■

(by the) skin of one's teeth

> *Laurie Miles writes:* **Can you tell me how the expression "by the skin of my teeth" came about? As far as I know, teeth never have had any skin!**

■ I suppose it depends on how frequently you brush them, but never mind that.

The expression **by** (or **with**) **the skin of one's teeth,** which means 'by an extremely narrow margin; just barely; scarcely' is an example of a literal translation of a phrase in another language. It's also another example of a biblical expression gaining currency in mainstream usage.

The biblical source of this phrase is the following passage, where Job is complaining about how illness has ravaged his body: "My bone cleaveth to my skin and to my flesh, and I am escaped with the skin of my teeth" (*Job* 19:20, in the King James Version). The point here is that Job is so sick that there's nothing left to his body. The passage is rendered differently in other translations; the Douay Bible, for example, which is an English translation of the Vulgate (St. Jerome's fourth-century Latin translation), gives: "My bone hath cleaved to my skin, and nothing but lips are left about my teeth."

The phrase, which first appears in English in a mid-sixteenth-century translation of the Bible, does not appear to become common until the nineteenth century. At this point **by the skin of one's teeth** is the usual form, as if the teeth actually have skin that is so fine you can barely tell. (An interesting parallel is the nineteenth-century Americanism *fine as frog's hair,* meaning 'very fine', based on a similar assumption.)

■ ■ ■

skirt

> *Kathy Hayden writes:* **What is the origin of the word "skirt," used as a verb, as in "skirting the issue"? Does it in any way derive from the clothing?**

■ Yes, it does. Like many words, one meaning is built on a number of figurative developments which are each clear, but the relationship of the final meaning to the original meaning is not clear if you don't know the intervening steps.

In this case, the original meaning of **skirt** is still the most common: 'the part of a dress or similar garment that extends downward from the waist; (hence) a garment extending downward from the waist, worn especially by women and girls'. An important figurative extension of this is 'the outlying or bordering parts of anything; border; boundary', which itself has a number of specific subsenses. Then, from this, we saw the development of **skirt** as a verb, meaning 'to form or lie along the border of', as in "The hills skirt the town." Next, there developed the sense 'to pass along the border or edge of (something)': "Traffic skirted the park." Finally, this generated a figurative sense 'to avoid or keep distant from (something potentially difficult or controversial)', which is your example "skirting the issue." And there you have it.

Skirt is from Middle English, first appearing around 1300. It is a borrowing from an Old Norse word that is cognate with our word *shirt.* The sense 'border' appeared by the fifteenth century, and the various verb senses by the seventeenth century.

■ ■ ■

skive

Janet Penny writes: **Could you tell the origins of the word "skive" as in "to skive off school/work" or "to be a skiver." I hadn't heard or used this word for ages until today.**

■ I haven't ever heard this word in America, but it's a fairly common piece of British slang.

Skive, which means 'to avoid work or responsibility', and which is usually used with *off,* was originally British military slang from World War I. The agent noun *skiver* 'a shirker' is first attested in 1941, and the noun **skive** 'an act of shirking' in 1958, although both of these are claimed to have been in use earlier.

As with many slang words, **skive** is of uncertain origin. The main etymological suggestions are that it is derived from French *esquiver* 'to dodge; shirk' (the French word is common and has the same meaning, and there are a number of French borrowings into British military slang in World War I); that it is an extension of an earlier dialect word **skive** 'to move quickly; dart' (the semantic change is plausible, but the dialect word, itself of unknown origin, does not seem to have had broad currency); or that it is an extension of an earlier word **skive** 'to shave leather; cut (leather) into strips', eventually from Old Norse (also a plausible semantic change, and a reasonably common word).

Barring a new discovery of early evidence for the term, it is unlikely that the precise origin of the word will be able to be pinpointed.

■ ■ ■

skulduggery

Tim Ellis writes: **In my daily dialogue with students, I try to enliven the conversation with words that they do not use often. It never ceases to cause a reaction, usually humorous. The word then becomes part of their vocabulary. For this reason, I really enjoy your word of the day. Can you explain the origin of "skulduggery"? Am I correct it's another Shakespeare usage?**

■ Not only is **skulduggery** not a Shakespearean usage, nor even a Dickensian usage, but—egad!—it's an Americanism.

Skulduggery (also spelled with two *l*s), which means 'dishonest or unscrupulous behavior; trickery' or 'an instance of devious behavior; a trick', is first attested in the 1860s. It was used primarily in America for many years before crossing over to England.

The origin of the word is uncertain. Most authorities relate it to an earlier Scots word *sculduddery,* which was a jocular euphemism for 'fornication', 'adultery', or 'obscenity'. (One source alleges a serious, rather than jocular use, for the word, but evidence for a serious use has never been found.) This word is first found in the early eighteenth century.

It's certainly plausible that the Scots word could be the origin of our U.S. word; there is a good amount of Scots influence on American English at the time, the semantic connection makes sense, and there is precedent for the phonetic change. The origin of *sculduddery,* however, remains unknown.

I'm sorry not to be able to give a more definite answer, but keep up the good work with your students. A word a day keeps the doldrums away.

■ ■ ■

sliding pond

Rachel Bunin writes: **Many children grow up playing on sliding ponds . . . those fun long metal (now plastic and not quite as much fun . . .) playground apparatus. Typically (and hopefully) there is no pond at the end of the slide. Is the origin from "slide upon"? I'm also wondering if this is a regional term and has other names in other playgrounds around the country.**

■ Your question will no doubt mystify anyone not from New York, since the apparatus you're asking about is known everywhere else as a *slide.* The expression **sliding pon(d)** is almost exclusively connected to the New York City area. An interesting observation about **sliding pond** is that many people who use the term are unaware of any other term. My mother, for example, didn't know that the apparatus could be called a *slide* (the term I grew up with) at all.

The origin of **sliding pond** is obscure. One problem with tracking down a source is that, like many words for children's games, **sliding pond** is not recorded in print until rather recently. Scholars are forced to work with memories of older people, since even common expressions or practices weren't regarded as important enough to study and record.

One possibility is, as you suggest, that it's from *slide-upon,* with the *pond* form arising by FOLK ETYMOLOGY. Two problems with this are that *upon* is a more formal word than children would normally use, and also of course that *slide-upon* is not known to have ever been used.

A somewhat more likely possiblity is that it comes from a Dutch source. A Dutch dictionary in 1599 gives the term *glijd-baene,* literally 'glide-road', for a children's slide (on ice, in this case), showing that the term was used at least in European Dutch around the time that Dutch had an influence on New York speech. **Sliding pond** could thus represent a partial translation of the Dutch term, with the *glijd* translated as *sliding* and the *baene* taken as *pond.*

A German word such as *Rutschbahn* ('slide; chute', or the phonologically more likely *Schlitterbahn,* with the same meaning, is also possible, and from a purely linguistic standpoint as likely as Dutch. The main objection to a German, rather than Dutch, source is the observation that **sliding pond** is found only in New York, and not in other areas with large concentrations of German speakers, such as Milwaukee, Minneapolis, St. Louis, and parts of Pennsylvania.

■   ■   ■

(up to) snuff

Richard Silvestri writes: **Why is something "up to snuff" when it's OK?**

■ It's hard to say exactly; the semantic explanation for phrases is often difficult to determine. The phrase **up to snuff,** meaning 'up to a certain standard; satisfactory', or in British English 'shrewd; sharp; knowing', dates to the early nineteenth century. One possible explanation is simply that snuff, then extremely popular, was considered a standard in its own right. The term refers either to powdered tobacco that's inhaled through the nose (the usual meaning) or to what we call "chewing tobacco." Someone or something **up to snuff** was sophisticated, participating in a common ritual of society. The problem with this interpretation is that **snuff** was also used at the time to denote something of small value, as in "not worth a snuff" or "don't care a snuff." It is possible that the same word could refer to something of high value and of low value, but it makes the argument more difficult.

Another suggestion is that it's connected to other "smell" expressions implying perception of discernment, such as "to smell out" as situation, or "to be on the right scent." This would attach **up to snuff** to the verb meaning 'to inhale' rather than the powder. A factor in favor of this argument is that almost all the early examples refer to people, so an early sense of 'discerning' could be followed by a later broadening to a figurative use meaning '(of anything) satisfactory'.

Snuff itself is a seventeenth-century borrowing from Dutch *snuiftabak* 'tobacco for snuffing'.

■ ■ ■

snuff (revisited)

Eric Schoenfeld writes: **I found your explanation of** UP TO SNUFF **very interesting, but what about "to snuff someone" (as in to kill them)? Is that related to tobacco in any way?**
And at the same time, Christopher Pratt writes: **I had to wonder today: why is it that the word "snuff" is also used to describe movies in which people are killed on-camera for "entertainment" purposes?**

■ The word **snuff** in the sense 'murder' is unrelated to the word **snuff** referring to powdered tobacco that we discussed earlier.

The 'murder' word is a figurative use of **snuff** as a verb meaning 'to cut the wick of a candle; extinguish a candle'. This in turn is based on the noun **snuff** 'the charred part of a candlewick', which is of Germanic origin but which is apparently unrelated to the tobacco word.

The figurative sense 'murder' is a standard type of sense shift; a parallel expression is *put (someone's) lights out* 'to knock unconscious or kill'; the word *extinguish* itself has meant 'to kill' since the sixteenth century. We first see **snuff** meaning 'to die' (usually in the expression "to snuff it") in the 1860s; the sense 'to murder' is found by the 1930s. The use of **snuff** to refer to the actual killing of a person in a movie (the reality of which is a debated issue) is first found in the mid-1970s. This use is a direct application of the murder sense.

■ ■ ■

sound

Hal Riley writes: **"Safe and sound"—what does the word "sound" have to do with safe? My only guess is the use of the word sound that means "solid" or "secure." Am I correct?**

■ There are, incredibly enough, at least four (count 'em) completely unrelated **sound** words, and the **sound** in "safe and sound" is one.

Of the others, we have **sound** meaning 'the perception on the auditory organs of vibrations of air or another medium', which has many different subsenses relating to hearing. This is ultimately from Latin *sonāre* 'to sound', by way of Old French.

We have **sound** meaning 'a narrow passage of water or inlet of the sea', as in Puget Sound or the Long Island Sound. This is from an Old English word *sund,* related to *swim.*

We have **sound** meaning 'to measure the depth of water' and hence 'to probe; elicit the views of', which is from Old French, ultimately of uncertain origin.

And we have your **sound,** meaning 'free from injury; healthy; robust', and with a number of derived senses: 'financially strong or stable' ("a sound investment"); 'sensible or competent' ("sound judgment"); 'of substantial or enduring character' ("sound moral values"); 'vigorous or severe' ("a sound beating"); and several others. This word is from Old English and is related to other Germanic words broadly meaning 'healthy'.

The idiom **safe and sound** is a very frequent set phrase that dates from the thirteenth century and is a good example of an idiom using alliteration for effect (others are "kitch and kin," "from pillar to post," and "pig in a poke").

■ ■ ■

soup to nuts

Kenneth Norton writes: **What's the origin of the phrase "from soup to nuts" to mean "running the gamut" or "from A to Z"?**

■ In the dim and distant past, when people still did such extravagant things as getting dressed up to go to the theatre, dinners could have a number of courses. The first course was traditionally soup; the meal could then run through any variety of goodies, such as oysters, fish, roasts, game, and dessert, and would finish with a serving of nuts. **Soup to nuts,** therefore, means 'from beginning to end; inclusive of everything' in the same way as *from A to Z* or *running the gamut* (which originally referred to the range of notes in the musical scale).

The phrase *from soup to nuts* is first found in the early twentieth century in America.

■ ■ ■

stemwinder

Cevza M. Zerkel writes: I am always distressed, and especially during each political silly season, to hear talking heads refer, with approbation, to a particularly stimulating speech as a "stemwinder." Isn't this bass-ackwards? Doesn't the term relate to a speech so dull that the listener checks to see if his (pocket)watch is still running?

■ Once upon a time, long before battery-operated quartz watches, before mechanical self-winding watches, before even wristwatches, and before pocket watches were wound through the stem, watches—pocket watches, of course—were wound with a key. In order to wind them, you had to carry the key around at all times. Something of a pain, I'm sure you'll agree.

When a watch was developed that wound through a stem (one permanently attached to the watch, that is, usually underneath the pendant (the ringed hook)), this was, naturally enough, seen as a great advance. The term **stemwinder,** originally referring to a stem-winding watch, was then broadened to mean 'anything that is a remarkable example of its kind', and the usual sense we see is 'a rousing speech or orator'. *Ace* and *cream* are two other words that have been broadened from senses referring to a particular good thing (the best card in the deck, the best part of milk) to mean 'something great', showing that this is a common process in slang.

Stemwinder in the sense 'a stem-winding watch' is first attested in 1875. The sense 'a rousing speech or orator', an Americanism, is first attested in 1892.

■ ■ ■

sthenic

Suzanne Whalen writes: The word "sthenic" seems to have an unlikely spelling and is a word I've not heard used. What is the origin and could you use it in a sentence?

■ **Sthenic,** like *phthisic,* is a word that seems to be used chiefly by doctors or by people trying to make a point about unusual spellings in English. The main sense of **sthenic** is 'marked by excessive energy, especially nervous energy'. This is often used of feverish states to mean 'having a high temperature, rapid pulse, etc.' **Sthenic** can also be used to mean 'strongly or sturdily built', and the noun form is *sthenia.*

The word is contrasted with *asthenia,* or 'lack of strength; weakness'. These words are of Greek origin, the root form being *sthénos* 'strength'. Both are first attested in English in the late eighteenth century.

Most real examples of **sthenic** are in medical contexts and are thus rather boring to nondoctors, and I don't want to invent a sentence. So this example from a major author should give a rough idea of what the word's use is like: "The next step is to characterize the feelings. To what psychological order do they belong? The resultant outcome of them is in any case what Kant calls a 'sthenic' affection, an excitement of the cheerful, expansive, 'dynamogenic' order which, like any tonic, freshens our vital powers."—William James, *Varieties of Religious Experience.*

■ ■ ■

stiff

> *Craig Silverstein writes:* **As a working stiff, I'm curious about the word "stiff." Am I supposed to be one of the living dead? For that matter, when I stiff a waiter, am I using the same sense of "stiff" or an unrelated one?**

■ All the slang senses of **stiff**—and for that matter, all other senses of **stiff**—stem from the same word. The earliest noun sense referring to people is, as you suggest, 'a corpse'. (Fave quote of this sense: "Ten thousand stiffs humped under the snow in the Ardennes take on the sunny Disneyfied look of numbered babies under white wool blankets"—Thomas Pynchon, *Gravity's Rainbow.*) This sense is first attested in the mid-nineteenth century.

By the late nineteenth to early twentieth centuries, several other derivative senses appear, including 'a tramp; bum'; 'a laborer' (which includes both unskilled migratory workers and regular blue-collar workers, or *working stiffs;* the word was later extended to a worker of any sort, as opposed to a management type); 'a drunkard'; 'a person' (used very broadly, as in *a lucky stiff*); and 'an unpleasant or obnoxious person'.

This last can carry a number of overtones, one of which is 'a miserly person; tightwad' and hence 'a poor tipper'. The verb **stiff** 'to fail to pay or tip; cheat' is a shift from this sense of the noun. It is first found in the middle of this century.

Stiff, originally an adjective meaning 'rigid; not flexible', goes back to Old English, and is related to various Germanic words. It is also related to English *stifle.*

■ ■ ■

stitch

Brynn Sandler writes: **The meaning of the word "stitch" generally refers to sewing. I'd like to know where the expression "in stitches" comes from when referring to laughter, and is "stitch" used in any other sense?**

■ While **stitch** is most often used in senses referring to sewing, this is actually a later development in the history of the word. Let's go back to the earliest forms and see where we end up.

Stitch is a word of Germanic origin, and cognates exist in Old Frisian, Old High German, Old Saxon, Gothic, and the modern languages descended from some of these. The etymological meaning of the word, and the earliest sense in English, is something like 'a thrust; a stab', and it is related to the English verb *to stick.*

The first important sense for our purposes is 'a sudden sharp pain, now especially in the side' (originally with the suggestion that the pain resulted from being stabbed). This sense is about a thousand years old. There are several meanings derived from this sense, one of which is 'a fit of laughter', usually in the expression *in stitches,* which derives from the idea that one is laughing so hard one's sides hurt. This expression is first found in the twentieth century.

The sewing meanings, beginning with 'one complete movement of a threaded needle through a fabric' and radiating out from there, are first attested in the late thirteenth century. These meanings are all derived from the original 'thrust or stab' sense.

Stitch has a number of other senses as well. Just sticking to the ones referring to sewing, we have 'the loop of thread left by a stitch', 'a complete movement of the needle or hook in knitting, crocheting, etc.', 'a particular method of making a stitch' (e.g., "knit" or "purl"), and a number of other progressively less interesting technical senses. Some extended senses include 'a piece of fabric or clothing' ("not wearing a stitch of clothes") and 'the least bit of anything' ("didn't do a stitch of work"). There are a few other unrelated words spelled **stitch** you'll never encounter, but we should mention *stich* 'a verse or line of poetry', an eighteenth-century borrowing from Greek. This is pronounced like "stick"; don't confuse the spelling.

■ ■ ■

straw man

Jeanne Woodward writes: **Can you please tell me the origin of the term "straw man"?**

■ **Straw man** is an expression one sees rather often lately, what with the frequency of rhetorical attacks. The usual sense of **straw man** is 'a weak or imaginary person, object, or issue set up in order to be triumphantly refuted'. The attacking of straw men is an easy way to score points in an argument, and so they have become something of a fixture.

Another common sense of **straw man** is 'a person whose only function is to cover the activities of another; a front'.

These senses, in this form, are first found in the late nineteenth century. The original, sixteenth-century sense of **straw man** is the literal 'a figure of a man stuffed with straw', in other words, 'a scarecrow'. Our figurative senses stem from the idea of 'a counterfeit', and, in the slightly different wording *man of straw,* are found in the seventeenth century in all senses.

In recent years we've also been collecting examples of the gender-neutral *straw person* and the specific *straw woman,* applied to women used as subjects of easy refutation.

■ ■ ■

subjunctive

edu@hess.com.tw writes: **Which one is correct? (A) If I was tall, I would play basketball. (B) If I were tall, I would play basketball. And if B is correct, why?**

■ B is correct, although A is becoming increasingly frequent in English, especially in informal speech.

This question depends on the use of the subjunctive in English. The subjunctive is a grammatical mood in many languages that is typically used to express uncertain, hypothetical, subjective, or grammatically subordinate statements or questions. It is contrasted with the *indicative,* which expresses ordinary statements or questions. The use of the subjunctive is a complicated question that generates much discussion, and I don't have the space here to mention more than the most basic points.

For most verb forms, the subjunctive has the same form as the indicative. The notable exception, and the one most likely to cause problems, is the verb *to be.* In the present tense, the subjunctive is *be,* in contrast with the indicative forms *am, is,* and *are:* some subjunctive examples are "Far be it for me to comment" and "She asked that I be ready at 7:00." In the past, the subjunctive is *were* throughout, in contrast with the indicative form *was* in the first and third person singular (the second person singular and all plural forms are also *were*).

In your example, the "If I . . . tall" clause expresses a hypothetical or contrafactual situation, and therefore takes the subjunctive, namely *were,* so "If I were tall, I would play basketball" is correct. There has been a tendency for several centuries to use the indicative in these contexts, especially in informal use or in speech. While the indicative is very common here, it is still often considered wrong, and my advice would be to stick with the subjunctive.

■ ■ ■

suffice

Allison Payne writes: **I hear people say "suffice it to say . . ." To my way of thinking, this should be "let it suffice to say that . . ." Is there a rule about this or am I getting irritated for no reason?**

■ You're getting irritated for no reason. There are a few things going on here, and the easiest thing to do would be to say it's just an established idiom, but we can look at it in some more detail.

Suffice has several meanings, of which the most important, and the only truly current one, is the intransitive 'to be enough or adequate': "Two hours should suffice"; "Why need I volumes, if one word suffice?" (Emerson).

In the expression *suffice it to say,* the word **suffice** is a subjunctive. In other words, it *does* mean "let it suffice to say . . ." In the past there were various ways **suffice** could be used in the subjunctive ("Suffise, that I haue done my dew in place"—Spenser; "My designs/Are not yet ripe; suffice it that ere long/I shall employ your loves"—Beaumont and Fletcher), but now it is effectively found only in this set phrase. This example is known as the *formulaic subjunctive:* an invariant expression found chiefly in independent clauses. Some other examples of the formulaic subjunctive are the phrases "Be that as it may . . ." (i.e., "let that be . . . ,"); "Come what may . . . ," "God save the Queen!" (i.e., "may God save the Queen"), and others, none of which excites any controversy.

The *it* in *suffice it to say* is an *impersonal* or *indefinite* pronoun, one that functions as a grammatical placeholder without supplying much real meaning. Relevant examples, which are assigned to various complex subcategories by grammarians, are "it's raining," "go it alone," or "it behooves you," discussed under BEHOOVE, itself an impersonal verb.

■ ■ ■

swan song

Les Aldridge writes: **I believe that "swan song" refers to the last great thing that someone does before sliding into obscurity or off this mortal coil. But why "swan song"? Does this refer to *Swan Lake* perhaps?**

■ No, in fact the expression **swan song** is a half-century older than the ballet *Swan Lake,* and the sentiment behind it is several millennia older than that.

The **swan**, a beautiful though quite unpleasant bird, has long been associated with music. In Greek mythology it was associated with Orpheus and Apollo; in English we use the word **swan** in reference to poets (Shakespeare as "the sweet swan of Avon," in Ben Jonson's phrase).

One of the most pervasive of swan legends is that a swan sings a beautiful song just before dying. Though it is a story with no basis in fact, it was believed by Plato, Euripides, Aristotle, Seneca, and Cicero. (Pliny, among others, disbelieved it, and the truth of the fable was debated at various times.) References to the legend are mentioned in the works of many English writers, including Chaucer (twice), Caxton, Shakespeare (twice), and Spenser. Coleridge, ever the wit, commented notably that "swans sing before they die; 'twere no bad thing/Did certain persons die before they sing."

Despite the age and pervasiveness of the legend, the phrase **swan song** itself doesn't appear in English until 1831, when Carlyle mentions it literally in his *Sartor Resartus;* he used it figuratively to mean 'the final work of a person's life' several years later. Carlyle was apparently translating the earlier German word *Schwanengesang* or *Schwanenlied,* the existence of which demonstrates the pervasiveness of the legend.

■   ■   ■

tank

Stanley Newman writes: **"Tank" as a verb, meaning "to decline rapidly," isn't in any of my dictionaries. I've heard it used re the stock market and business conditions in general. What've you got on this usage?**

■ It's not surprising that you can't find **tank** in most dictionaries, since it's a rather new word in this and related meanings. The original sense is from sports, where it meant 'to lose a match deliberately; throw'. The earliest example I know of is only from the mid-1970s, and it was mostly confined to tennis in the early period. This verb is based on the equivalent noun expression *to go into the tank,* which is somewhat older, and which is itself based on the common expression *to take a dive,* which dates from the 1910s.

Your sense 'to decline; do poorly; fail' is a logical broadening of meaning. It first appears around 1980, but only became notably common in the last few years. Some recent examples: "Eleven new shows were unveiled last September; eight of them tanked" (*Esquire*); "He lost more than $40 million last week when Intuit's stock tanked (*Newsweek*).

It's interesting to note that there's a meaning of **tank** in Scottish slang of 'to overwhelm; defeat decisively; thrash', but this is probably a coincidental use.

■ ■ ■

tarnation

Dave Smith writes: **Can you shed some light on the meaning and origin of "tarnation"? It isn't even listed in my dictionary.**

■ The exact meaning of **tarnation** is hard to pinpoint, because it's used as an oath in relatively vague constructions.

But in many cases, "hell" or "the devil" would be a good substitute. It can be used as an interjection (just "tarnation!," like "damn!"); as an intensive in various ways ("What in tarnation are you talkin' about?"); as a substitute for "hell" or "the devil" ("Well, tarnation strike me!"—James Joyce, *Ulysses*); as an adjective meaning 'damned' ("I'm in a tarnation hurry"); or as a vaguely intensive adverb like "damnably" ("He's tarnation bad").

Tarnation is probably a blend of *tarnal,* which is a dialect pronunciation of *eternal* and which was used as a mild oath, and *darnation,* a euphemistic variant of *damnation*. (*Darn* itself is also a euphemism for "damn"; its origin is obscure.)

Tarnation is originally and chiefly an Americanism. It is first attested in the late eighteenth century in New England.

■ ■ ■

tartar sauce

Jesse Costello writes: **I just got out of my Classical Mythology class, and need to purge myself of a curiosity. Does the word tartar, as in "tartar sauce," have any root in the word Tartarus, as in "realm of the underworld"? If so, why in hell would someone want to associate their condiment with such a place?**

■ **Tartar sauce** is not directly connected with *Tartarus,* although such an association, if true, would be perfectly normal and has many parallels.

Tartar sauce is a mayonnaise flavored especially with chopped capers, dill pickles, and olives. It is now usually served with deep-fried fish. The term is a translation from French *sauce tartare* (the English term occasionally preserves the French spelling with the *-e*). In French, *tartare* originally referred to a dish covered with breadcrumbs and grilled and served with a seasoned sauce; now it can refer to a variety of dishes, including such raw dishes as steak tartare (which purists think should only be made with horsemeat, by the way).

In French, this *tartare* is the equivalent of *Tartar* 'a member of any of various Mongolian or Turkic groups who ruled parts of Asia and Eastern Europe under Genghis Khan'. The use of regional or ethnic terms to describe foods is common—we have *Russian dressing, Cajun catfish,* and the like—and *tartare* falls into this family. The ethnic name *Tartar* is apparently from Persian *Tatar,* from a Turkic name; the form *Tartar* found in Western languages is probably influenced by *Tartarus* 'the Greek underworld' but not ultimately derived from it.

As to why a sauce would be named after *Tartarus* if that were the origin, it would be to emphasize the spiciness. That's why we (and other languages) have *deviled eggs,* or hot sauces with *hell* as part of the name, or *diabolic* referring to foods made with mustard.

■ ■ ■

taxi

Don Willmott writes: Last night it was raining, and I couldn't get a taxi. "No taxis, no taxis, no taxis," I thought to myself until I noticed that "taxi" is a strange little word. Can I flag down an explanation? I assume that it comes from the same place as "taxation"?

■ Yes. **Taxi** is ultimately short for *taximeter* 'device used in a vehicle for automatically computing the fare'. (The words **taxi** and *taxicab* entered the language at the same time, so it is uncertain whether **taxi** is short for "taxicab" or short for "taximeter" or "taximeter cab.")

Taximeter is borrowed from the French *taximètre*, meaning "tax meter" (*tax* here used in the broad sense 'charge; fee'). The French word is probably based on an earlier German word *Taxameter* in the same sense; this German word was also used in English.

Taxi and *taxicab* are first recorded in 1907. The form *taxameter* is first recorded in 1894, and *taximeter* in 1898.

■ ■ ■

therefor/therefore

Kari Cornelius writes: I have a question about the word I always thought was spelled "therefore." Writing a paper with a friend for class, she insisted that you spell the word "therefor" which looked horribly wrong to me. But the spell-checker didn't correct it. Is my spell-checker fallible after all, or has there been some change in the word and I didn't get the memo? And how did the *e* get there then?

■ *All* nonhuman spell-checkers are fallible, and this anecdote is an extremely good example of why they should only be used with great caution.

There exist two related adverbs, **therefor** and **therefore.** The words are spelling variants of the same word from the same origin, *there + fore.* The spelling has varied at different times, but in modern use (for the last two hundred years, roughly) the two are distinct.

Therefor is a relatively formal word meaning 'for it' or 'in exchange for it': "a refund therefor"; "parts and pieces therefor." The much more common word **therefore** means 'consequently; hence; as a result'. It's very likely that this second word, **therefore,** is the one you want to use.

Most spell-checkers are unable to make distinctions based on meaning; they only compare a word to a list, and if it shows up it's OK. They can't tell if you are using *there, their,* or *they're* correctly. The larger its word list is, the worse it gets for you, since a larger word list is more likely to include obscure forms which could be errors. For example, *oo* exists as a variant of "you" or "who," and as a rare Hawaiian songbird, but if you wrote "oo" in a document, you'd probably want your spell-checker to flag it. So the only thing this program is telling you is that there is a word **therefor**—it's up to you to realize that it's not the *right* word.

There is no simple way to rely on a spell-checker. If you're unsure about the spelling of a word, look it up in a dictionary. All current American dictionaries will tell you that the only current spelling of the word meaning 'consequently' is **therefore.**

■ ■ ■

there's

Phil Grandsard writes: Is the contraction "there's" short for 'there are' and for 'there is'? I often hear it used both ways.

■ It's not that **there's** is a contraction of "there is" and "there are," it's that *there is*—in full or contracted form—is often used with a singular or plural subject. Shakespeare example: "Honey, and milk, and sugar: there is three" (*Love's Labour's Lost*). This tendency also applies to other linking verbs, like *appear* or *seem,* although these don't contract. (Example: "There seems to be about twenty guys outside.")

While this use goes back to the fifteenth century, it is especially common in informal use today. In some cases, there are plausible explanations for the tendency. For instance, if you have a compound subject, the verb is likely to agree with the first subject following it: "There's a table and eight chairs you might want to look at." And if the subject is plural but considered as a collective whole, the verb can also be singular: "There's five more miles to go before we can rest."

Other cases can't be justified like this. The simplest explanation might just be that "there is" is used as a tag opener to any likely statement, regardless of what the statement is. According to the standard rule, these examples are wrong, but they are so common that it's hard to avoid them. In informal use, where it usually occurs, you probably shouldn't worry about it if it seems natural.

■ ■ ■

thigmotropic

Kathy Green writes: "Thigmotropic" is a word that's supposed to mean "fond of pressure or contact," but I would like a more thorough definition, if possible.

Thigmotropism is a biological term meaning 'oriented growth of an organism in response to mechanical contact, as a plant tendril coiling around a string support'. The adjectival form **thigmotropic** means pretty much 'of, pertaining to, or exhibiting thigmotropism'.

The word is formed from the Greek word *thígma* 'touch' and the English *tropism* 'the orientation of an organism toward or away from a stimulus, as light'. It is first found in scientific literature around 1900.

Thigmotropic seems to be pretty much restricted to science. It's not hard to imagine a figurative use meaning 'fond of touch', as you suggest, but I'm not aware of any such use. There's probably an example in Pynchon somewhere. I have, on the other hand, seen a figurative example of the related *thigmotaxis* 'movement of an organism in response to contact with a solid': "The cat's sleeping in my chair again, honey—pass me the broom and I'll try a little thigmotaxis." This is from a humorous book of interesting words, but it works for me.

■ ■ ■

thunk

> *JP Weisenberger writes:* **Please settle this tiny disagreement between my girlfriend and me. She believes it proper to use the word "thunk" in certain circumstances, for example: "Who'd have thunk it?" She seeks vindication in her belief. I seek to put the entire nonsense behind us and move on. . . . (She says I'm a pedantic self-righteous piglet . . . she may be right.)**

■ There are two issues here. The first is the status of the word **thunk**, and the second is its appropriateness.

Thunk is a dialectal form of the past tense and past participle of *think*. In America, it is characteristic of the South and South Midland dialect areas, but it's also found in England and Ireland; Joyce uses it in *Finnegans Wake*. **Thunk** is about a hundred years old, and is formed by analogy with strong verbs such as *drink, drank, drunk*. As dialect, **thunk** could be considered nonstandard and inappropriate for formal circumstances.

Though **thunk** is a genuine dialectal form, it probably occurs most often in the frozen jocular expression *Who'd a thunk it?*, which is itself found as early as the 1880s. Since this expression is clearly jocular when used by most people, I feel that there's nothing wrong with using it as a joke. After all, when Harvard professor Henry Louis Gates, Jr., wrote in the *New York Times Book Review*, "The literary canon—now that ain't chopped liver," neither Harvard nor the *Times* was (to my knowledge) flooded with calls complaining that Gates was too stupid to know that *ain't* is wrong.

In sum, while I wouldn't call it quite "proper" to use **thunk** freely as a past or past participle, I certainly think it acceptable in jocular contexts.

And if you still think it's absolutely never, ever OK, well . . . what was it your girlfriend said?

■   ■   ■

tit for tat

Arthur Zura writes: **Why is retribution or a fair exchange "tit for tat"?**

■ Both **tit** and **tat** are archaic words meaning 'a light blow'. The entire expression thus means 'a blow for a blow', like 'an eye for an eye'. Both words were used as verbs, too: a popular song of the late sixteenth century had a refrain, "Come tit me, come tat me,/Come throw a kiss at me."

These words are probably of imitative origin, with a vowel variation found in other words expressing striking such as *tip* and *tap* or *pit-a-pat*. The **tit** is not related to other **tit** words, such as the ones (each of independent origin) meaning 'a small bird' (e.g., "titmouse"), 'a breast', or the first element of "tit-bit" (in America usually euphemized to "tid-bit," but not related to the 'breast' word).

The phrase **tit for tat** is first found in the sixteenth century. It is probably a variant of *tip for tap,* of similar origin but found a century earlier. The *tip* in this earlier phrase is the same word as in the baseball expression "a foul tip."

■   ■   ■

titillate

DeWane Stone writes: **Ok, I'm sure that everyone has a good assumption for this one, but where did "titillate" come from?**

■ Not from *that,* but thanks for reminding us all of high school. . . .

Titillate, which usually means 'to excite agreeably', is from the Latin word *titillare* 'to tickle'. Note, semantically, that the English word *tickle* is also used in this 'excite' sense, as in "to tickle someone's fancy."

The earliest form in English was *titillation* 'mental excitation or stimulation', first recorded in the early fifteenth century. The regular verb **titillate,** probably a back formation from *titillation,* is from the early seventeenth century.

While your imagination is running wild, perhaps you'd be interested to know of the existence of the word *titivate,* which means 'to make smart; spruce up'. This nineteenth-century favorite, an alteration of an earlier form *tidivate,* apparently formed from *tidy* with the *-vate* ending as in *captivate* or *cultivate,* lends itself to such delightfully suggestive wordplay that I'll forget I ever mentioned it.

toothsome

Abrupt NYC writes: **A friend writes: "And if you ever get the chance to try some of those Buffalo Wing Flavored Potato Chips, you shouldn't pass up the opportunity. I've found that each of the available brands are all equally toothsome." This "toothsome" is such a ticklish word, I just have to know more about it.**

■ **Toothsome,** a nice word indeed, is first found in the sixteenth century, in two senses. The literal sense is 'pleasing to the taste; delicious; appetizing'. This is formed from a special sense of *tooth* meaning 'the sense of taste; tastiness', first attested in Chaucer in the late fourteenth century. (Compare the technical senses of *nose* 'the smell of a wine', and *hand* 'the properties (especially of fabric) that can be sensed by touching it', as in "that silk has a wonderful hand.")

The suffix *-some* is used to form adjectives from nouns; it has a broad range of meanings including 'like'; 'tending to'; and 'characterized by a certain quality, condition, action, etc.'. (Bonus word: *clipsome,* meaning 'fit to be embraced; huggable', from the mostly archaic *clip* 'to hug'. *Please* use this word in print and send it to me! It's a personal favorite, and I'd like to get printed examples. A friend tried to use it in a major national magazine, but her editor spiked it.) **Toothsome,** to return to the topic at hand, thus etymologically means 'characterized by tastiness; tending to be tasty'.

The other important sense of **toothsome** is the figurative sense 'pleasing; delightful' (with no reference to taste), which has its own derived sense 'sexually attractive' ("a toothsome redhead"). This figurative sense is actually attested slightly earlier in the sixteenth century than the literal sense, but that is presumably due to a gap in the evidence.

■　■　■

tour, tourist

Abe VanDuelmen writes: **I need the origin of the word "tourist," and not having an etymological dictionary handy, I turn to you for help. I believe that it is connected to the city of Tours, either as a destination or starting point for pilgrims.**

■ We'll get **tourist** itself out of the quickly by noting that it's from **tour** and the suffix *-ist* 'person who practices, is concerned with, or holds principles of (that specified in the initial element)'.

Tour itself is connected to France, but not to the city of *Tours.* The original meaning of **tour,** found in English from the thirteenth century, is, broadly, 'one's turn to do something in an orderly fashion'. A natural development is our sense, 'a long journey usually including the visiting of a number of places', which stems from the idea of visiting these places in order. This sense dates from the mid-seventeenth century.

Tour is a borrowing from Old French, where it meant 'turn', and is a borrowing from Latin *tornus* from Greek *tórnos* 'a tool for making a circle'. Our word *turn* derives from the same source (it is partly from the French word and partly continues an Old English word that's itself from the Latin source of the French word); **tour** and *turn* are thus doublets.

The city of *Tours*, which was an important city in medieval times but which was not an important pilgrimage center, is of unrelated origin: it is from the name of the people who lived there, in Latin called the *Turones*.

■ ■ ■

toward/towards

Charles Knapp writes: **Is there any subtle distinction (semantically, U/non-U, regional, Brit/US) between "toward" and "towards"?**

■ In modern use, there is only a regional distinction: **toward** is the more common form in the United States, and **towards** is the more common form in Great Britain. However, both variants are used in both places. Some people prefer a form based on the phonetic environment, using the "-s" before vowels.

There is no semantic distinction between the variants, although some language critics have tried to find or invent one.

Toward(s) has been in the language since the Old English period. It is formed from the preposition *to* and the suffix *-ward(s)*, which denotes spatial or temporal direction, as in *afterward, backward,* or *seaward.* As with **toward(s),** all of these words can be used with an *s* in the adverbial form, with the non-*s* variant being more common in American English. In adjectival forms (as in "a backward glance"), only the non-*s* variant is used.

■ ■ ■

traipse

Jerry Schwartz writes: **I am interested in the etymology of the word "traipse." I thought it was a Yiddish word similiar to "schlep" as in "schlep around," but my wife says no way.**

■ The time-honored advice "listen to your wife" is applicable here, for there's no chance of a Yiddish origin for **traipse.** Its origin is, unfortunately, unknown, but there are a few possibilities to explore.

Traipse, meaning roughly 'to walk aimlessly or idly', is first found in the late sixteenth century, which itself would invalidate any claim of Yiddish origin (it's too early for there to be a possibility of Yiddish influence; there's also no Yiddish source that would work). The usual form in the early history of the word is *trapse.*

A simple solution, adopted by many dictionaries, is to say "origin unknown," and this is not without its merits. But this won't satisfy anyone except a nervous etymologist, so we'll move on. The most likely possibility is that it's a variant of *trape* or *trappe,* an earlier word with the same meaning. This word is probably from Middle Dutch or Middle Low German *trappen* 'to trample; tread'. The biggest problem with this suggestion is that the -*s*- is difficult to justify; a usual answer is to write it off as an "unexplained variant." There is, however, a word in Frisian (a West Germanic language similar to Dutch) *trapsen,* apparently an intensive of the *trappen* mentioned above, that is likely to be either the source of the English word or a close relation.

Another possibility, given some credence by dialectal forms *trapass* or *traipass,* is that it's a borrowing from French *trappasser* 'to pass over or beyond', related to English *trespass.* The problems here are that the English dialectal forms aren't found until the nineteenth century, and that the senses of **traipse** and the French *trappasser* aren't really that similar.

Schlep, on the other hand, is a fairly straightforward borrowing from Yiddish, where it means 'to drag', and which itself comes from Middle Low German; it's ultimately related to English *slip.*

■ ■ ■

truffle

> **Frank Wright writes: I am curious about the derivation of the word "truffle" meaning a potato-like fungus that grows beneath the ground. I'm puzzled how a chocolate has the same name. Is there any relationship in their derivation?**

■ Yes, and in this case the relationship is a simple one: the chocolate **truffle** is named after the fungus.

There are a large number of related fungi known as **truffles,** but two of them are especially important: the *black truffle* (*Tuber melanosporum*), found particularly in the Perigord region of France, and the *white truffle* (*Tuber magnatum*), found particularly in the Piedmont region of Italy. Both are used in cooking, both are found in the wild by trained dogs (pigs are rarely used, despite what you're heard), both have resisted most attempts at cultivation, and both are spectacularly expensive. Both are also small, dark, roughly spherical, and rough-textured.

A *chocolate truffle,* to use its full name, is a confection made with chocolate, butter or cream, and other flavorings, such as liqueurs or coffee, rolled into a ball and often coated with cocoa, nuts, or more chocolate. It is so named because the finished candy somewhat resembles the famous fungus.

The word **truffle** comes (by way of Dutch and Middle French) from Old Provençal *trufa,* from an unattested Vulgar Latin word *tufer,* a variant of Latin *tuber,* which is the source of the Modern English word *tuber.*

■   ■   ■

try and

> *Adam Davies writes:* **"Try and stop me" or any other "try and" configuration. This favorite taunt of the about-to-be-stopped archvillain seems to have gotten comically out of whack. I guess people mean "Just try to stop me" but I hear a lot of people using "and" instead of "to." There must be similar misusages of "and" (to say nothing of people writing "of" when they mean "have"—"should of done that," etc), but I can't think of any right now.**

Actually, this so-called mistake is found *earlier* than the "proper" construction with *try to.* Not that that makes it right, but in this case there's a huge amount of evidence for **try and**: authors who have used it include Austen, Dickens, Thackeray, Henry Adams, Melville, Twain, Fitzgerald, and many others. The evidence shows that it's often colloquial—it's found in letters or representations of speech more often than in formal writing—but is still widespread at all levels of usage.

The fact is, the infinitive in English (such as the "stop" in your example "Try and stop me") does not necessarily require "to," and "and" can often be used for emphasis—granted, typically in colloquial use. Some examples of verbs taking infinitives with "and" are *be sure* ("Be sure and tell me when you're leaving"), *go,* and *come* ("What's he want to go and do that for?").

Try is different—it really does require a following verb, while "go" and "come" can often be considered to be used independently of the next verb (that is, "Come and get it!" could mean "Come to get it," but "come here, and then get it" is a valid interpretation). For this reason, you can use **try** *to* when appropriate, but **try and** is very common and there's no reason to avoid it when it feels right.

■   ■   ■

𝒰, 𝒱, 𝒲

Uriah Heep

Guy Cox writes: **Say, can you help me with the term "Uriah Heep," as in "to Uriah Heep one's way through life." Using the band name made no sense to me. Thanks.**

■ Long before **Uriah Heep** was adopted as the name of one of history's most talentless, plodding heavy metal bands, the name was that of one of the most famous characters in English literature.

In Charles Dickens's great novel *David Copperfield* (1850), **Uriah Heep** is a clerk of Mr. Wickfield, a lawyer whose daughter Agnes eventually marries David. Heep aggressively presents himself as " 'umble," but in fact he is malicious and designing, and blackmails Mr. Wickfield. The name **Uriah Heep** has thus become a symbol of someone who is hypocritically humble but dangerously malignant. The verb means 'to act like Uriah Heep', so that "to Uriah Heep one's way through life" would mean 'to go through life pretending to be humble while actually being ruthlessly calculating'.

This symbolic use of **Uriah Heep** began in the mid-nineteenth century, soon after the novel was published.

The other great character in *David Copperfield* who became a word is *Mr. Micawber*. Micawber, whom David lived with briefly and who helped foil Heep, was an incurable optimist whose schemes to get rich were always ending in failure. Despite his poverty, he never lost faith. A *Micawber* is used to refer to an optimistic person who always thinks that something good will turn up.

■　■　■

vamp

Stanley Newman writes: **My local weekly newspaper routinely uses the word "vamp" as a synonym for volunteer firefighter. I can't find this usage of the word in any of my dictionaries. Can you shed any light on this?**

■ I'm guessing that you're from Long Island or another suburb of New York, since that's where we have most of the examples of **vamp**. While fairly rare, the word has been around for quite some time—the earliest example I know of is from the 1870s. It always refers to volunteer, as opposed to professional, firefighters.

Its origin is unknown. A recent explanation is that it's an acronym for "Voluntary Association of Master Pumpers," but this is almost certainly false. Like most suggested acronymic etymologies, there is no supporting evidence for the claim, and acronyms were extremely rare before the 1920s in any case. It could conceivably be a clipping of *vampire,* but it's hard to give a good explanation for this. (The word **vamp** meaning 'a seductive woman who uses her looks to exploit men', which *is* from *vampire,* is first found in the early 1900s.)

■　■　■

walm

Paige Everhart writes: **Browsing through a facsimile of an eighteenth-century cookbook, I saw references to "walm," evidently a unit of time. Such as directions to boil something "for a few walms." How long is a walm and what's its derivation?**

■ **Walm** is a long obsolete word with several senses related to boiling; its use as a measure of time is incidental.

The word **walm** goes back to an Old English word meaning '(of water) the action of bubbling or boiling', related to words in several other Germanic languages in the same general sense. It was used to refer to the surging motion of waves, to the gushing of a fountain, or the motion of boiling water, for example.

A specific application of this is 'one individual motion of boiling water; a period of boiling', and this was often used as a vague measure of time in cooking or chemistry instructions. Presumably it meant 'an especially vigorous surge of boiling water', and "three or four walms" would not be very much time.

This sense of **walm** is first found in the mid-sixteenth century.

■　■　■

wanker

Mary Cresswell writes: **What about the etymology of the word "wanker"? Or don't Americans use the word?**

■ No, Americans in general don't use the word. In fact I'm not sure I've ever heard it actually used by an American, though it is recognized as a piece of British/Australian slang. It is somewhat more offensive in British use than Americans typically realize.

That said, **wanker,** which means roughly 'a contemptible person', is a figurative use of the earlier meaning, 'a person who masturbates', which in turn is from *wank,* which means as a noun 'an act of masturbation' and as a verb 'to masturbate'. This roughly parallels the semantic development of words like *jerkoff* in American slang.

The origin of the word is uncertain. The only likely suggestion is that it is a development of an English dialect word *whang* which means 'to beat or strike'. Note that there are various other expressions for masturbation which are based on senses of striking, such as "beat off" or "whack off." Note also that *whang* is used to mean 'penis' in American slang; this may be a coincidence.

■　■　■

warhorse

aw399@lafn.org writes: **Can you trace the origin of the expression, "an old war horse," when used to describe a seasoned expert?**

■ The original meaning of **warhorse** is what you'd expect: 'a horse used in war'. The next sense to develop was 'a veteran of many conflicts, as a soldier or a politician'. This is simply an extension of the idea of combat from the literal to a directly figurative one. This sense was then broadened to 'an experienced person (without any suggestion of combat or struggle)', which is what you're asking about. Finally, the word expanded beyond people to mean 'something, as a musical composition, that is extremely familiar through excessive performance, viewing, etc.'.

These senses are all in use today, though the original meaning of 'a horse used in war' is now largely historical, for obvious reasons.

Warhorse first appears in the mid-seventeenth century. The senses referring to people are found by the early nineteenth century, and the sense referring to overfamiliar musical pieces by the middle of this century.

■　■　■

wheelbarrow

Adam Sachs writes: **Can you please inform us as to the origin of the word "wheelbarrow"? I have recently learned that a lot of my friends believe that the name of this piece of equipment is "wheelbarrel." Of course, there is no such word. Is this a common mistake?**

■ **Wheelbarrow,** which is indeed the correct form, means 'a frame or box for carrying a load, supported by a wheel at one end and pushed by a handle at the other'. The word has been in the English language since the fourteenth century. It is formed from *wheel,* of course, and *barrow,* a descendant of the Old English word *bearwe,* which referred to a similar, hand-held device for carrying loads. This Old English word is related to our word *bear* in the sense 'to carry'.

The form "wheelbarrel" is an example of a FOLK ETYMOLOGY in progress. A folk etymology is a modification of a word to associate it with a more common or easily understood word. For example, the word *bridegroom* was originally something like *bridegome,* the second element being the Old English word for 'man'. When *gome* fell out of use, *bridegome* was changed to *bridegroom* on the analogy of the common and familiar word *groom,* which is at least a plausible substitute.

Errors where similar words are confused are extremely common, as you might imagine. One encounters such errors every day; this morning, for example, I noticed that the package for a very expensive brand of shaving soap announces that using the soap will leave "the skin sleek, smoothe and soft." In this case the adjective *smooth,* while very common, is mistakenly spelled with a final *e,* probably by association with the verb *soothe,* which is sensible in this context. When the proper word is uncommon, this type of error is even more likely to happen. In your example, the "barrow" element is rare in modern English, and *barrel* makes some sense—the trough of a wheelbarrow does resemble the inside of a barrel—so the word was changed to "wheelbarrel." Though the correct **wheelbarrow** is so common that a lasting change is unlikely, the "wheelbarrel" form represents a historically common process. The only remedy for such problems is education: make sure that people, whether they're your friends with "wheelbarrel" or the marketing department of a fancy cosmetics company with "smoothe," know what the truth is. They'll thank you for it.

■　■　■

whinge

Denise writes: I've seen this word "whinge" several times in the recent past but I don't find it in my dictionary. Folks are swearing it's a legit word—any help?

■ If you think that British and Australian English are legit, then yes, **whinge** is a legit word. In America, however, it's very rarely encountered, which is why it's omitted from most American dictionaries; I had never heard the word before I went to England.

Whinge is pronounced *(h)winj* and means pretty much 'to whine', in the sense of 'to complain in a peevish manner'. It's quite frequent in British and related varieties of English (though not in Canadian English). A few examples from this century: "Forgive this contemptible sort of whinging. I am so lonely and miserable I cant [sic] help it" (John Millerton

Synge); "If that girl didn't stop her wingeing [sic], the neighbours would be banging on the wall" (Beryl Bainbridge).

The word **whinge** is of Germanic origin; its ultimate root is the same as the source of *whine*. **Whinge** is a northern form, and in early use was a form used by Scottish and northern English writers.

Whinge is a continuation of the Old English verb *hwinsian;* though **whinge** is not found in Middle English, this is presumably due to a gap in the evidence.

■ ■ ■

whipping boy

> *Stephen A. Edwards writes:* **I've just read your archive discussion of the origin of** SCAPEGOAT. **It reminded me of "whipping boy," which has a similar meaning. I've always heard that it refers to the boy who had to take the punishment for misbehavior by a prince (who could not himself be touched by a commoner). Is that right?**

■ Yes. **Whipping boy,** like SCAPEGOAT, has a specific literal meaning and a more general and now more common meaning.

The literal meaning of **whipping boy** is, as you say, 'a boy educated with a young prince or other aristocrat and physically punished in his place'. This sense is first attested in the mid-seventeenth century. One could certainly question the effectiveness of such a punishment as far as the prince is concerned, but there you have it. A punishment known to boot camp graduates in the modern world is, when a person has made a mistake, forcing the rest of the unit (but not the person who made the mistake) to do push-ups. There are similar practices reported in the folklore of various cultures—the scapegoat itself being an excellent example—where less important people or animals are punished in place of the more important.

The figurative use of **whipping boy** is identical to that of *scapegoat:* 'a person or group made to bear the blame for others or to suffer in their place'. Recent example, from the *New York Times:* "George Stephanopoulos, the one-time 'war room' Wunderkind who has functioned as Clinton's all-purpose adviser, conscience, mind-reader and occasional whipping boy for nearly five years."

■ ■ ■

white

George Bredehorn writes: **In the expression, "That's very white of you," is the "white" reference one of hue, race, purity, or something else?**

■ The word **white** in the sense 'honorable; fair; upright; decent' has racial origins. It is first found in the late nineteenth century, and reflects the belief, current at the time, that whites were morally superior to people of other races. This sense is an Americanism, and has been used by Mark Twain and Edith Wharton.

Since the underlying assumption of this sense is racist and considered repugnant today, the word is usually avoided by those aware of its origins.

There was another sense of **white**, 'morally or spiritually pure; innocent', that dates back to the tenth century and is not connected with racial notions. The word **white** in the racial sense, '(of people) having a relatively light pigmentation of the skin' is first attested in the early seventeenth century.

■ ■ ■

who/whom

Janet Slifer writes: **Now that you have covered the "between you and I" question, could you set us straight on the correct usage of "who" and "whom"?**

■ I knew this was coming.

The traditional rule holds that **who** is used as the subject of a sentence ("Who sent you?") or of a clause ("The editor who hired me took me out to lunch"). **Whom** is used as the object of a verb ("The writer whom I met at the party called today") or of a preposition ("To whom did you send the letter?").

In current usage, these rules apply largely to formal, written prose. In most speech, **whom** is quite rare; **who** is used in most constructions. Few would quibble with, say, "Who did you see?" Directly after a preposition, **whom** is almost always used ("everyone with whom you've spoken"; "I've got a date." "With whom?"), but this is itself relatively rare in informal speech—people are more likely to say "everyone you've spoken with," "Who's this package from?", and the like. (Naturally, these constructions are themselves criticized for ending a sentence with a preposition, but that's a question for another day.) The use of **whom** in speech can often be considered overly formal, if not pretentious.

There are two main current concerns with the use of **who** and **whom**. The first is the "incorrect" use of **who**—the use, that is, of **who** in objective positions. This type of construction is, as noted, very common in informal use, and it has been for centuries; here are three examples from Shakespeare alone: "Who wouldst thou strike?" (*Two Gentlemen of Verona*); "What do you read, my lord? "Words, words, words." "What is the matter, my lord?" "Between who?" (*Hamlet*); "Run, run, O, run!" "To who, my lord?" (*King Lear*). You're almost always safe using something like this informally, but if the use of "whom" comes naturally, by all means stick with it. The claim " 'Whom' is correct, and I'm not being pretentious" is a strong one.

The second concern is the hypercorrect use of **whom**—the use of **whom** where **who** is expected. This is normally based on the fact that subjective/objective distinctions depend on the use of the pronoun in its own clause, not in the overall sentence. Thus, the sentence "Whom shall I say is calling?" is regarded as incorrect, since the status of the pronoun as the subject of "is calling" takes precedence over its status as the object of "I shall say." Similarly, "A person whom everyone agrees is brilliant" is incorrect, since the relevant clause is "who is brilliant"; a slight change to "A person whom everyone admires" renders the pronoun correct, since **whom** is then the object of "admires." An extreme example, showing why this can cause so much confusion, is the correct "I'll give it to whoever wants it," where "whoever" is called for since it's the subject of "whoever wants," even though it immediately follows the preposition "to," which would seem to require "whomever." Grammarians have written at great length about this issue. This hypercorrect use seems to be increasing, since people feel uncertain when to use **whom** and end up using it even when it doesn't belong.

The pronouns *whoever* and *whomever* follow the same pattern as **who** and **whom**.

■　■　■

wiseacre

cdthom@echonyc.com writes: **What is a "wiseacre"? Why is it wise? And is it just another way of saying wise ass?**

■ A **wiseacre** is pretty much equivalent to a *wise guy* or *smart aleck* or even, yes, a *wise ass*—a guy who thinks he knows everything and is cocky about it. But **wiseacre** is by far the earliest of these terms, dating from the late sixteenth century, as opposed to the 1890s for *wise guy,* the 1860s for *smart aleck,* and just the 1960s for *wise ass,* so if anything the others are just variants of **wiseacre.**

Wiseacre is a borrowing of a Middle Dutch word *wijssegger,* which meant 'prophet; soothsayer', and which is itself a borrowing or translation of Old High German *wizzago* 'wise person', assimilated in Dutch to the Dutch words for "wise-sayer." The first element is indeed related to the

English word *wise,* filtered through a bunch of other Germanic languages and ending up in the same place.

■   ■   ■

withers

Karen Seriguchi writes: **A surprisingly young coworker (admittedly one who reads nineteenth-century English literature) exclaimed today, "Well, wring my withers!" in response to a whine of some kind. Now I find that Shakespeare unwrung someone's withers in *Hamlet.* Do I have withers too? Are they like a dowager's hump? Why are they wrung if I cry?**

I've never met you, but I highly doubt you have **withers.** The **withers** (a singular referent, but in -*s* and always taking a plural verb) are the highest part of the back, found at the base of the neck bewteen the shoulder blades, of a horse or other quadruped.

The *wring* here is an application of the usual sense 'to twist', meaning something like 'to injure' (though not necessarily through twisting—compare the expression "it wrings my heart"). Figurative use of a wring/withers connection seems to have been a fave of our friend Bill; he uses it first in *Henry IV, Part I:* "[The] poor jade is wrung in the withers" (2.1.7). The *Hamlet* example is particularly obscure: in the great players scene (3.2), Hamlet says to Claudius, "Let the galled jade winch: our withers are unwrung." The first bit means 'let the chafed horse wince', and the second part means 'my back is unchafed' and hence 'I am uninjured'; 'I am not guilty'. (Hamlet is trying to get Claudius to react guiltily when the players perform a version of Claudius's murder of Hamlet's father.)

There are various allusions to this phrase in literature. Dickens, in *Dombey and Son,* has "Rob the Grinder, whose withers were not unwrung, caught the words as they were spoken." William James notes, " 'External relations' stand with their withers all unwrung, and remain, for aught he proves to the contrary, not only practically workable, but also perfectly intelligible factors of reality." (We'll take "perfectly intelligible" on faith here.)

I am not aware of the interjectional use of *wring my withers!,* and I've searched through a big heap of nineteenth-century literature to find it. But it sounds like a plausible phrase, and I'm sure it's somewhere out there. I can't tell exactly how your friend is using the phrase, but "Twist my arm!" could be a valid comparison. It's worth noting that *wring my withers!* itself is not necessarily a Shakespearean allusion; writers discussed horses literally being wrung in the withers by a poor saddle about twenty years before Shakespeare wrote.

The usual explanation for the origin of **withers,** which is first attested in the late sixteenth century, is that it's from the obsolete *wither* 'against' (ultimately related to *with*), in reference to the strain against the withers when a horse pulls a load.

■ ■ ■

words ending in -gry

A whole lot of people over the months have written something like: **What's the third word ending in "-gry"?**

■ This insidiously annoying riddle has been around for many years, but over the last six months or so it has really taken off. Every other person on the street has heard that in addition to *angry* and *hungry* there's a third **word ending in -gry.** And they all know that it must be obvious—because the question's phrased to make it seem so—and none of them can think of it, no matter how hard they try.

The reason none of them can think of it is simple: *there is no third word ending in* **-gry**. At least, there's no *common* word ending in **-gry**; there are a number of words ending in **-gry**, but they're so rare that if this puzzle weren't around you could spend ten lifetimes reading without ever encountering one. One of these words is *puggry,* a rare spelling variant of *pugree* (or *pugaree,* or a few others), which is a type of turban worn in India. Another is *aggry,* a type of glass bead found in Africa. Another is *gry* itself, a unit of measurement proposed by John Locke, equal to a tenth of an inch. These words are not the answer to the puzzle.

The answer to this question depends on the phrasing, but every version involves a trick question of some sort. The version I've seen most often is: "There are three words in the English language that end with '-gry.' One is hungry and the other is angry. What is the third word? Everyone uses this word every day, everyone knows what it means, and knows what it stands for. If you have listened very closely I have already told you the third word." Thus phrased, there are a few possible answers: "three" (the question "What is the third word?" being taken to mean "What is the third word of this puzzle itself?"), "language" ("There are three words in the English language" being intended to read "There are three words in 'the English language'," and "language" is the third word of that phrase), or "what" (the question "What is the third word?" being intended to read " 'what' is the third word," thus supplying its own answer). There are other possibilities, depending on how loosely you want to interpret the question, and depending on what form it actually takes.

So there is, in short, no satisfactory answer. Either the whole thing is a shaggy-dog riddle that has nothing to do with the **-gry** question, leading to the stupid answers we've just discussed, or the thing is an actual question about **-gry**, which has no real answer because there's no common third word. The reason, I think, that the question is so annoying is that most people really think there's an answer that they just can't figure out. There isn't. Don't spend any more time on it.

■   ■   ■

(the) worm has turned

Rex writes: **Where does the phrase "the worm has turned" come from?**

■ It's one of many derived forms of an old proverb, the base of which is either *tread on a worm and it will turn* or *even a worm will turn*. It means 'even the most humble will strike back if abused enough'.

The proverb is first recorded in John Heywood's 1546 collection of proverbs in the form: "Tread a woorme on the tayle and it must turne agayne." Shakespeare uses it, of course: "The smallest worm will turn, being trodden on" (*Henry VI, Part III*). It has remained common in all sorts of literature: "He's a very meek type. Still, the worm will turn, or so they say." (Agatha Christie, *The Mirror Crack'd*).

The proverb's first American attestation is in 1703, and there are a number of eighteenth-century American examples, showing that it has been popular here for some time.

In the form **the worm has turned,** the proverb is often used in the broad sense 'the situation has changed', which suggests that people aren't really clear about what it actually means: "The day was one long, sometimes poignant reminder of how the worm has turned for Mr. Cuomo—whose approval ratings now lag Mr. Clinton's in the state by 10 percentage points" (*New York Times,* 1994).

■   ■   ■

worrisome

Ken Kurson writes: **I want to say that someone is worrisome. But I want it to mean both that the person tends to worry a lot, and also that he produces much worry in others. May I?**

■ Yes, but you have to make sure that other people will interpret it that way too, which is the hard part.

Worrisome does mean both 'causing worry; annoying' and 'inclined to worry'. Both of these senses are standard and have existed since the nineteenth century, when the word is first used. (The adverb *worrisomely,* however, goes back to around 1700.) This type of dual interpretation is common in English; *nauseous,* for example, can mean both 'causing nausea' and 'affected by nausea' (though people often criticize the latter).

The problem here is that context will determine how the word is interpreted. If your goal is to suggest both meanings at the same time, you have a burdensome task: it's difficult to construct a use of **worrisome** in a context ambiguous enough that people will naturally think of both meanings. You'd have to point it out explicitly, which will look very awkward, since most people wouldn't normally think that it even has two meanings. Another possibility is to use variants based on *worry:* "He's a worry—and a worrier too."

Both senses of **worrisome** exist; how to use them effectively is your challenge as a writer.

■   ■   ■

yawning

Liz Lesnick writes: **In the lead of the lead article of a recent** ***New York Times,*** **Serge Schmemann writes, "Israeli voters confirmed their country's** *yawning* **divisions in elections on Wednesday by splitting their ballots almost evenly between the candidates for Prime Minister and, in the separate balloting for Parliament, abandoning the two major parties in droves for small religious ethnic and other groupings." While I can figure out what "yawning" means from the context of the piece, I was curious about the origins of this use of "yawning."**

■ This use of **yawning** actually preserves the original, etymological sense of the word (albeit in a figurative use). It's the "main" sense, 'to open the mouth wide with a heavy breath, usually involuntarily, as from fatigue or boredom', that is something of a specialization.

The earliest meaning of *yawn,* which goes back to the Old English period, is 'to open the mouth wide while eating or gaping'. The fundamental semantic aspect is the "open wide" part; *yawn* is etymologically related to such other words as *chasm* and *hiatus* that also refer to gaps or openings. As a verb, this sense is obsolete, but it's still current in the adjectival form **yawning,** which thus means 'gaping', both literally and figuratively. So your sentence could have been written ". . . their country's *gaping* divisions" instead.

The specialization of *yawn* to refer specifically to the involuntary reaction to tiredness or boredom didn't occur until the fifteenth century.

■   ■   ■

yonic

Andrew Van Schaack writes: **When one refers to an object that bears a resemblance to a certain part of the male anatomy, one could describe that object as "phallic." (I tend to shy away from people that have a keen eye for this sort of thing.) Now, what is the equivalent word for an object that bears a resemblance to the woman's . . . ahem . . . anatomy? P.S. Please hurry with your reply, I'm going to a Georgia O'Keeffe showing soon.**

No reason to be shy, Andrew. We're all adults here, and you've asked a very serious question—a question, indeed, that I've been expecting someone to ask for quite some time now.

The feminine counterpart of *phallic* is *doughnutish.* No, just kidding. There really is a word, and it is **yonic.** This word is the adjectival form of *yoni,* which is a term used in Hinduism to refer to the external female genitalia regarded as a symbol of Shakti; it's from Sanskrit, and first appears in English in the late eighteenth century. My all-time favorite example of *yonic* is found in Kevin Wald's recent take off of Gilbert and Sullivan, in which TV's Xena, Warrior Princess parodies "I am the Very Model of a Modern Major-General":

> *My armory is brazen, but my weapons are ironical;*
> *My sword is rather phallic, but my chakram's rather yonical*
> *(To find out what that means, you'll have to study Indo-Aryan).*
> *I am the very model of a heroine barbarian!*

The word **yonic** is quite rare. Presumably this concept was previously considered either irrelevant or undiscussable. It is, however, an extremely useful word, and now that we're pulling ouselves out of the mire of phallo-centrism, our cultural vocabulary has been—ahem—enlarged by the increasing currency of this word. In general the only people who are familiar with it are those of us who have very big, um, dictionaries, but that's changing, and one can now find it in serious academic discussions as well as parodies, manuals of Wicca (modern witchcraft), and other sources.

And, of course, at Georgia O'Keeffe showings.

■　■　■

young lion

V. N. Rains writes: **Please explain to me the meaning of the phrase "young lions."**

A **young lion** is simply 'a young and vigorous man'; in plural the phrase often implies a connected group of young and vigorous people. ("Young lion" usually refers to men, but can refer to women as well, especially as part of a group.) An example, from Henry James: "Frederic Harrison . . . one of [Matthew Arnold's] too confidently roaring 'young lions' of the periodical press."

The use of **lion** meaning 'a person who is strong or courageous' dates back to the twelfth century. The sense 'a prominent or influential person sought after as a celebrity' is from the eighteenth century. The phrase **young lion** itself is first attested in the mid-nineteenth century. Its ultimate source is the Bible. **Young lions** is a translation of Hebrew *kefirim,* which appers in numerous biblical verses: "The young lions roared upon him, and gave tongue" (Jeremiah 2:15); "The young lions roar after their prey" (Psalms 104:21); "And she brought up one of her whelps; it became a young lion, and it learned to catch the prey; it devoured men" (Ezekiel 19:3).

The Young Lions is also the title of the American novelist Irwin Shaw's first novel, published in 1948. It dealt with the experiences of young American soldiers in World War II.

■ ■ ■

young Turk

babglad@aol.com writes: **I wonder about the expression "young Turk." I know what it means, but where does it come from? Is it from a work of literature, or was it a particular Turk in history?**

■ The main meaning of the expression **young Turk** is 'a member of an insurgent, usually liberal faction within a political group or other organization'. The expression is a figurative application of the *Young Turks,* which was the popular name for the Committee of Union and Progress, a revolutionary reformist group that led a successful rebellion in (yes!) Turkey in 1908 and held power for another decade or so.

The word **Turk** has been used since the sixteenth century to mean 'a person having characteristics traditionally applied to the Turks; (specifically) a cruel or tyrannical person'; there is an isolated example in 1904 of the phrase **young Turk** which is probably just an application of this sense.

■ ■ ■

Zeitgeist

yoden@ibm.net writes: **Could you tell me what the word "zeitgeist" means? I thought that it was an adjective, but it is used as a noun. How is it used as a noun?**

■ **Zeitgeist** is certainly a noun. It means literally 'the spirit of the age', that is, 'the general trend of thought or feeling characteristic of a particular period of time'.

A few recent examples: "If a dozen movies, television dramas and memoirs are any indication, incest, one of humanity's last taboos, is taboo no longer. Incest is the plat du jour in the '90s marketplace, the sudden *Zeitgeist* zapping a jaded American audience." (*New York Times*); "A few years ago, I described the author of *Maigret and the Man on the Bench* as the Zola or Balzac of suspense, but it seems to me now that his books would have to teem with more life, provide a denser ambiance, come closer to the *zeitgeist* for him to qualify as a naturalist of the *roman policier* [detective novel]" (Anatole Broyard).

The word **Zeitgeist** is from German, a compound formed from *Zeit* 'time' and *Geist* 'spirit'. Its written form varies; it is sometimes considered a fully German word, and is thus printed in italics with an intial capital letter (all German nouns begin with capitals); it is occasionally given in lowercase italics (still considered foreign, but conformed to English capitalization standards); and it is sometimes considered fully Anglicized and printed like a regular word.

Zeitgeist was first used in English in the mid-nineteenth century; it seems to have been a favorite of Matthew Arnold.

■   ■   ■

Other English-Language Resources on the Net

Aside from Jesse's Word of the Day (http://www.jessesword.com), there are a great many other on-line resources of interest to English language buffs. Here are a few of my favorites, in alphabetical order; many of these have additional links to more language sites.

alt.usage.english
news:alt.usage.english

The main Usenet group for discussions of English. Enormously high-volume, the quality of information on alt.usage.english varies, but there's always something useful to be found here. Virtually every English-related topic, simple to complex, is discussed here.

alt.usage.english FAQ
http://www.scripps.edu/pub/dem-web/misrael/usage.html

An exceptionally useful FAQ (Frequently Asked Questions) document, written by Mark Israel, covering everything from the etymology of common phrases to advice on reference works to the use of ASCII to represent International Phonetic Alphabet symbols. Perhaps the best single document on the Net devoted to English. The above address is for Mark Israel's language page, which has links to several versions of the FAQ.

American Dialect Society
http://www.jerrynet.com/ads/index.htm

The American Dialect Society is the premier scholarly organization for the study of the English language in North America. Their Web site provides background about the ADS, an index to its journal, *American Speech*, information about and archives of ADS-L, the Society's very active electronic mailing list, and more.

American Name Society
http://www.wtsn.binghamton.edu/ANS/

A brief description of the American Name Society, devoted to the study of names—both personal and geographical—and naming practices in the U.S. and abroad.

Copy Editor
http://www.copyeditor.com

The Web site for *Copy Editor,* an outstanding newsletter for publishing professionals. Especially good in its coverage of cutting-edge language issues.

Dictionary of American Regional English
http://polyglot.lss.wisc.edu/dare/dare.html

The Dictionary of American Regional English, or DARE, is an ongoing project (three volumes, covering the letters A through O, have been published) to catalogue the regional variations in American English. The DARE site provides a general introduction to this most important dictionary project.

The Eclectic Company
http://www.lsa.umich.edu/ling/jlawler/lingmarks.html

An array of links to sites, resources, and articles on many aspects of English (and other languages) by University of Michigan linguist John Lawler. Includes Lawler's own excellent articles on usage, and the great ChomskyBot, which randomly generates surprisingly believable linguistics articles.

Grammar and Style Notes
http://www.english.upenn.edu/~jlynch/Grammar/

A large collection of essays by Jack Lynch, a graduate student in English, covering grammar, usage, and style. Concise and sensible.

The Jargon File
http://www.wins.uva.nl/~mes/jargon/

An extremely comprehensive guide to the language of the on-line world. Has existed in various forms for many years, and has been published in print as (most recently) *The New Hacker's Dictionary.* Detailed, accurate definitions, masses of historical information, zesty writing. Indispensable.

Oxford English Dictionary
http://www.oed.com

Though still under development and not fully accessible to the public, the Oxford English Dictionary's site has much fascinating material about the greatest historical dictionary ever produced.

The Scots Haunbuik
http://www.umist.ac.uk/UMIST_CAL/Scots/haunbuik.htm

A short introduction to the Scots language. Includes historical background, pronunciation guidelines, grammar, spelling, vocabulary, and references.

The Word Detective
http://www.word-detective.com

The online version of Evan Morris's syndicated newspaper column. Morris's consistently witty and knowledgeable writing shouldn't be missed. As a very rare bonus, this is an exceptionally well-designed Web site.

World Wide Words
http://clever.net/quinion/words/index.htm

A collection of short essays by Michael Quinion on a wide variety of topics. Sections on new words, newsworthy words, old obscure words, and usage notes. Consistently interesting and reliable.

Index of Contributors

Index of Sources

Index of Words, Phrases, and Concepts

Terms printed in **boldface** appear as main entries in the text.

tooth (long in the), 124
toothsome, 198
tour, 198–199
tourist, 198–199
toward, 199
towards, 199
traipse, 199–200
tread on a worm and it will turn, 211
triskaidekaphobia, 5
triskaidekaphobiaphobia, 5
truffle, 200–201
try to, 201
try and, 201
Turk, 215
t'aint, 67

U

Uriah Heep, 202
uvula, 66

V

vamp, 202–203
vampire, 203

W

walm, 203
wank, 203
wanker, 203–204
wanna, 78
warhorse, 204
whang, 204
what for, 31
wheelbarrow, 115, 204–205
whine, 206
whinge, 205–206

whipping boy, 206
white, 207
who, 207–208
whoever, 208
whole kit and caboodle, the, 114
whom, 207–208
whomever, 209
who'd a thunk it, 196
Wicca, 214
wise ass, 208
wise guy, 208
wiseacre, 208–209
withers, 209–210
withershins, 43
without let or hindrance, 52, 65
woe betide…, 17
words ending in -gry, 210–211
working stiff, 187
worm has turned, (the), 211
worrisome, 211–212
worrisomely, 211
worry, 212
wring, 209

Y

yawn, 213
yawning, 213
yen, 110
yonic, 213-214
young lion, 214–215
young Turk, 215
Young Turks, 215
y'all, 63

Z

Zeitgeist, 215–216